BE ✝
SPEN✝

WINNING THE FIGHT FOR FREEDOM'S SURVIVAL

MARIO DIAZ

BE SPENT

Winning the Fight for Freedom's Survival

Mario Diaz

ISBN: 978-1-927684-24-5

To Mrs. Beverly LaHaye

who, in obedience to God, gave her life to the noble task of equipping the Christian citizen in America, inspiring a generation of Christians to live out their faith in public policy service.

Acknowledgments

Many have contributed to this effort who will not yet be found in the footnotes. My wife Jennyffer (perfect for me in every way) and children Mia Raquel, Mario Alessandro, Cara Danielle and the little one still in the womb are without parallel in that regard. I am deeply grateful for them. But there are many others like my parents Mario and Raquel, my brother and his precious family, my in-laws, my pastor, my fellow "New Inklings," my publishers and my colleagues at Concerned Women for America (CWA); a big thank you to all of them and those who will have to remain unmentioned.

Endorsements

"God has a plan for your life and for America. *Be Spent* is a tool that can help you to better understand God's plan. This book is both educational and inspirational, Mario Diaz writes in a style you will enjoy. I highly recommend it."

—Dr. Tim LaHaye
Best-selling author, minister, Christian educator

"Liberty is not just the right to do what we want. That is libertinism. True liberty is the right ordering of society so that we are able to honor God and protect the dignity, the inherent worth, of God's 'image bearers:' every human being in that society. Mario Diaz does us a great service with *Be Spent*: Winning the Fight for Freedom's Survival. He calls us back to this beautiful idea of 'ordered liberty.' If the prophet's gift is to remind us of "known but forgotten things," as the poet Marion Montgomery said, then this book is profoundly prophetic. I found it deeply nourishing and pray it finds a wide audience."

—Warren Cole Smith
WORLD Magazine

"We know our Lord can make something good out of any evil, but sometimes we wonder what good He could have brought out of the attacks on life and family and now religious freedom. It is, of course, the great coming together of His children who have largely put aside our differences in order to fight for life and faith and family. Mario Diaz is such a fighter and His spirit permeates this very fine book on our current travails."

—Austin Ruse
President, Center for Family & Human Rights

CONTENTS

Part I: Worldview

Part II: Governing Principles

Part III: Practical Application

Part IV: Preserving Freedom

FOREWORD

It gives me great pleasure to present to you Mario's first book. Just like many products proudly display a "Made in America" tag, *Be Spent* should proudly bear a "Made at CWA" mark. As was the case with me and countless others, Mario's call to serve in public policy came through the vision God entrusted more than 35 years ago to one woman: Beverly LaHaye, the founder of Concerned Women for America (CWA).

It all started when Mrs. LaHaye watched in disbelief as the founder of the radical National Organization for Women, Betty Friedan, said in television that she spoke for the women of America. "Well, she doesn't speak for me!" thought Mrs. LaHaye. The Biblical principles God had placed in Mrs. LaHaye's heart were far away from the feminist ideology espoused by Friedan and others like her. The groundwork was set then for God's call to land on Mrs. LaHaye to start an organization in order to represent the voice of Christian conservative women who believed in the wonderful Biblical principles of America's founding. From a handful of women in 1978, CWA has grown to become the nation's largest public policy women's organization with half-a-million members around the country.

Many great women and like-minded men (we always joke that CWA is the women's group that actually likes and appreciates men) have been touched by Mrs. LaHaye's vision. From Minnesota Representative Michelle Bachman to former Alaska Governor and vice-presidential candidate Sarah Palin to the Founder of the Homeschool Legal Defense Fund Michael Farris to Jordan Lorence of the Alliance Defending Freedom and of course Mario, the Christian conservative public policy world has been forever changed by Mrs. LaHaye's faithfulness to God, and more importantly, by God's faithfulness to Mrs. LaHaye and CWA.

Here is the way President Ronald Reagan spoke about CWA and Mrs. LaHaye when he came to speak at our 4th National Convention on September 25, 1987:

> In just a few short years, you've become the largest politically active women's organization in the nation. A lot of the credit, of course, has to go to one woman. She is one of the powerhouses on the political scene today and one of the reasons that the grassroots are more and more a conservative province. Because of her the great majority of women once again have a voice on the issues of the day. You can no longer be ignored by the media or by their elected representatives. Beverly LaHaye is changing the face of American politics and she deserves our thanks and congratulations.

My own journey to lead CWA as its CEO and President also started with Mrs. LaHaye's vision and commitment to God's principles some 24 years ago. I was a recent college grad working on Capitol Hill with a deep passion to serve God in public policy. I applied to CWA not knowing anyone there, though I had been a member years earlier and, as Providence would have it, I was given a legislative position. I enjoyed every minute of it, but my time would come to an end (or so I thought) when I got married and took some time to start a family. Years later, Mrs. LaHaye's vision still burned within me and led me to start my own organization and a business. I served on CWA's board during that period, until I went to work to promote those family values at the Federal Communications Commission. Unbeknownst to me God was preparing me every step of the way to receive that call from Mrs. LaHaye a short time later to lead CWA after she stepped down as President and remain Chairman of our Board.

Isn't God amazing? His ways are beyond our comprehension, but we stand on solid ground when we trust His judgments above all—even above our own desires. He is always faithful to those who diligently seek Him.

That is the ultimate vision you will discover in *Be Spent*. That the God in whom our forefathers trusted to establish our great nation is the same yesterday, today and forever. He is still knocking at our doors. It is up to us to answer. That's the key to freedom's survival that Mario will present to you.

That vision grabbed Mario at a young age, before he had his four precious children or married his beautiful wife or was even an accomplished attorney. Fourteen years ago, a young Hispanic man came to CWA to produce our nationally syndicated radio show. He did not even know much about the issues we dealt with (CWA's core issues are: religious liberty, sanctity of human life, defense of the family, sexual exploitation, education, national sovereignty, and support for Israel), but he had an especially deep commitment to the Word of God. Mario describes it as a "pilot light," that small flame that helps ignites a furnace in the winter. He has said he had that pilot light for all the principles we care about deep within him – for the sanctity of every human life as created in the image of God, for the family and marriage as the model God uses to describes His relationship to the church, for religious liberty as born out of Biblical soil – as you will discover reading the pages of this book. "Coming to CWA," Mario says, "was like throwing kerosene onto that small pilot light, igniting a fire and a passion for God's principles to be displayed in public policy that has never stopped since." It drove him to law school and to the ministry at his home church. It has kept him at CWA for fourteen years in faithful service to God. And it has fueled the countless hours spent translating that passion into the words you will read in the pages ahead.

So you can be assured of one thing. What you are about to read is Mario's sincere passion and life. You can expect an honesty and realness that is seldom seen today. And I hope it ignites in you a similar passion to see God's principles restored in America again. For I stand with him in saying that freedom's survival depends on it.

As my favorite Ronald Reagan quote says:

> "Freedom is never more than one generation away from extinction. We didn't pass it to our children in the bloodstream. It must be fought for, protected, and handed on for them to do the same, or one day we will spend our sunset years telling our children and our children's children what it was once like in the United States where men were free."

Enjoy.

-Penny Nance

INTRODUCTION

America stands at the edge of suicide. We are slowly turning away from everything that made us a uniquely blessed people—a free people. We are moving towards a state that will put us in direct conflict with the very God we relied on to establish this great nation. This is a frightening thought. Just as in our personal lives, there is an internal struggle within the soul of America that is more dangerous than any threat we face from the outside. No one can hurt us more than we can hurt ourselves.

What you are about to read are a series of principles that represent the source of America's freedom and the only soil upon which our liberties can survive in the years to come. High among these critical principles is the fact that you, as an individual, are important, indeed vital, to freedom's survival. Without you taking ownership of these principles and making them a reality for your daily life, promoting them in public policy, teaching them to your children and standing for them among those around you, freedom will surely die in our land. We stand at a crucial time in history where we are in danger of losing the very idea of America to a distorted, corrupted, selfish and self-destructive view of freedom that has taken root among a significant part of the population. The reasons for this are varied, but chief among them is the fact that we have lost our faith in God.

There can be no question that America has been incredibly blessed throughout our short history. The problem is that we have absolutely no idea why. We have tasted God's blessings, so that we can see and feel they are slipping away fast, but we do not know what to do about it, or even if there is anything that can be done. Maybe it's just random; it's just life. Perhaps it's the natural processes of evolution, the much sought after "progress" (or is it regress?). Isn't it interesting that for all our technological, scientific, and philosophical advances, we are still as unfulfilled as ever and our hopelessness continues to grow? We have progressed to a big empty nothing. Our spirits are to a very significant degree (as they always are without freedom) broken, disorganized, and anxious, without any sort of lasting joy or peace.

I want us to recapture our faith in God as individuals, a people and a nation. I believe we still can. I am hopeful because of the object of our faith: God. He is merciful and gracious. I am truly optimistic because I believe what I am about to present to you throughout the pages of this book can be used by God in ways we cannot even imagine.

Our refusal to abide by God's statutes reflects a deeper problem. It reflects a loss of confidence in God himself. Notice I want us to recapture our faith *in God*, not just faith in the abstract, which is the modern idea. It is not about "spirituality." We are probably as spiritual today as we were at any other point in our history. Our country is full of very spiritual people that feel connected to "the universe" or "each other's energy" or "karma." We have seen the rise in popularity of many disciplines for meditation and self-discovery. Even atheists today routinely say they are "spiritual" people and even talk about their deep "faith." But faith, by its very definition, requires an object; "faith in what?"

I am especially weary of those who fall for the modern mantra of "believe in yourself." Of all the things to fall for, you know yourself! You know how weak and unstable you are. You are going to put your trust in you? Really? Trusting yourself more does not change who you are and the struggles you have. Think of it in terms of someone else. If you have a friend that you know is completely untrustworthy, will entrusting him with more things make him more trustworthy? Even if you try that a few times, maybe to inspire him, will you continue to put him in charge of that which you value most when he continues to betray you time and again? "Fool me once," goes the old saying, but we don't seem able to apply that to ourselves. Somehow, we have fallen for a trap that says, "If we believe in ourselves, things will happen for us." Well, what will happen? What are we trying to accomplish? Where are we trying to get to? I have the suspicion this sort of rhetoric is truly tied to money in the end or to material "things" at least. When we say "things will happen" for us, we really mean we will get something: a new job, a new car or house, or that big break at fame and fortune. Belief in your abilities and skills is what we used to call confidence, and yes, confidence is a real thing. If you are confident in your work, you will project that and it will help you in your career advancement. But to somehow extrapolate from that simple concept, a gigantic worldview to direct our entire lives is absurd, for we know how unreliable we are. If you feel confident right this minute, just wait an hour or two. You can be as confident in your skills as you want and one simple car accident and "bam!" Where will you be then?

Besides, once "things happen" for us, what do we think we will find? Fulfillment? Our theory is that if we had what that other unhappy person has then somehow we would not be as unhappy as they are? Surely you see that we deceive ourselves. Isn't it interesting we are always once step away from being "happy"? If you just had, "that," then everything would be good. But once "that" comes, you just need that other thing. When in school, we just want to graduate and we'd be happy. When we graduate, we just want to get into that university to be happy. When in the university, we just want to graduate and get a job. When in the job, we just need to get married. When married, we just need kids. When kids come, we just need a house and everything would be good. But by that time we are tired of the old job and if only we could get a better job, we'd be happy. And on and on we go, always living our lives one step away from happiness. Always looking at what others have and thinking if we only had "that." We must come to terms with the fact that our happiness does not come from bettering our circumstances, but from bettering ourselves. And the only way to be a better person (or a better country) is to put our trust in something outside of us. Something steady. Something true.

There is a reason we continue to go around in circles and feel trapped. It has nothing to do with our circumstances and everything to do with the object of our faith. I submit to you that the Founding Fathers had it right when they put their trust in God—in seeking after Truth. That is the key to breaking out from the monotonous, unhappy routines of this world and rediscover freedom. It has to do with the seriousness with which we take our Maker and His Word. "[T]ruth will set you free," says John 8:32, and "your word is the truth," John 17:17. It doesn't mean we get everything right, but living in pursuit of Truth will force us to self-examination and correction when we fail to live up to the standard.

This book is meant to encourage you to break out of the typical cycle and find lasting joy. It is meant to reveal the true source of freedom. If I am successful, you will feel both convicted and inspired to spend your life in service to God and others. My prayer is that we all turn from the "believe in yourself" propaganda of the world. For far too long Christians have compartmentalized God, so that we are trying to live with faith in God on one box and the world's wisdom on another. No surprise we have failed miserably, as the two are mutually exclusive. "Do you not know that friendship with the world is enmity with God?" (James 4:4). It is time we let God out of the box, so to speak. He wants us to trust Him and Him alone. It is time we allow Him to shine through us, even in the ugliest, darkest parts of our lives, including in the way we engage the culture through public policy. It is what King David spoke of in Psalms 16:8 when he said, "I have set the Lord always before me; because He is at my right hand I shall not be moved" (NKJV). Setting the Lord always before us will bring such sweetness and depth to our lives that we will be transformed into a deeper vessel where God can pour even more of Himself. Our cup will overflow in service to our neighbor, if we were to set the Lord always before us in the way we govern in America. I contend this is the key to freedom's survival.

I speak here primarily to those who believe in objective truth. For that belief carries with it a reverence and sincerity that cannot be easily disposed. It provides a standard from where we can take measure. It is a belief that, as we will see, the Founders relied on to establish, against all odds, one of the greatest, freest, most prosperous nation in history. More to the point, I want to inspire and challenge the Christian citizen in America, so that we know who God is more fully and, through His Word, are able to assess the ways in which He relates to us, His creation in a more profound way. The Bible, therefore, will serve us as a lamp to our feet as we walk through the many peaks and valleys of our Christian citizenship.

The fact that our aim is to persuade Christians to live out what they purport to believe in every area of their lives, including as citizens, does not mean that the result of the ideas presented is to benefit Christian citizens alone. By no means. If Christian citizens were to live this way, the result will be to the benefit of all citizens in this country, not just Christians.

It is my contention that many of us have neglected to always set the Lord before us when it comes to many areas of our lives, including in government and public policy specifically, and we are feeling the consequences of that neglect. There is a clear disconnect between what some of us say we believe, the way we live, and the policies we support. We must therefore question whether we really believe what we say we believe. There seems to be an internal struggle in the hearts and minds of many Christians (for those of us who actually stop to consider the problem) in part because we want to be "good persons;" we really want to bring peace and good news, not to upset people and be seen as "antagonists." These are good intentions that may be rooted in the love of God and others, but we have to be careful not to neglect God's Commandments in order to make ourselves and others feel good. We cannot ignore the self-serving nature of that internal struggle. Pride plays a major role. My prayer is that this book will help us strengthen our reliance on Truth and embolden us to live out God's principles, for His glory, whatever the cost. That it may enable us to "spend and be spent," as Paul said in 2 Corinthians 2:15, for our fellow men, in true, unselfish, humble service to God.

Everything I write to you I have learned from others, so that I present these ideas, not as my own but only as my way of expressing the eternal truths that have transformed the life of millions before, including the lives of many of the men and women who established our great nation. May we follow in their footsteps.

—Mario Diaz, Esq.
Washington, D. C., 2015

PART ONE
WORLDVIEW

CHAPTER ONE

THE HAND OF PROVIDENCE

Our journey must start where everything starts. "In the beginning, God..." (Genesis 1:1). Or, from America's Declaration of Independence, "We hold these truths to be self-evident that all men are created equal, that they are endowed by their *Creator* with certain unalienable Rights... "[1] Our understanding of the world and everything in it hinges on this one assertion: God "Is"[2] (Praise His name!), therefore, we must drive this stake deep into the soil. As Saint Augustine (354-430) said, "The higher your structure is to be, the deeper must be its foundation."[3] God is the Alpha and the Omega, Beginning and End.[4] Everything was created by Him and without Him nothing would have been created.[5] He is

---

1   The Declaration of Independence para. 2 (U.S. 1776) (emphasis mine).

2   "God said to Moses, 'I am who I am.' And he said, 'Say this to the people of Israel, I am has sent me to you,'" (Exodus 3:14).

3   Josiah H. Gilbert, *Dictionary of Burning Words of Brilliant Writers: A Cyclopædia of Quotations from the Literature of All Ages* 330 (Wilbur B. Ketcham, 1895).

4   "And He said to me, "It is done! I am the Alpha and the Omega, the Beginning and the End. I will give of the fountain of the water of life freely to him who thirsts," (Revelations 21:6, NKJV).

5   "All things were made through Him, and without Him nothing was made that was made," (John 1:3, NKJV).

the One not created but who has always been and will be forever.

Freedom's underpinnings

For the Christian citizen God alone lies at the foundations. We live by Him, through Him and for Him. He is both the Subject and Object of life. He reigns above all and is in ultimate control of all. Jesus told His disciples that not even a sparrow "falls to the ground apart from [our] Father's will," (Matthew 10:29). We stand at His mercy and depend completely on Him for our very beings. Every breath we take happens because He allows it to happen. This truth applies to everything in life, including the way we engage the culture and government. That is the approach we take as we humbly work to influence our society through our involvement as Christian citizens. All our efforts are only worthwhile if they function within God's overall purposes. Any efforts apart from Him amount to nothing. No Scripture brings this point home better than Psalm 33:

> [T]he word of the LORD is upright,
> and all his work is done in faithfulness.
> He loves righteousness and justice;
> the earth is full of the steadfast love of the LORD.
>
> By the word of the LORD the heavens were made,
> and by the breath of his mouth all their host.
> He gathers the waters of the sea as a heap;
> He puts the deeps in storehouses.
>
> Let all the earth fear the LORD;
> let all the inhabitants of the world stand in awe of him!
> For he spoke, and it came to be;
> He commanded, and it stood firm.
>
> The LORD brings the counsel of the nations to nothing;
> He frustrates the plans of the peoples.
> The counsel of the LORD stands forever,
> the plans of his heart to all generations.
> Blessed is the nation whose God is the LORD,
> the people whom He has chosen as his heritage!

The LORD looks down from heaven;
He sees all the children of man;
from where He sits enthroned he looks out
on all the inhabitants of the earth,
He who fashions the hearts of them all
and observes all their deeds.
The king is not saved by his great army;
a warrior is not delivered by his great strength.
The war horse is a false hope for salvation,
and by its great might it cannot rescue.

Behold, the eye of the LORD is on those who fear him,
on those who hope in his steadfast love,
that He may deliver their soul from death
and keep them alive in famine.

Our soul waits for the LORD;
He is our help and our shield.
For our heart is glad in him,
because we trust in his holy name.
Let your steadfast love, O LORD, be upon us,
even as we hope in you (Psalm 33:4-22).

The Christian citizen knows God is always in control and therefore can rejoice at all times.[6] God never "loses an election" or is absent when a catastrophe hits or is disinterested in us when we fail Him. We take great comfort in knowing God loves us despite our shortcomings and will bring about His purposes above human caprices. Did you hear the psalm? "The LORD brings the counsel of the nations to nothing; He makes the plans of the peoples of no effect." Our plans are of no consequences when compared to the overall plan of Almighty God. The counsel of the nations (*all* nations), including the most powerful ones, cannot alter what God traced from eternity. Proverbs says it this way, "Many are the plans in the mind of a man, but it is the purpose of the LORD that will stand," (Proverbs 19:21). Our vision is so skewed, so limited, that we know not what we do. We are simply powerless when it comes to ulti-mate reality, even though we see ourselves as high, mighty and strong,

---

6   "Rejoice in the Lord always; again I will say, rejoice," (Philippians 4:4).

capable of anything. Listen to the words of the Prophet Isaiah:

> Remember this and stand firm, recall it to mind, you transgressors, remember the former things of old; for I am God, and there is no other; I am God, and there is none like me, declaring the end from the beginning and from ancient times things not yet done, saying, "My counsel shall stand, and I will accomplish all my purpose," calling a bird of prey from the east, the man of my counsel from a far country. I have spoken, and I will bring it to pass; I have purposed, and I will do it (Isaiah 46:8-11).

If you ever find yourself doubting God's power to bring about His purposes, think about Christ. Do you really believe God sent His Son to earth to see what would happen? No! God sent His son to die for our sins and even those who were planning to get rid of Him and His teachings by crucifying Him were only accomplishing what God had pre-ordained from the beginning. Listen to the words of the Apostle Paul in Acts:

> For truly against Your holy Servant Jesus, whom You anointed, both Herod and Pontius Pilate, with the Gentiles and the people of Israel, were gathered together to do whatever Your hand and Your purpose determined before to be done (Acts 4:27-28, NKJV).

Jesus himself told us that He, as the Good Shepherd, gave His life for us:

> I am the good shepherd. The good shepherd gives His life for the sheep. But a hireling, he who is not the shepherd, one who does not own the sheep, sees the wolf coming and leaves the sheep and flees; and the wolf catches the sheep and scatters them. The hireling flees because he is a hireling and does not care about the sheep. I am the good shepherd; and I know My sheep, and am known by My own. As the Father knows Me, even so I know the Father; and I lay down My life for the sheep. And other sheep I have which are not of this fold; them also I must bring, and they will hear My voice; and there will be one flock and one shepherd.

Therefore My Father loves Me, because I lay down My life that I may take it again. No one takes it from Me, but I lay it down of Myself. I have power to lay it down, and I have power to take it again. This command I have received from My Father (John 10:11-18, NKJV).

Our confidence

The effects of this assurance are immeasurable. We do not lose heart. We do not despair. We do not lose hope. Our immediate circumstances are but a blink in the eyes of history; a history that will ultimately proclaim the glory of God. I know that we often just focus on tragedies to question the existence of God or His love for us, but why are we not so willing to attribute to Him all the good that we see around us? The psalmist said, "The earth is full of the goodness of the LORD," (Psalm 33:5, NKJV). Have you ever taken time to think about that? Most people have not. We simply do not pay attention to the manifold wonders of God. When was the last time you stopped and looked up? Listen to Psalm 19:1-4:

> The heavens declare the glory of God,
> and the sky above proclaims his handiwork.
> Day to day pours out speech,
> and night to night reveals knowledge.
> There is no speech, nor are there words,
> whose voice is not heard.
> Their voice goes out through all the earth,
> and their words to the end of the world.

Where is all this speech going? Who is listening? Have you seen it or heard it? The passage says the firmament reveals knowledge. That's knowledge straight from God. Knowledge of God. Knowledge of Truth.[7] This is a crucial question for us, "Can truth be known?" Not subjective truth, but objective, never-changing, all-satisfying, true truth. The Christian citizen believes it is absolutely possible and this has enormously liberating implications for us. It is pivotal that truth can indeed be ascertained. The Christian citizen seeks after it. We depend on it. We

---

7   "Jesus said to him, 'I am the way, and the truth, and the life. No one comes to the Father except through me,'" (John 14:6).

accept it. We submit to it. We submit all our plans, desires, complaints and preoccupations to the One Who is Truth. That's the idea presented in James 4:13-15:

> Come now, you who say, "Today or tomorrow we will go into such and such a town and spend a year there and trade and make a profit"— yet you do not know what tomorrow will bring. What is your life? For you are a mist that appears for a little time and then vanishes. Instead you ought to say, "If the Lord wills, we will live and do this or that."

Sounds new and radical today, but these truths were once understood and celebrated in our land. We all know them to be true deep inside, even if we don't attribute our happenings to a god. Have you noted more and more people saying they are "spiritual," even if they don't want to believe in God? Many times this happens because, they simply cannot deny the presence of the supernatural in their daily lives, the evidence is so obvious. They can't even explain themselves, apart from the spiritual. We know all our life-plans turn to dust when visited by the unforeseen: a tragedy, a diagnosis, friendship, love… The Christian citizen trusts in a God who directs our paths. We do not make plans and ask God to bless them. We seek His plan for us and the world and move from that to work within His purposes. Abraham Lincoln (1809-1865) touched on this Truth when he famously said as he struggled with the enormous issues of the Civil War, "Sir, my concern is not whether God is on our side; my greatest concern is to be on God's side, for God is always right"[8] It is in grace that we receive any blessings we get from God, with thanksgiving. This is the attitude of the Christian citizen, and it is the attitude that we as a people and as a country should have. It is the same mindset we see reflected in the history of America's founding. Listen to George Washington's (1732-1799) *Thanksgiving Proclamation* on October 3, 1789:

> Whereas it is the duty of all Nations to acknowledge the providence of Almighty God, to obey his will, to be grateful for his benefits, and humbly to implore his protection and favor -- and whereas both Houses of Congress have

---

8   Dee J. Rammell, *The Next President: How the Man Defines the Office* 19 (Tate Publishing, LLC 2012).

by their joint Committee requested me "to recommend to the People of the United States a day of public thanksgiving and prayer to be observed by acknowledging with grateful hearts the many signal favors of Almighty God especially by affording them an opportunity peaceably to establish a form of government for their safety and happiness."

Now therefore I do recommend and assign Thursday the 26th day of November next to be devoted by the People of these States to the service of that great and glorious Being, who is the beneficent Author of all the good that was, that is, or that will be -- That we may then all unite in rendering unto him our sincere and humble thanks -- for his kind care and protection of the People of this Country previous to their becoming a Nation -- for the signal and manifold mercies, and the favorable interpositions of his Providence which we experienced in the tranquility [sic], union, and plenty, which we have since enjoyed -- for the peaceable and rational manner, in which we have been enabled to establish constitutions of government for our safety and happiness, and particularly the national One now lately instituted -- for the civil and religious liberty with which we are blessed; and the means we have of acquiring and diffusing useful knowledge; and in general for all the great and various favors which he hath been pleased to confer upon us.

And also that we may then unite in most humbly offering our prayers and supplications to the great Lord and Ruler of Nations and beseech him to pardon our national and other transgressions -- to enable us all, whether in public or private stations, to perform our several and relative duties properly and punctually -- to render our national government a blessing to all the people, by constantly being a Government of wise, just, and constitutional laws, discreetly and faithfully executed and obeyed -- to protect and guide all Sovereigns and Nations (especially such as have shewn [sic] kindness onto us) and to bless them with good government, peace, and concord -- To promote the knowledge and practice of true religion and virtue, and the encrease [sic] of science among them and us -- and generally to grant unto all Mankind such a degree of temporal prosperity as he alone knows to be best.

Given under my hand at the City of New York the third day of October in the year of our Lord 1789.

George Washington[9]

Washington believed it is our duty to acknowledge Almighty God. When was the last time you heard a politician speak this way? Many would actually vehemently criticize him for it. I wonder how their record would stand up against Washington's. Not very well, I imagine. But that's a debate for another occasion. The important thing to note is that this was not mere rhetoric for Washington; he lived it. Washington knew he had been spared when he was just 23 at the Battle of Monongahela on July 9, 1755, at the beginning of the French and Indian War (1754-1763). Reports of their defeat and even his death where spreading all over the country when he wrote to his brother John on July 18, 1755:

Dear Brother,

As I have heard, since my arrival at this place, a circumstantial account of my death and dying speech, I take this early opportunity of contradicting the first, and of assuring you, that I have not as yet composed the latter. But, by the all-powerful dispensations of Providence, I have been protected beyond all human probability or expectation; for I had four bullets through my coat, and two horses shot under me, yet escaped unhurt, although death was leveling my companions on every side of me![10]

Mindful of the ramifications of his assertion, Washington not only attributed his survivals to Providence, but his defeats as well. He wrote

---

9   George Washington, *General Thanksgiving By the President of the United States Of America, A Proclamation*, The Massachusetts Centinel, Wednesday, October 14, 1789, available at http://lcweb2.loc.gov/ammem/GW/gw004.html.

10   Jared Sparks, *The Writings of George Washington*, American Quarterly Review, Volume 15, No. 30, p. 301 (T.K. Collins & Co.).

this account a few weeks later on August 2, 1755:

> It is true, we have been beaten, shamefully beaten, by a handful of men, who only intended to molest and disturb our march. Victory was their smallest expectation. But see the wondrous works of Providence, and the uncertainty of human things! We, but a few moments before, believed our numbers almost equal to the Canadian force; they only expected to annoy us. Yet, contrary to all expectation and human probability, and even to the common course of things, we were totally defeated, and sustained the loss of every thing.[11]

In that letter Washington also acknowledges how incredible his account sounds:

> I join very heartily with you in believing, that when this story comes to be related in the future annals, it will meet with unbelief and indignation, for had I not been witness to the fact on that fatal day, I should scarcely have given credit to it even now.[12]

Our faith

Young Washington's worldview and these early experiences would develop in him a faith that would prove indispensable as he took on liberty's cause many years later. Everyone knew that it was not humanly possible for those farmers-turned-soldiers, alongside whom Washington fought the American Revolutionary War (1775-1783), to defeat arguably the greatest military force in the world at the time, Great Britain. Yet Washington would lead them to victory, against all odds, perhaps knowing the role that Providence can play in such matters. It seems Washington knew first-hand what young David meant when he wrote: "No king is saved by the multitude of an army; a mighty man is not delivered by great strength. A horse is a vain hope for safety; neither shall it deliver any by its great strength," (Psalm 33:16, NKJV). David, who is said to have written most of the Psalms, was certainly not only saying things either, he lived them too. Remember the story of Goliath,

---

11   *Id.*

12   *Id.* at 301-02.

the mighty Philistine warrior who terrorized Israel for forty days, morning and night, challenging someone to dare confront him?[13] Everyone knew David could not defeat Goliath.[14] The Bible tells us everyone, including the bravest soldiers and even the King himself, was afraid of "the giant." He was almost 10 feet tall, armed with a 15 pounds-plus spear, covered with a bronze helmet and armor. His coat of mail alone weighted over 125 pounds. He also had a shield-bearer before him.[15] Yet young David wanted to fight him, alone? The Great King Saul said to him, "You are not able to go against this Philistine to fight with him; you are a youth, and he a man of war from his youth," (1 Samuel 17:33). But David spoke as Washington would centuries later. "I have seen it. God has delivered me in the past. He will do it again. It's not about my might but His. Providence will see me through." The cynic would say, "With such a worldview, why fight? If God is in control, let Him handle it." But this is a most jejune view of the world, for God chooses to work through us and we must still be intelligent, astute and use our reason, not only to trust Him fully, but also to use the God-given talents and capacities He has given us for His Glory. Here is David striking that divine balance in response to Saul:

> "Your servant used to keep sheep for his father. And when there came a lion, or a bear, and took a lamb from the flock, I went after him and struck him and delivered it out of his mouth. And if he arose against me, I caught him by his beard and struck him and killed him. Your servant has struck down both lions and bears, and this uncircumcised Philistine shall be like one of them, for he has defied the armies of the living God." And David said, "The LORD who delivered me from the paw of the lion and from the paw of the bear will deliver me from the hand of this Philistine" (1 Samuel 17:34-37).

No delusions of grandeur for David. He used rational arguments to convince Saul that he could take on this impossible task. He knew Who saved him when he defeated the lion and the bear. It wasn't his might or skill. God had delivered him, even as David used his own skills. Now, he

---

13   1 Samuel 17.

14   *Id.* 17:11.

15   *Id.* 17:4-7.

was able to apply that experience to this new foe. It doesn't matter that Goliath is bigger, stronger, more intelligent, better trained and protected by an impressive armor. If you remember, David couldn't even wear any armor himself for it was too heavy and he couldn't walk with it.[16] But God is still God. And David knew Him and trusted Him. Far from the "blind" faith Christians are accused of practicing many times, David was acting on what he had already seen. He was actually seeing things clearer than anyone else at the camp. "If God is for us, who can be against us?"[17] he asked. In a similar way, Washington saw clearer at our nation's birth. He trusted that hand of Providence, whatever the outcome. It is imperative we understand that the Christian citizen in America speaks of what we have seen and heard; what we have experienced time and again as a people and a nation; that we are not blind, but see clearly; that we attribute honor and glory only where honor and glory are duly placed. Washington and David's victories were not theirs ultimately.

Freedom's victory

America's Founders went to battle with a full understanding of the impossibility of their task. They knew they needed more than military might to achieve the freedom and liberty they sought. From the human perspective, they simply lacked the resources to take on this cause in such a manner. And everyone else knew it too. The entire world knew it. That is why many patriots were opposed to what they considered a senseless endeavor, a suicidal mission. Here is how Patrick Henry (1736-1799) responded to the criticism in his "Give me Liberty or Give Me Death" speech addressing the Virginia Convention just months before signing the Declaration of Independence:

> They tell us, sir, that we are weak; unable to cope with so formidable an adversary... Sir, we are not weak if we make a proper use of those means which the God of nature hath placed in our power. Three millions of people, armed in the holy cause of liberty, and in such a country as that which we possess, are invincible by any force which our enemy can send against us. Besides, sir, we shall not fight our battles alone. There is a just God who

---

16   *Id.* 17:38–39.

17   Romans 8:31.

presides over the destinies of nations, and who will raise up friends to fight our battles for us. The battle, sir, is not to the strong alone; it is to the vigilant, the active, the brave.[18]

Sounds a lot like David's appeal to reason, but with ultimate confidence in that hand of Providence. The Founders went into battle, largely on faith, believing that if they aligned themselves on God's side, that Just, Supreme Being would come to their aid. And He did! Time and again during these years of conflict Providence came just in time when they were in the most perilous situations. Weather played an especially vital role in their survival at several pivotal points. On one occasion, British General Howe had Washington and his troops cornered on Brooklyn Heights on Long Island. Disaster loomed. But for some "fortunate" bad weather the war would have been lost little over a month after the Declaration of Independence was signed. Colonel William Douglas (1742-1777) wrote to his wife about the weather's role on that crucial day, August 23, 1776:

Night before last we had a most terrible thunderstorm. One capt., two liuts. Of the first battalion of York troops were killed with lightning in one place. Also two men in two different places. The wind and wether [sic] has been remarkable [sic] in our favour [sic] for this sometime past, has brought on our troops and kept back the enemy and we begin to shew like a formidable [sic] army and I hope the same kind Providence that has wonderfully carried us thus far will shew his power in bringing us off victorious, and take to himself the glory.[19]

The colonel attributes their preservation to the glory of God. Washington then decides their only option was to retreat across the East River, but they did not have enough time to do that, aside, again, from Providential intervention. On his memoirs, Colonel Benjamin Tallmadge (1754-1835) described the scene:

---

18   Patrick Henry, Virginia Delegate, Address at the Second Virginia Convention: *Give Me Liberty or Give Me Death* (Mar. 23, 1775).

19   Henry Steele Commager & Richard B Morris, *Spirit of '76* 431 (New York, Harper & Row, 1975).

To move so large a body of troops with all their necessary appendages, across a river full a mile wide, with a rapid current, in face of a victorious, well disciplined army, nearly three times as numerous as his own, and a fleet capable of stopping the navigation, so that not one boat could have passed over, seemed to present most formidable obstacles.[20]

Still, Washington was unshakable in his resolve, and they spent the whole night taking men across the East River. The next day, they still had many soldiers to bring across who were now completely exposed. General Howe and his army were closing in, and they would be trapped. But wouldn't you know it, a heavy fog "fortunately" descended right where they were crossing, allowing them time to complete the task and escape unharmed. Col. Tallmadge recalled the event:

In the history of warfare I do not recollect a more fortunate retreat. After all, the providential appearance of the fog saved a part of our army from being captured, and certainly myself, among others who formed the rear guard. Gen. Washington has never received the credit which was due to him for this wise and most fortunate measure.[21]

These are amazing first-hand accounts, recognizing God's hand on the historical events that gave birth to our nation. And that was just one incident. There are many others. The crossing of the Delaware River also presented similar odds for Washington. In December of the same year (1776), he planned a surprise attack at Trenton, New Jersey. Washington's army was demoralized by recent defeats and morale was very low. Many were leaving because conditions were so poor. Washington needed a victory, and he was convinced a surprise attack by crossing the Delaware River would surely provide it. But there was "no way." Conditions were so bad that he would need nothing short of a miracle. And that's exactly what he got. Again. The plan should have never worked under that type of weather, that's the reason why it would be so surpris-

---

20   Benjamine Tallmadge, *Memoir of Col. Benjamin Tallmadge* 10 (Thomas Holman, 1858).

21   Henry Steele Commager & Richard B Morris, *Spirit of '76* 446 (Harper & Row, 1975).

ing to the enemy. Washington wrote about his preoccupation with the river. It was not completely frozen, so they could not cross on foot, yet it was frozen enough to make it extremely difficult to cross by boat. And things got worse. Here is a description from David Hackett Fischer's *Washington's Crossings*:

> As they marched along snowy roads in the gathering darkness, the sky clouded over. A little after sunset, [John] Greenwood wrote, "it began to drizzle or grow wet." By the time they reached the river, the drizzle had become a driving rain. About eleven o'clock, a howling nor'easter hit them with terrific force. Greenwood remembered that "it rained, hailed, snowed and froze." He forgot to mention sleet ...[22]

> Another problem was the darkness of the night. A bright moon had risen after sunset but was obscured by the storm. Visibility grew so poor that boatmen could barely see the opposite shore. Wilkinson recalled that "the force of the current, the sharpness of the frost, the darkness of the night, the ice which made during the operation and a high wind, rendered the passage of the river extremely difficult."[23]

Howe never expected such a bold move (on Christmas Eve!) and his men were not prepared for battle when Washington showed up with his men. The implausible move is said to have turned the entire momentum of the war and changed the course of human history. Washington dared cross the river two more times after that, all of them under extraordinary conditions. Having lived through those remarkable events, among others, it is not surprising at all to hear Washington say this at his Inaugural Address as the first president of the United States:

> No people can be bound to acknowledge and adore the Invisible Hand which conducts the affairs of men more than the people of the United States. Every step by which they have advanced to the character of an independent

---

22   David Hackett Fischer, *Washington's Crossing* 212 (Oxford University Press, 2004).

23   *Id.* at 218.

nation seems to have been distinguished by some to-
ken of providential agency... We ought to be no less per-
suaded that the propitious smiles of Heaven can never be
expected on a nation that disregards the eternal rules of
order and right which Heaven itself has ordained.[24]

It is no coincidence that under such leadership as that of Washington
the United States of America would grow to become one of the greatest
nations in history. A nation is its people and its leaders. And the American people, right from their infancy, experienced and, therefore, trusted
in God. Our motto "In God We Trust" is a testimony to this historical
fact. Although the official motto was adopted in 1956, the phrase had
appeared on most coins since 1864 and it was part of the fourth stanza
of "The Star-Spangled Banner," our national anthem, written in 1814 by
Francis Scott Key (1779-1843). Though only the first stanza is usually
sung at public events today, there are really four stanzas reflecting the
character of America. The whole fourth stanza proclaims our reliance
on Almighty God:

Oh! thus be it ever, when freemen shall stand
Between their loved home and the war's desolation!
Blest with victory and peace, may the heav'n rescued land
Praise the Power that hath made and preserved us a nation.

Then conquer we must, when our cause it is just,
And this be our motto: "In God is our trust."
And the star-spangled banner in triumph shall wave
O'er the land of the free and the home of the brave![25]

Francis Scott Key wrote the poem, originally titled "Defence of Fort
McHenry" after the fort's bombardment by the British Royal Navy in
the Chesapeake Bay during the War of 1812. The acknowledgment and
appreciation of Providence is palpable. But as is often the case, we have
slowly forgotten all about that. Those men who experienced the hand
of God so intimately are long gone and our generation has no idea what
these references to Providence mean. "We did it!" we proclaim today.

---

24   George Washington, *Inaugural Address* (April 30, 1789).

25   Francis Scott Key, *The Star-Spangled Banner* (1814), available at http://www.
usa-flag-site.org/song-lyrics/star-spangled-banner.shtml (accessed Sept. 8, 2014).

"American ingenuity," we cry. The contemporary politician believes he has the ideas that will get us out of the hole we find ourselves in. Yet, we continue to fall deeper into immorality and self-destruction. Oh, that we had leaders who would call on the nation, as Washington did, to pray to Almighty God as our ultimate hope! Someone to recognize he or she does not have the answers, but knows He who does. Well, regardless of what our leaders do, we need the Christian citizens to stand in unison and proclaim these truths once again, if freedom is to survive our current turmoil.

The challenge

I'm afraid we are nowhere near that type of vision. We are suffering from an almost complete blindness. In fact, those who dare bring that type of vision to the forefront are shunned as "extremists" in today's America. Do you believe Americans would choose "In God We Trust" as their motto, if we were voting on it nowadays? Today's leaders want to be "sensitive" to those who do not believe in God and are extra careful not to upset the apparently terribly frail "wall of separation between church and state." So they see best not to mention the "G"-word in public.[26] In our time, the mere acknowledgment of God's existence (as reality) is met with, not just apathy, but outright hostility. The cry for "tolerance" in today's culture is so strong that we are prepared to ignore reality to create our own fictions to live out. Isn't that what we say, "What's true for you might not be true for me?" Creating our own "truths," we've ended up worshiping the lies that lead to our own destruction. As Romans 1:23 tells us, "[T]hey exchanged the truth about God for a lie and worshiped and served the creature rather than the Creator..." The result is troubling, "[S]ince they did not see fit to acknowledge God, God gave them up to a debased mind to do what ought not to be done," (Romans 1:28).

We have become experts in doing what ought not to be done, especially when it comes to God. Legal groups are ready at every corner to file law suits to remove any mention of God in public. The latest trend is to say that if you "enter the stream of commerce"— if you want to make a living that is— then you must leave your Christian beliefs out

---

26   "For I am not ashamed of the gospel of Christ, for it is the power of God to salvation for everyone who believes..." (Romans 1:16, NKJV).

of it.[27] You cannot conduct business in a Christian manner. You must betray your Christian values if you want to open any type of business that caters to the public.[28] These efforts are funded, if only in part, by our own tax dollars. Therefore, we effectively reward groups that work to erase our history and try to make God an enemy of the state. The distortion and exploitation of the "wall of separation between church and state" language, never found in the U.S. Constitution but adopted by the U.S. Supreme Court, has actually brought government hostility towards religion, turning our First Amendment and our history on its head. The Pledge of Allegiance has been attacked because a few find it repulsive to say we are "one nation, under God."[29] Religious symbols like the Ten Commandments or crosses or nativity scenes or Christmas carols have all been targeted for eradication.[30] We have restricted children's prayer in schools and at public events.[31] We have even restricted prayer for those in the military, including chaplains.[32] When we allow public prayer, we try to control their content and even to whom they are praying. In a famous case, a judge ordered the Speaker of the Indiana House to immediately stop the practice of "sectarian prayers" at the opening of the legislative session because the prayers were too Christian.[33] The judge argued that praying in the name of Jesus is unconstitutional, but praying to "Allah" is perfectly fine. And the downward spiral continues. At President Barack Obama's Second Presidential Inauguration, Pastor Louie Giglio was forced to withdraw from bringing the invocation be-

---

27　　"There can be a conflict between religious liberty and sexual liberty, but in almost all cases the sexual liberty should win because that's the only way that the dignity of gay people can be affirmed in any realistic manner." *Chai Feldblum On Sexual Liberty vs. Religious Liberty*, Hot Air, October 5, 2009, available at http://hotair.com/greenroom/archives/2009/10/05/chai-feldblum-on-sexual-liberty-vs-religious-liberty/ (accessed Sept. 26, 2014).

28　　See *Ingersoll v. Arlene's Flowers*, *State of Washington v. Arlene's Flowers*, and *Arlene's Flowers v. Ferguson*, available at http://www.adfmedia.org/News/PRDetail/8608 (accessed March 20, 2015). Also, *Elane Photography v. Willock*, available at http://www.alliancedefendingfreedom.org/News/PRDetail/5537.

29　　*Elk Grove Unified School District v. Newdow*, 542 U.S. 1 (2004).

30　　*Van Orden v. Perry*, 545 U.S. 677 (2005); *Lynch v. Donnelly*, 465 U.S. 668 (1984); *Florey v. Sioux Falls School District*, 619 F.2d 1311 (1980).

31　　*Engel v. Vitale*, 370 U.S. 421 (1962) and *Abington School District v. Schempp*, 374 U.S. 203 (1963).

32　　*Mellen v. Bunting*, 327 F.3d 355 (4th Circuit. 2003).

33　　*Hinrichs v. Bosma*, 400 F. Supp. 2d 1103 (Dist. Court, SD Indiana 2005).

cause of his Biblical beliefs on sexuality.[34] In other words, not only will modern America interfere with prayer as to whether, how, and to whom it is offered, but now they will require that anyone who is selected to bring an invocation in public embraces the latest "moral" standard of the day, regardless of what their consciences dictate. Not only does a powerful group reject the Providence of our birth, they also require universal rejection. And even though it is true that these impositions have been pressed on the culture by a very small group of anti-religious militants, "*We the people*" have allowed it to happen, and our silence has become the loudest approval; a tacit endorsement of the rejection of our Creator. But make no mistake about it, we are paying the price of our indifference and unfaithfulness with a continued moral and spiritual decay in our nation. That decay is by no means limited to morality alone. As General Douglas MacArthur (1880-1964) of the U.S. Army said, "History fails to record a single precedent in which nations subject to moral decay have not passed into political and economic decline. There has been either a spiritual awakening to overcome the moral lapse, or a progressive deterioration leading to ultimate national disaster."[35] We fail to see that connection. The concept has become completely foreign to us.

Will we be able to avoid ultimate disaster? The only way to answer that question is to answer whether the Christian citizen in America will be able to embrace once again the Biblical principles of our founding. Will we recover our faith in God? Will we recognize and honor the hand of Providence, as our Founders did? That belief, and only that belief, provides the fertile soil needed for the American ideal to be reborn and to flourish once again. It is up to us. Christians. The Body of Christ. The Church. There would simply be no America without God's principles— only those principles bring true freedom and liberty, for they come from He who created us in His image. Neither freedom nor liberty can survive, much less thrive, without God's principles. As John Adams (1735-1826), one of our Founding Fathers and the Second President of the United States, recognized, "Our Constitution was made only for a moral and religious people. It is wholly inadequate to the government

---

34   Jonathan Capehart, *Louie Giglio out from Inaugural: Good*, Washington Post, January 10, 2013, available at http://www.washingtonpost.com/blogs/post-partisan/wp/2013/01/10/louie-giglio-out-from-inaugural-good/ (accessed Sept. 8, 2014).

35   General Douglas MacArthur quoted in John Stormer, *The Death of a Nation* 128 (Liberty Bell Press, 1968).

of any other."[36]

We are no longer a moral people. Therefore, it is no wonder why we are having so much troubling accepting the principles envisioned in our Constitution. But these are the principles of freedom and they are uniquely Christian. The Christian worldview is America's worldview. It is freedom's worldview. Therefore the Christian citizen in America, who espouses, preserves and promotes those principles, is essential for the country's survival as a free nation. It is up to us to articulate these principles in a clear, precise, winsome way and, perhaps more importantly, to live them out for the world to see the marvelous fruits of abiding by them.

---

36   John Adams, *The Works of John Adams,* Second President of the United States: with a Life of the Author, Notes and Illustrations Vol. 9. of 10 (Charles Francis Adams ed., Little, Brown and Co. 1856), available at http://oll.libertyfund.org/titles/2107#lf1431-09_head_222 (accessed Sept. 8, 2014).

CHAPTER TWO

KINGDOM FOCUS

We concern ourselves with the Christian citizen in America and not the American citizen who is a Christian. Scripture is clear, we have but one citizenship:

> [O]ur citizenship is in heaven, and from it we await a Savior, the Lord Jesus Christ, who will transform our lowly body to be like his glorious body, by the power that enables him even to subject all things to himself (Philippians 3:20–21).

Wherever we are on earth, we are sojourners. Pilgrims. This has been the experience of the Christian faith ever since Adam and Eve were taken out of the Garden of Eden.[37] It was the shadow which covered Abraham, the father of our faith, in Old Testament time. The Book of Hebrews explains it this way:

> By faith Abraham obeyed when he was called to go out to a place that he was to receive as an inheritance. And he went out, not knowing where he was going. By faith he

---

37   Genesis 3.

went to live in the land of promise, as in a foreign land, living in tents with Isaac and Jacob, heirs with him of the same promise. For he was looking forward to the city that has foundations, whose designer and builder is God (Hebrews 11:8-10).

Pilgrimage

We too live "as in a foreign country," wherever we are physically born, wherever life takes us. We are born again into a new citizenship when Christ draws us to Him. Jesus explained it to Nicodemus, a Pharisee and ruler of the Jews, this way:

> "Truly, truly, I say to you, unless one is born again he cannot see the kingdom of God." Nicodemus said to him, "How can a man be born when he is old? Can he enter a second time into his mother's womb and be born?" Jesus answered, "Truly, truly, I say to you, unless one is born of water and the Spirit, he cannot enter the kingdom of God. That which is born of the flesh is flesh, and that which is born of the Spirit is spirit (John 3:3-6).

As the ram God provided to take the place of Isaac,[38] Abraham's son, mirrored the Lamb of God who takes away our sins by dying in our place on the cross, so Abraham's journey mirrors the struggle of all Christians as pilgrims in foreign lands, in a fallen world where we await the place that God has promised to those who believe: the New Jerusalem. Hebrews again:

> These all died in faith, not having received the things promised, but having seen them and greeted them from afar, and having acknowledged that they were strangers and exiles on the earth. For people who speak thus make it clear that they are seeking a homeland. If they had been thinking of that land from which they had gone out, they would have had opportunity to return. But as it is, they desire a better country, that is, a heavenly one. Therefore God is not ashamed to be called their God, for he has prepared for them a city (Hebrews 11:13-16).

---

38   *Id.* at 22:13-14.

Augustine called it the "City of God."[39] It is our ultimate hope, through our Lord and Savior Jesus Christ. But this is not just a future promise bearing no influence on our lives today. This reality is of utmost importance to how we live now. What we do today reflects on eternity. Our earthly, human actions have a spiritual, eternal impact. Therefore, living for eternity impacts the way we relate to government, culture, yea even our own bodies today.

> [W]e do not lose heart. Though our outer self is wasting away, our inner self is being renewed day by day. For this light momentary affliction is preparing for us an eternal weight of glory beyond all comparison, as we look not to the things that are seen but to the things that are unseen. For the things that are seen are transient, but the things that are unseen are eternal (2 Corinthians 4:16-18).

It is this "eternal weight of glory" which produces in us a perspective that is indispensable to a free people. I call it "Kingdom focus:" living today in light of eternity. We do not fear death. "For [us] to live is Christ, and to die is gain," (Philippians 1:21). We have a hope that is not dependent on our immediate circumstances. We have a confidence that cannot be explained. We have a peace that "surpasses all understanding," as Paul described:

> Rejoice in the Lord always; again I will say, rejoice. Let your reasonableness be known to everyone. The Lord is at hand; do not be anxious about anything, but in every-thing by prayer and supplication with thanksgiving let your requests be made known to God. And the peace of God, which surpasses all understanding, will guard your hearts and your minds in Christ Jesus (Philippians 4:4-7).

Unshakable assurance

Again, this assurance is not based on "blind faith" as is sometimes por-trayed by the culture. It is based on a strong, confident faith placed in a God that has come to the aid of His people time and again. It is an "eyes-wide-open" kind of faith. God sustained our ancestors in the past

---

39   Augustine of Hippo, *City of God* (426 AD).

and we know He will also come to our aid today. Take the example of Job. God sustained Job through incredible adversity. He was a "blameless and upright man, who fear[ed] God and turn[ed] away from evil," (Job 1:8). Then, life:

> [T]here was a day when [Job's] sons and daughters were eating and drinking wine in their oldest brother's house, and there came a messenger to Job and said, "The oxen were plowing and the donkeys feeding beside them, and the Sabeans fell upon them and took them and struck down the servants with the edge of the sword, and I alone have escaped to tell you." While he was yet speaking, there came another and said, "The fire of God fell from heaven and burned up the sheep and the servants and consumed them, and I alone have escaped to tell you." While he was yet speaking, there came another and said, "The Chaldeans formed three groups and made a raid on the camels and took them and struck down the servants with the edge of the sword, and I alone have escaped to tell you." While he was yet speaking, there came another and said, "Your sons and daughters were eating and drinking wine in their oldest brother's house, and behold, a great wind came across the wilderness and struck the four corners of the house, and it fell upon the young people, and they are dead, and I alone have escaped to tell you" (Job 1:13-19).

Despair should've followed. Hopelessness. Yet Job's response is illuminating: "Naked I came from my mother's womb, and naked shall I return. The LORD gave, and the LORD has taken away; blessed be the name of the LORD," (Job 1:21). Amazing! That is that peace that surpasses all human understanding. If Job would have turned away from his beliefs in God, the world would've understood. In fact, his own wife tells him, "Do you still hold fast your integrity? Curse God and die," (Job 2:9). That is an understandable statement from the world's perspective. The world's math says, "You followed God, things didn't go well, try something else." But Job's faithfulness was not of this world, his understanding came from above. He knew true wisdom and Scripture tells us that, "The fear of the LORD is the beginning of wisdom; all those who practice it have a good understanding," (Psalm 111:10). In that wisdom Job rebukes his wife:

"You speak as one of the foolish women speaks. Shall we indeed accept good from God, and shall we not accept adversity?" (Job 2:10, NKJV). Behind these understandings stand the world's assumptions of what is "good" versus what truly is good for us. Job trusted God and His judgment above all. So should we.

The Bible tells us, "In all this Job did not sin with his lips," (Job 2:10). Was this an extremely difficult time in Job's life? That would be an understatement. Did he hurt? You bet he did. Did he have questions? That is what the whole book is about. But he remained faithful. He had Hope. And Hope does not disappoint because it is about where we place our Hope. More precisely, Who is that Hope for us? Listen to Paul:

> Therefore, since we have been justified by faith, we have peace with God through our Lord Jesus Christ. Through him we have also obtained access by faith into this grace in which we stand, and we rejoice in hope of the glory of God. Not only that, but we rejoice in our sufferings, knowing that suffering produces endurance, and endurance produces character, and character produces hope, and hope does not put us to shame, because God's love has been poured into our hearts through the Holy Spirit who has been given to us (Romans 5:1-5).

Therefore, Job's faithfulness was commended, "[T]he Lord blessed the latter days of Job more than his beginning," (Job 42:12). And that was just the earthly blessings, the eternal blessings, which are the most precious of all, were still to come.

Think of Joseph. Sold into slavery by envious brothers.[40] Tempted.[41] Slandered.[42] Imprisoned.[43] Joseph had every reason to be bitter and complain about his "bad luck." It seemed as if God had abandoned him. Yet, he never relented. He knew his God. He knew his faith was not in vain, whatever his immediate circumstances. It is not faith itself, but the God in whose character we place our faith. Joseph knew a real God

---

40   Genesis 37:12-36.

41   *Id.* at 39:1-10.

42   *Id.* at 39:11-18.

43   *Id.* at 39:19-23.

who spoke to him through dreams.[44] He believed in Yahweh, the Great I Am. And putting his trust in Yahweh, he prospered in the middle of all the adversity thrown at him. In Egypt, he went from being in prison to being second only to Pharaoh. He got that opportunity in the most unlikely of manners, being the only man able to interpret Pharaoh's dreams. Genesis 41 tells the story. Pharaoh dreamed he saw "seven cows attractive and plump," and then seven "ugly and thin." And the seven ugly cows ate the attractive ones. He also dreamed he saw seven ears of grain that were "plump and good" and then seven more that were "thin *and* blighted." And the thin ears swallowed up the good ones. The Bible tells us Pharaoh's spirit was in distress and he called for all the magicians and wise men, but there was none who could interpret them, until Joseph was given the chance. Joseph was shown by God what both dreams meant. Here is the account of what he told Pharaoh:

> "The dreams of Pharaoh are one; God has revealed to Pharaoh what he is about to do. The seven good cows are seven years, and the seven good ears are seven years; the dreams are one. The seven lean and ugly cows that came up after them are seven years, and the seven empty ears blighted by the east wind are also seven years of famine. It is as I told Pharaoh; God has shown to Pharaoh what he is about to do. There will come seven years of great plenty throughout all the land of Egypt, but after them there will arise seven years of famine, and all the plenty will be forgotten in the land of Egypt. The famine will consume the land, and the plenty will be unknown in the land by reason of the famine that will follow, for it will be very severe. And the doubling of Pharaoh's dream means that the thing is fixed by God, and God will shortly bring it about. Now therefore let Pharaoh select a discerning and wise man, and set him over the land of Egypt. Let Pharaoh proceed to appoint overseers over the land and take one-fifth of the produce of the land of Egypt during the seven plentiful years. And let them gather all the food of these good years that are coming and store up grain under the authority of Pharaoh for food in the cities, and let them keep it. That food shall be a reserve for the land

---

44   *Id.* at 37.

against the seven years of famine that are to occur in the land of Egypt, so that the land may not perish through the famine.

This proposal pleased Pharaoh and all his servants. And Pharaoh said to his servants, "Can we find a man like this, in whom is the Spirit of God?" Then Pharaoh said to Joseph, "Since God has shown you all this, there is none so discerning and wise as you are. You shall be over my house, and all my people shall order themselves as you command. Only as regards the throne will I be greater than you" (Genesis 41:25-40).

The story is an amazing display of God's power and faithfulness. When Joseph's brothers came to him to be saved because of the famine that plagued the land and were afraid of him retaliating, Joseph tells them why his heart is not full of bitterness and vengeance for those who had betrayed him long ago:

Joseph said to [his brothers], "Do not fear, for am I in the place of God? As for you, you meant evil against me, but God meant it for good, to bring it about that many people should be kept alive, as they are today. So do not fear; I will provide for you and your little ones." Thus he comforted them and spoke kindly to them (Genesis 50:19-21).

The outpouring of hope

Could this attitude help a society or a culture today? Imagine a people who exalt mercy and goodness, kindness and righteousness. Imagine if we were able to forgive as Joseph.

If we have learned anything throughout history, it is that pain, suffering and calamity are a big part of our experience on earth. War, famine, disease, betrayal… We don't understand it all, but we have all experienced that pain in one form or another. How we cope with these realities, how we think of them, determines also the way we behave through those realities— how we act in culture (that is in relation to one another) and in society (as to the type of government that is needed to deal with these issues appropriately). The Christian citizen knows God has a purpose for what happens in his life. We never suffer in vain. "Kingdom focus" looks to our immediate circumstances through the lens of the promises of God. We look at our struggles through the promise of Revelations 21:

> Then I saw a new heaven and a new earth, for the first heaven and the first earth had passed away, and the sea was no more. And I saw the holy city, new Jerusalem, coming down out of heaven from God, prepared as a bride adorned for her husband. And I heard a loud voice from the throne saying, "Behold, the dwelling place of God is with man. He will dwell with them, and they will be his people, and God himself will be with them as their God. He will wipe away every tear from their eyes, and death shall be no more, neither shall there be mourning, nor crying, nor pain anymore, for the former things have passed away."

> And he who was seated on the throne said, "Behold, I am making all things new" (Revelations 21:1-5).

What hope! Only a Christian perspective provides us with adequate materials to deal with the harsh realities of this world. To the Christian, wordily things are secondary, including worldly sufferings. Kingdom focus brings internal peace and stability. There is no fear of the future, immediate or long term. There is confidence. The classic verse to illustrate comes from the Gospel according to Mathew. Jesus tells us:

> Therefore I tell you, do not be anxious about your life, what you will eat or what you will drink, nor about your body, what you will put on. Is not life more than food, and the body more than clothing? Look at the birds of the air: they neither sow nor reap nor gather into barns, and yet your heavenly Father feeds them. Are you not of more value than they? And which of you by being anxious can add a single hour to his span of life? And why are you anxious about clothing? Consider the lilies of the field, how they grow: they neither toil nor spin, yet I tell you, even Solomon in all his glory was not arrayed like one of these. But if God so clothes the grass of the

field, which today is alive and tomorrow is thrown into the oven, will he not much more clothe you, O you of little faith? Therefore do not be anxious, saying, 'What shall we eat?' or 'What shall we drink?' or 'What shall we wear?' For the Gentiles seek after all these things, and your heavenly Father knows that you need them all. But seek first the kingdom of God and his righteousness, and all these things will be added to you.

Therefore do not be anxious about tomorrow, for tomorrow will be anxious for itself. Sufficient for the day is its own trouble (Matthew 6:25-34).

This belief is not just lip service. This is true inner peace and joy. It is internal and therefore social stability. I love the word Paul uses, "contentment:"

I have learned in whatever situation I am to be content. I know how to be brought low, and I know how to abound. In any and every circumstance, I have learned the secret of facing plenty and hunger, abundance and need. I can do all things through him who strengthens me (Philippians 4:11-13).

True fulfillment

Do not confuse this with complacency or mediocrity. The Christian worldview is a meaningful worldview that will produce incalculable benefits for every person who adheres to it and the society where they live. In light of that reality, what contributions can be expected from the Christian citizen in America when we go through difficult times? What could be expected in an economic crisis from a society that accepts such a life philosophy? Resilience is the word that comes to mind; hope, most assuredly, generosity, and good productive works. A common mistake of those looking at this from the outside is to think that there should be no desire for the Christian citizen to work hard, since "God will provide for us." But that simplistic look at the works of God will always fall short of His glory. We are called to excellence. The Christian citizen must labor hard, for we labor ultimately for God. "[W]hatever you do, do all to the glory of God," 1 Corinthians 10:31 tells us.

Some erroneously think of this way of life as diminished living but, on the contrary, it is joyful living. It is fulfilled living. It is not distorting reality, but seeing true reality. It is a matter of value placement or value judgment; holding as most valuable, that which truly is most valuable: God himself. It is seeing with spiritual eyes. The famous atheist-turn-believer C.S. Lewis (1898-1963) shared a similar sentiment when he said, "I believe in Christianity as I believe that the Sun has risen: not only because I see it, but because by it I see everything else."[45] The Christian worldview helps you see clearer, to establish proper priorities in your life. This spiritual awakening happens only through what Paul calls the renewing of the mind. "[D]o not be conformed to this world, but be transformed by the renewing of your mind, that you may prove what is that good and acceptable and perfect will of God," (Romans 12:2, NKJV). Through this mind renewal we are able to give proper value to everything around us; both the material and the spiritual. This is immensely helpful when dealing with the excesses of capitalism and the free enterprise system we have in America.

The financial crisis of 2008 is a good example. It was predicated in no small measure on a few elites (in the corporate world and government) who abused the system for personal gain. The love of money and dishonesty were the problem. How can we fight that? How can we fight dishonesty? With government regulations? Hardly. Or is the government immune to dishonesty? The problems our society faces stem from something much deeper than mere politics or economics. Therefore, it takes much more than economic or political ideas to deal with these issues. It takes a vision as that of our Founding Fathers whose reliance on Providence proved so profitable. It takes a vision as that of John Adams who wrote to the officers of the First Brigade of the Third Division of the Militia of Massachusetts in October 11, 1798:

> Gentleman,
>
> While our country remains untainted with the principles and manners which are now producing desolation in so many parts of the world; while she continues sincere, and incapable of insidious and impious policy, we shall have the strongest reason to rejoice in the local destina-

---

45   C.S. Lewis, *Weight of Glory* 14 (Harper Collins 2001).

tion assigned us by Providence. But should the people of America once become capable of that deep simulation towards one another, and towards foreign nations, which assumes the language of justice and moderation while it is practicing [sic] iniquity and extravagance… this country will be the most miserable habitation in the Nvorld [sic]; because we have no government armed with power capable of contending with human passions unbridled by morality and religion. Avarice, ambition, revenge, or gallantry, would break the strongest cords of our Constitution as a whale goes through a net. Our Constitution was made only for a moral and religious people. It is wholly inadequate to the government of any other.[46]

Why is morality and religion so important in Adams' mind? He knows something that not many realize. That true freedom actually comes from restraint, not political or military prowess. In our example of the economic crisis, the Christian citizen knows he must guard against the love of money. The warning of 1Timothy 6:9-10 serves as an ever-present caution:

[T]hose who desire to be rich fall into temptation and a snare, and into many foolish and harmful lusts which drown men in destruction and perdition. For the love of money is a root of all kinds of evil for which some have strayed from the faith in their greediness, and pierced themselves through with many sorrows (NKJV).

We must guard against such evil. Notice, much of this mind renewal relates to the way we look at ourselves. To know that we are prideful and overly ambitious, that we lie and cheat to get our way. Therefore our laws should deal with man as he is and not as we wished he would be. We must reject utopian ideas that seek to establish a "heaven on earth." Those are mere fantasies that, whether by deception or ignorance, only worsen man's condition by shackling his feet and longings on a lie. A more robust discussion of this topic will be dealt with in chapter six.

---

46   John Adams, *The Works of John Adams, Second President of the United States: with a Life of the Author, Notes and Illustrations* Vol. 9. of 10 (Charles Francis Adams ed., Little, Brown and Co. 1856), available at http://oll.libertyfund.org/titles/2107#lf1431-09_head_222 (accessed Sept. 8, 2014).

An impossible standard

"Kingdom Focus" requires a revolutionary view of money, as with many other issues. Listen to Proverbs 23:4-5: "Do not overwork to be rich; because of your own understanding, cease! Will you set your eyes on that which is not? For riches certainly make themselves wings; they fly away like an eagle toward heaven" (NKJV). Material things are part of that which is not, spiritual matters are truly important and will be with us forever. "[W]hat does it profit a man to gain the whole world and forfeit his soul?" asked Jesus, (Mark 8:36). He also warned us against covetousness in our hearts:

> "Take care, and be on your guard against all covetousness, for one's life does not consist in the abundance of his possessions." And he told them a parable, saying, "The land of a rich man produced plentifully, and he thought to himself, 'What shall I do, for I have nowhere to store my crops?' And he said, 'I will do this: I will tear down my barns and build larger ones, and there I will store all my grain and my goods. And I will say to my soul, "Soul, you have ample goods laid up for many years; relax, eat, drink, be merry."' But God said to him, 'Fool! This night your soul is required of you, and the things you have prepared, whose will they be?' So is the one who lays up treasure for himself and is not rich toward God" (Luke 12:15-21).

Jesus admonished us to seek ruthlessly after heavenly blessings in "The Parable of the Dishonest Manager:"

> "There was a rich man who had a manager, and charges were brought to him that this man was wasting his possessions. And he called him and said to him, 'What is this that I hear about you? Turn in the account of your management, for you can no longer be manager.' And the manager said to himself, 'What shall I do, since my master is taking the management away from me? I am not strong

enough to dig, and I am ashamed to beg. I have decided what to do, so that when I am removed from management, people may receive me into their houses.' So, summoning his master's debtors one by one, he said to the first, 'How much do you owe my master?' He said, 'A hundred measures of oil.' He said to him, 'Take your bill, and sit down quickly and write fifty.' Then he said to another, 'And how much do you owe?' He said, 'A hundred measures of wheat.' He said to him, 'Take your bill, and write eighty.' The master commended the dishonest manager for his shrewdness. For the sons of this world are more shrewd in dealing with their own generation than the sons of light. And I tell you, make friends for yourselves by means of unrighteous wealth, so that when it fails they may receive you into the eternal dwellings.

"One who is faithful in a very little is also faithful in much, and one who is dishonest in a very little is also dishonest in much. If then you have not been faithful in the unrighteous wealth, who will entrust to you the true riches? And if you have not been faithful in that which is another's, who will give you that which is your own? No servant can serve two masters, for either he will hate the one and love the other, or he will be devoted to the one and despise the other. You cannot serve God and money (Luke 16:1-13).

The Christian citizen lives by a higher standard than that of the world. A Christian worker cannot take advantage of his boss' shortcomings. Colossians 3:23 tells us "Whatever you do, work heartily, as for the Lord and not for men, knowing that from the Lord you will receive the inheritance as your reward. You are serving the Lord Christ." Therefore, our "Boss," who sees everything will hold us accountable to that standard, regardless of what we can "get away with" here on earth. If a Christian is able to steal form his company "without anyone finding out," he still knows that he will give an account for his actions before a Holy God and that is a great incentive to resist what might be his natural impulse to take advantage of any particular situation. These ideals, serve a great practical purpose for society. They alone can serve as the foundation for justice and freedom.

The French Historian Alexis de Tocqueville (1805-1859), who came to America to study its extraordinary freedom and success, noticed the practical application of this worldview on his visit to America:

> While I was in America, a witness called at assizes of the county of Chester (state of New York) declared that he did not believe in the existence of God and the immortality of the soul. The judge refused to allow him to be sworn in, on the ground that the witness had destroyed beforehand all possible confidence in his testimony. Newspapers reported the fact without comment.[47]

It makes perfect sense, doesn't it? The person who believes he will ultimately give an account before Almighty God for his testimony will naturally be more likely to resist the temptation to alter his testimony for personal gain. Christian citizens are called to be peacemakers,[48] to love their neighbors,[49] to love even our enemies and pray for those who wish to harm us,[50] to be charitable,[51] and productive.[52] These are all good, practical principles that only benefit our society and bring the blessings of God to our nation.

De Tocqueville again on the American spirit to strive for this ideal and

---

47   Alexis de Tocqueville, *Democracy in America* 343 (Penguin Classics 2003 (1835–1840)).

48   "Blessed are the peacemakers, for they shall be called sons of God," (Matthew 5:9).

49   "You shall love your neighbor as yourself," (Mark 12:31); see also 1 John 4:21, "And this commandment we have from him: whoever loves God must also love his brother."

50   "You have heard that it was said, 'You shall love your neighbor and hate your enemy.' But I say to you, Love your enemies and pray for those who persecute you... For if you love those who love you, what reward do you have?" (Matthew 5:43-46).

51   "And if anyone would sue you and take your tunic, let him have your cloak as well. And if anyone forces you to go one mile, go with him two miles. Give to the one who begs from you, and do not refuse the one who would borrow from you," (Matthew 5:40-42).

52   "In all things I have shown you that by working hard in this way we must help the weak and remember the words of the Lord Jesus, how he himself said, 'It is more blessed to give than to receive,'" (Acts 20:35).

its unbreakable link to freedom:

> Thus whilst the law permits the Americans to do what they please, religion prevents them from conceiving, and forbids them to commit, what is rash or unjust.
>
> Religion in America takes no direct part in the government of society, but it must nevertheless be regarded as the foremost of the political institutions of that country; for if it does not impart a taste for freedom, it facilitates the use of free institutions. Indeed, it is in this same point of view that the inhabitants of the United States themselves look upon religious belief. I do not know whether all the Americans have a sincere faith in their religion, for who can search the human heart? but I am certain that they hold it to be indispensable to the maintenance of republican institutions. This opinion is not peculiar to a class of citizens or to a party, but it belongs to the whole nation, and to every rank of society.[53]

DeTocqueville is spot on. If you would like to enjoy the blessings of an apple, you need an apple tree. The bond between freedom and religion is unmistakable. We simply cannot separate the blessings of liberty and freedom apart from religion. For true religion is the pursuit of the true God, the pursuit of Truth. And knowing Truth is what sets us free.[54] Freedom's survival in America, therefore, will go hand in hand with the relative health of religion (of the church, the body of Christ). The greatness of America is not its own, but God's. Those who seek for freedom apart from God will only to discover despair and oppression, the inevitable fruits of rejecting Truth; of rejecting God.

---

53   Alexis de Tocqueville, *Democracy in America* 333-34 (Henry Reeve, Esq. trans., Edward Walker 1847).

54   John 8:32.

CHAPTER THREE
PRELIMINARY OBJECTIONS

Before we delve any deeper, let us deal with some common objections I receive when approaching freedom in American in this way. Getting these out of the way will give us a better understanding of our purpose and aim in talking in these terms and it will also help us focus on real issues rather than chasing after the wind, so to speak.

Providence or coincidence?

Some may be skeptical of stories attributing God's hand to weather events and other Providential accounts. Does God really work in this way? Or are we just attributing simple coincidences to God? Here is what God Himself told Job when he finally responded to the crushed man's plea for an explanation of his bad fortune: "Have you entered the storehouses of the snow, or have you seen the storehouses of the hail, which I have reserved for the time of trouble, for the day of battle and war?" (Job 38:22-23). At first glance the passage does not make much sense. But when you direct your attention to our experiences here on earth in our relationship with God (when you read Washington's accounts, for example) we know exactly what God means, even though we can't fully comprehend His ways. That is God telling us He indeed works in the way Washington experienced. He has and does use weather to direct the course of history. The Bible is full of those accounts, further confirming the principle for us. The most obvious example is Genesis' account of the Great Flood. God told Noah:

> I have determined to make an end of all flesh, for the earth is filled with violence through them. Behold, I will destroy them with the earth... For behold, I will bring a flood of waters upon the earth to destroy all flesh in which is the breath of life under heaven. Everything that is on the earth shall die (Genesis 6:13, 17).

And He did, sparing only two of each kind of animal, and Noah and his family, with whom He had established His covenant.[55] Therefore, David declared in psalm, "The LORD sat enthroned at the Flood, And the LORD sits as King forever," (Psalm 29:10, NKJV). David's son King Solomon, of whom God said there would be none wiser, asked rhetorically in proverb: "Who has ascended to heaven and come down? Who has gathered the wind in his fists? Who has wrapped up the waters in a garment? Who has established all the ends of the earth? What is his name, and what is his son's name? Surely you know!" (Proverbs 30:4).

God used weather in Exodus to help Moses bring God's people out of captivity. Remember the plagues? Here is how the eight plague, the locusts, came: "So Moses stretched out his staff over the land of Egypt, and the LORD brought an east wind upon the land all that day and all that night. When it was morning, the east wind had brought the locusts," (Exodus 10:13). He would later take the locust away in the same manner, "And the LORD turned the wind into a very strong west wind, which lifted the locusts and drove them into the Red Sea. Not a single locust was left in all the country of Egypt," (Exodus 10:19). In Leviticus, He promised, "If you walk in My statutes and keep My commandments, and perform them, then I will give you rain in its season, the land shall yield its produce, and the trees of the field shall yield their fruit," (Leviticus 26:3-4, NKJV). Jonah tried to run from the presence of the Lord on a ship, "But the LORD hurled a great wind upon the sea, and there was a mighty tempest on the sea, so that the ship threatened to break up," (Jonah 1:4). Samuel discovered God's power in nature also, saying:

---

55   Noah's story can be found in Genesis chapters 6-10.

'I will call upon the LORD, that he may send thunder and rain. And you shall know and see that your wickedness is great, which you have done in the sight of the LORD, in asking for yourselves a king.' So Samuel called upon the LORD, and the LORD sent thunder and rain that day, and all the people greatly feared the LORD and Samuel (1 Samuel 12:17-18).

Those are just a few of the many accounts we find in Scripture. The Biblical evidence is simply overwhelming. Remember Jesus calming the storm?[56]

And lest some object that these accounts had nothing to do with war, as in the examples of the Founders, let's recount the story of Joshua. After Moses died, God called Joshua to lead the people into the Promised Land. God promised He would be with Joshua as He was with Moses.[57] The land God was giving them was not uninhabited. Joshua would have to take it by facing the Canaanites, Hittites, Hivites, Perizzites, Girgashites, Amorites and Jebusites.[58] The first miracle God did had to do with nature, though not weather specifically. To show the people that He was with Joshua as He was with Moses, God opens the Jordan for the Israelites[59] as He did with Moses on the Red Sea.[60] One cannot help but acknowledge the similarities with Washington's crossings. Here is the account starting with Joshua's instructions:

"Now therefore take twelve men from the tribes of Israel, from each tribe a man. And when the soles of the feet of the priests bearing the ark of the LORD, the Lord of all the earth, shall rest in the waters of the Jordan, the waters of

---

56   "And when he got into the boat, his disciples followed him. And behold, there arose a great storm on the sea, so that the boat was being swamped by the waves; but he was asleep. And they went and woke him, saying, "Save us, Lord; we are perishing." And he said to them, "Why are you afraid, O you of little faith?" Then he rose and rebuked the winds and the sea, and there was a great calm. And the men marveled, saying, "What sort of man is this, that even winds and sea obey him?" (Matthew 8:23-27) (*See also,* Mark 4:35-41).

57   Joshua 1:5.

58   *Id.* at 3:10.

59   *Id.* at 3:17.

60   Exodus 14.

the Jordan shall be cut off from flowing, and the waters coming down from above shall stand in one heap."

So when the people set out from their tents to pass over the Jordan with the priests bearing the ark of the covenant before the people, and as soon as those bearing the ark had come as far as the Jordan, and the feet of the priests bearing the ark were dipped in the brink of the water (now the Jordan overflows all its banks throughout the time of harvest), the waters coming down from above stood and rose up in a heap very far away, at Adam, the city that is beside Zarethan, and those flowing down toward the Sea of the Arabah, the Salt Sea, were completely cut off. And the people passed over opposite Jericho. Now the priests bearing the ark of the covenant of the LORD stood firmly on dry ground in the midst of the Jordan, and all Israel was passing over on dry ground until all the nation finished passing over the Jordan (Joshua 3:12-17).

Then our all-loving, merciful God, who knows us better than anyone else, told Joshua to ask twelve men from every tribe to gather a stone from the river:

[T]hat this may be a sign among you. When your children ask in time to come, 'What do those stones mean to you?' then you shall tell them that the waters of the Jordan were cut off before the ark of the covenant of the LORD. When it passed over the Jordan, the waters of the Jordan were cut off. So these stones shall be to the people of Israel a memorial forever (Joshua 4:6-7).

God knew the Israelites would soon forget the miracle He had just performed before their eyes, just as they had forgotten the many before it. No surprise this is exactly what we have experienced in our own country's history. We have forgotten the many miracles we experienced as a country and a people.

But back to Joshua's story. News of what the Lord had done at the Jordan spread throughout the region and everyone became afraid of the

Lord and Joshua, His servant. Israel encamped at Gilgal, at the foot of Jericho, with its mighty walls protecting the city. No way they could penetrate the city and remain alive. But the Lord delivered Jericho into Israel's hand, bringing down the walls simply by their obedience. He told them to march around the city once a day for six days and seven times on the seventh day. As they marched for the seventh time, on the seventh day, "the wall fell down flat, so that the people went up into the city, every man straight before him, and they captured the city," (Joshua 6:20). Joshua took Jericho and then he took the city of Ai. Afraid of Israel's growing power, the Hittites, Amorites, Canaanites, Perizzites, Hivites, and Jebusites all "gathered together as one to fight against Joshua and Israel," (Joshua 9:2). But when the people of Gibeon heard of Joshua's victories they struck a peace treaty with Israel. This brought panic among their enemies because Gibeon was a mighty city. Therefore, they sent out for reinforcements to attack Gibeon. Joshua came from Gilgal to help defend Gibeon and the Lord delivered all those mighty armies into His hand. How? With some extremely opportune whether:

> And as they fled before Israel, while they were going down the ascent of Beth-horon, the LORD threw down large stones from heaven on them as far as Azekah, and they died. There were more who died because of the hailstones than the sons of Israel killed with the sword (Joshua 10:11).

Think about that. Yes, the people fought in the battle, but more of them died by the hailstones than by all their efforts. The hand of Providence intervened then as it did at our country's founding and as it does today. The prophet Daniel certainly understood God's involvement in the affairs of men, "[T]he Most High rules the kingdom of men and gives it to whom he will and sets over it the lowliest of men," (Daniel 4:17). "He changes times and seasons; he removes kings and sets up kings; he gives wisdom to the wise and knowledge to those who have understanding," (Daniel 2:21).

God rules above all. The evidence is hard to refute. Consider Proverbs 21:1, "The king's heart is in the hand of the Lord, like the rivers of water; He turns it wherever He wishes," (NKJV). The real problem we have is one of unbelief. We simply do not truly believe what we read in

Scripture. We do not believe God. That's the real problem. We fail to see His hand in our everyday life, even as we convince ourselves that we trust Him and believe that He did act in that way in the days of old. We say we believe God helped David defeat Goliath, but we don't believe He can help us defeat our own giants. We say we believe Jesus healed the sick but we are not sure He can do that in our case today. This, despite when He does heal many of our friends and family right in front of our eyes. We say advances in medicine did it. A person is diagnosed with cancer, he or she is put in prayer at their local church, goes for further testing and the doctors can't find any trace of the cancer (something I've experience several times in my life), but we do not attribute that to the work of God. Sure, we might give thanks to God in a general way, but we don't testify of Him and give Him glory for His many miracles. Not really. That is a big deal. It reveals the true condition of our hearts and our lack of faith. Are not all things possible with God?[61]

I am always amazed at the vast oceans of unbelief we navigate in our lifetime. I tend to think generally that it has always been that way, for we live in a broken down, fallen world. Yet it is also true that there are certain periods throughout history where we see in the Bible that people strayed so far, God had to intervene in drastic measure. When we compare our culture's level of skepticism to that of those periods in the Old Testament, even among those who profess to believe in God, it is scary to think about. We seem to be completely blind to His majesty. Worse, we live with our eyes closed, willingly. We refuse to acknowledge the evidence before us. Remember the story of Daniel in the lion's den? King Darius was conned into sending Daniel, whom he admired greatly, to be put to death in the lion's den. The king tried to find a way to spare Daniel through the law, but having found none, he gives the order. Let's read carefully:

> Then the king commanded, and Daniel was brought and
> cast into the den of lions. The king declared to Daniel,
> "May your God, whom you serve continually, deliver
> you!" And a stone was brought and laid on the mouth
> of the den, and the king sealed it with his own signet
> and with the signet of his lords, that nothing might be

---

61   "But Jesus looked at them and said, 'With man this is impossible, but with God all things are possible,'" (Matthew 19:26).

changed concerning Daniel (Daniel 6:16-17).

Isn't it amazing? It is King Darius, who does not serve the Lord, who tells Daniel that God will deliver him. Notice, he says, "your God," not "our God." How can that be? How can this king believe Daniel's God can save Daniel if he doesn't truly believe and serve that God? Well, the king has seen the Lord at work in Daniel's life. The evidence is there, he can't refute it. He had seen first-hand the evidence of God's power in Daniel's life and it was undeniable. So the king throws Daniel into the lion's den and goes to his palace where he is unable to sleep all night, overwhelmed with guilt. In the morning, he goes to the lion's den and, here is what happened:

> "O Daniel, servant of the living God, has your God, whom you serve continually, been able to deliver you from the lions?" Then Daniel said to the king, "O king, live forever! My God sent his angel and shut the lions' mouths, and they have not harmed me, because I was found blameless before him; and also before you, O king, I have done no harm" (Daniel 6:20-22).

I want us to see this clearly. God had preserved Daniel from the lions, as the king had predicted, and the king's reaction is a most reasonable one:

> Then King Darius wrote to all the peoples, nations, and languages that dwell in all the earth: "Peace be multiplied to you. I make a decree, that in all my royal dominion people are to tremble and fear before the God of Daniel, for he is the living God, enduring forever; his kingdom shall never be destroyed, and his dominion shall be to the end. He delivers and rescues; he works signs and wonders in heaven and on earth, he who has saved Daniel from the power of the lions" (Daniel 6:25-27).

In other words the king says, "I have seen that Daniel's God is real. The evidence cannot be refuted." That almost never happens in today's day and age. Today's culture rejects Daniel's testimony. Something else must have happened. Part of King Darius' recognition prior to seeing Daniel delivered from the lion's den might have come from seeing and/or hearing about the Lord's deliverance of Daniel's friends, Shadrach, Meshach, and Abednego, from the fiery furnace in Daniel 3. After throwing Shadrach, Meshach, and Abednego into the fire for refusing to bow down to King Nebuchadnezzar's image of gold, the king was surprised to see that they were not consumed by the fire but saw a fourth "person," an angel of God, preserving them. His reaction was similar to that of King Darius:'

> Nebuchadnezzar answered and said, "Blessed be the God of Shadrach, Meshach, and Abednego, who has sent his angel and delivered his servants, who trusted in him, and set aside the king's command, and yielded up their bodies rather than serve and worship any god except their own God. Therefore I make a decree: Any people, nation, or language that speaks anything against the God of Shadrach, Meshach, and Abednego shall be torn limb from limb, and their houses laid in ruins, for there is no other god who is able to rescue in this way" (Daniel 3:28-29).

This sort of honesty is unheard of in our days. Today's skeptic stands before a clear blue sky and says, "Who can define what the color blue is, ultimately? Your blue is not my blue. And who are you to define what color the sky is for the rest of us? Stop imposing your views on everyone else." What we have lost is that honest, sincere approach to finding truth. That is to say, today's skeptic will not see the evidence and take it as it is. They will deny reality and create a fantasy to fit the wants of their hearts. If Daniel is spared from the lion's today, the world would say there must have been some "logical" explanation and would dismiss outright any divine intervention. They would dismiss the testimony of the only one who was there in the lion's den when the angel appeared. The fourth person in the fiery furnace must have been just a shape from the flames. The assumption is that there is no god. There are no angels. Therefore reality must adapt to those assumptions. No question our blindness is much worse today. We choose not to see. Or choose to see what we want to, regardless of the evidence before us. The modern secularist boasts of open-mindedness and objectivity, while rejecting God outright, as deserving no consideration whatsoever.

It is not that there is no evidence of Providence, but that its very consideration is rejected from the outset and therefore another explanation must exist. We are not satisfied with God, even when it is hard work to deny His hand in our lives. C.S. Lewis said that he had to work extremely hard in order to remain an atheist. He wrote, "When I was an atheist I had to try to persuade myself that most of the human race have always been wrong about the question that mattered to them most... "[62] So sure, if you are committed to unbelief, then perhaps you can continue to deny the evidences of God and the testimony of millions. You can choose to believe they are just not as smart as you. But to boast of openness is a fallacy. If one dares not consider God, any number of absurd explanations will suffice. Say, aliens directing our weather from another planet. Professor Richard Dawkins, one of the most forceful atheists of our time (author of *The God Delusion*) famously told the *New York Times*, "Certainly. It's highly plausible that in the universe there are God-like creatures. It's very important to understand that these Gods came into being by an explicable scientific progression of incremental evolution."[63] In the movie "Expelled" by Ben Stein, Dawkins offered a similar idea for the beginning of our universe:

> It could be that at some earlier time, somewhere in the universe, a civilization evolved, probably by some kind of Darwinian means, probably to a very high level of technology, and designed a form of life that they seeded onto perhaps this planet. Um, now that is a possibility, and an intriguing possibility. And I suppose it's possible that you might find evidence for that if you look at the details of biochemistry, molecular biology, you might find a signature of some sort of designer.[64]

The modern skeptic is actually willing to consider some alien form in order to explain the evidence pointing to God, yet it will never consider the idea of God. It will consider god-like creatures, but not a god-like god. But, if one dares consider God, one would find the evidence very

---

62   C.S. Lewis, *Mere Christianity* 35 (Harper 2009 (1952)).

63   Michael Powell, *A Knack for Bashing Orthodoxy*, N.Y. Times September 20, 2011, D1.

64   Expelled: No Intelligence Allowed (Premise Media Corporation, Rampant Films 2008).

clearly points, not only to His existence, but to His involvement and concern for His creation. That is what Benjamin Franklin (1706-1790) referred to when he said at the constitutional convention in 1787:

> I have lived, Sir, a long time, and the longer I live, the more convincing proofs I see of this truth- that God Governs in the affairs of men. And if a sparrow cannot fall to the ground without his notice, is it probable that an empire can rise without his aid? We have been assured, Sir, in the sacred writings, that "except the Lord build the House they labour in vain that build it." I firmly believe this; and I also believe that without his concurring aid we shall succeed in this political building no better than the Builders of Babel.[65]

You have your truth, I have mine

Let us dispel also with the nonsense that truth can never be ascertained. St. Augustine suffered from this, what he called, "illusion." He said, "My rashness and impiety lay in the fact that what I ought to have verified by investigation I had simply asserted as an accusation."[66] G.K. Chesterton (1874-1936) discovered the same thing. He said, "The Christian ideal has not been tried and found wanting. It has been found difficult and left untried."[67] Most people who reject the Biblical principle today do so out of some sort of "indignation" at Scripture's revolutionary, exclusive claims, plain disinformation or ignorance of the principles in the first place. I have yet to meet a consistent skeptic. Most simply do not like God, especially the God of the Bible. But they have yet to confront the possibility that He is real. They have questions, but as Augustine, they have not answered them, they just state them as accusations. Perhaps the most well-known example of this was Pontius Pilate. Remember his reaction to the claims of Jesus as he questioned "the King of the Jews"? Here is the scene. Jesus had been making the most outrageous claims. He claimed to be the Son of the Living God. Listen to this account from

---

65   Benjamin Franklin, *The Constitutional Convention of 1787: A Comprehensive Encyclopedia of America's Founding,* Vol. I 593 (John R. Vile ed. ABC-CLIO, 2005).

66   Saint Augustine, Confessions 93 (Henry Chadwick trans., Oxford University Press 2009).

67   G. K. Chesterton, *What's Wrong With The World* 39 (Forgotten Books 2010) (1910).

the Gospel according to John, starting with the words of Jesus:

"My Father is working until now, and I am working."

This was why the Jews were seeking all the more to kill him, because not only was he breaking the Sabbath, but he was even calling God his own Father, making himself equal with God.

So Jesus said to them, "Truly, truly, I say to you, the Son can do nothing of his own accord, but only what he sees the Father doing. For whatever the Father does, that the Son does likewise. For the Father loves the Son and shows him all that he himself is doing. And greater works than these will he show him, so that you may marvel. For as the Father raises the dead and gives them life, so also the Son gives life to whom he will. The Father judges no one, but has given all judgment to the Son, that all may honor the Son, just as they honor the Father. Whoever does not honor the Son does not honor the Father who sent him. Truly, truly, I say to you, whoever hears my word and believes him who sent me has eternal life. He does not come into judgment, but has passed from death to life.

"Truly, truly, I say to you, an hour is coming, and is now here, when the dead will hear the voice of the Son of God, and those who hear will live. For as the Father has life in himself, so he has granted the Son also to have life in himself. And he has given him authority to execute judgment, because he is the Son of Man. Do not marvel at this, for an hour is coming when all who are in the tombs will hear his voice and come out, those who have done good to the resurrection of life, and those who have done evil to the resurrection of judgment.

"I can do nothing on my own. As I hear, I judge, and my judgment is just, because I seek not my own will but the will of him who sent me (John 5:17-30).

Everyone knew what Jesus meant and that's why they wanted to kill

Him. He claimed to be God. Here is another passage:

> "Let not your hearts be troubled. Believe in God; believe also in me. In my Father's house are many rooms. If it were not so, would I have told you that I go to prepare a place for you? And if I go and prepare a place for you, I will come again and will take you to myself, that where I am you may be also. And you know the way to where I am going." Thomas said to him, "Lord, we do not know where you are going. How can we know the way?" Jesus said to him, "I am the way, and the truth, and the life. No one comes to the Father except through me. If you had known me, you would have known my Father also. From now on you do know him and have seen him."

> Philip said to him, "Lord, show us the Father, and it is enough for us." Jesus said to him, "Have I been with you so long, and you still do not know me, Philip? Whoever has seen me has seen the Father. How can you say, 'Show us the Father'? Do you not believe that I am in the Father and the Father is in me? The words that I say to you I do not speak on my own authority, but the Father who dwells in me does his works. Believe me that I am in the Father and the Father is in me, or else believe on account of the works themselves.

> "Truly, truly, I say to you, whoever believes in me will also do the works that I do; and greater works than these will he do, because I am going to the Father. Whatever you ask in my name, this I will do, that the Father may be glorified in the Son. If you ask me anything in my name, I will do it.

> "If you love me, you will keep my commandments. And I will ask the Father, and he will give you another Helper, to be with you forever, even the Spirit of truth, whom the world cannot receive, because it neither sees him nor knows him. You know him, for he dwells with you and will be in you.

> "I will not leave you as orphans; I will come to you. Yet a little while and the world will see me no more, but you will see me. Because I live, you also will live. In that day you will know that I am in my Father, and you in me, and I in you. Whoever has my commandments and keeps them, he it is who loves me. And he who loves me will be loved by my Father, and I will love him and manifest myself to him" (John 14:1-21).

The claims were incredible, yet the works that He performed, the many miracles and the lives transformed, were undeniable. They did not know what to do with Him. He was arrested and taken to Annas, the former High Priest, first. Annas then sent him to Caiaphas, the then current high priest. And then they sent Him to Pilate who really wanted no part of it either. But after the religious leaders insisted on his demise, Pilate went to talk to Jesus. Here is the amazing interaction as described by the Gospel of John:

> So Pilate entered his headquarters again and called Jesus and said to him, "Are you the King of the Jews?" Jesus answered, "Do you say this of your own accord, or did others say it to you about me?" Pilate answered, "Am I a Jew? Your own nation and the chief priests have delivered you over to me. What have you done?" Jesus answered, "My kingdom is not of this world. If my kingdom were of this world, my servants would have been fighting, that I might not be delivered over to the Jews. But my kingdom is not from the world." Then Pilate said to him, "So you are a king?" Jesus answered, "You say that I am a king. For this purpose I was born and for this purpose I have come into the world—to bear witness to the truth. Everyone who is of the truth listens to my voice." Pilate said to him, "What is truth?" (John 18:33-38).

An amazing turn of events, isn't it? Pilate stands before Truth itself and yet fails to pursue the answer to his own question. That's because, as the skeptic today, he was making an argument, not really asking the question seeking an honest answer. He assumes no answer exists. He finds no fault in Jesus, yet he fails to pursue whether His claims are true.

What is this kingdom Jesus speaks about? Scripture tells us that if Pilate would have sought the answer he would have found it. Jesus said:

> [A]sk, and it will be given to you; seek, and you will find; knock, and it will be opened to you. For everyone who asks receives, and the one who seeks finds, and to the one who knocks it will be opened (Luke 11:9-10).

This is true for us today. If we seek after truth, we shall find truth. It is when we assume that truth is unattainable and proclaim God simply cannot "be" that we fall into a self-imposed blindness. Just as Pilate turned around and left without an answer, many today turn their back on the mere quest for truth as they are faced with the claims of the Christian faith. They cannot explain the millions of changed lives, so they turn their backs and reject all of it outright. They refuse the invitation of the psalmist to come "taste and see that the LORD is good!" (Psalm 34:8). They refuse to taste, yet they feel perfectly comfortable to talk about how sweet or sour it is. Even those who talk about their sour experiences, usually refer to a bad experience with a church or religious group, which is by no means the same as an experience with Christ Himself. We must experience and base our investigation of truth on a relationship with Truth; an experience with the God of the people and not merely the people of God. For we know that all men are broken, imperfect beings, all in desperate need of salvation and intervention by that loving, merciful God of the universe. We all fail. We are all frail. And any reliance on men will inevitably end in disappointment.

This reality is in perfect harmony with Biblical teaching. The failures of men only prove the claims of Scripture. They prove that truth can be found within the Bible's pages. May your eyes be open to witness that truth in the person of Jesus Christ. If you don't know where to start, I suggest you start with the Gospels, perhaps with the *Gospel of John*, where we have been reading. And leave all pre-conceptions behind, even those you would consider "good" ones. Let the words on the page speak for themselves and allow Christ to reveal Who He is. Taste and see. But don't reject Him beforehand. If you do, then truth will always remain an elusive abstract concept that can never be attained, even as your whole self, your spirit, your conscience testifies to you from within that there is more to life than the meaningless, empty pursuit of worldly pleasures.

You just want to impose your beliefs on everyone else

The short, simple answer to this objection is, "no." First of all, no man can be forced to believe in Christ by another man. Salvation by compulsion is no salvation at all. If you believe in Christ because the government and society will punish you if you don't, you are not really believing in Christ for who He is, and hailing Him as Lord. Still, wouldn't it be better if we imposed what we know to be good on all people? Well, no. There is only one righteous king: Jesus. This was the folly of the people of Israel when they insisted on a king. We are not about establishing a theocracy, as some critics would charge, for it solves nothing. Contrary to popular belief, it will not make things better for Christians, as we have already established. Our kingdom is not of this world. Every attempt, therefore at establishing such a kingdom on earth is bound to fail. Sure, we argue the principles of Heaven, God's principles, Biblical principles, are better than any other for all people, not just Christians. But the caricature the modern secularist draws of the Christian "zealots" imposing their views is just that, a caricature, and not the least bit real. The Christian citizen is not interested in forcing anyone to believe. Persuade? Yes. That is different. We believe Scripture is true and good. Its principles are eternal and bring blessings to those who heed its commands. Forcing people, however, would in itself require a violation of the very principles we want to promote, bringing ourselves into judgment.

There is no fooling God in this regard. The story of David being chosen king can help us on this topic. The Bible tells us Saul, who was king at the time, was rejecting the Word of the Lord and Samuel the prophet is deeply distressed when God tells him, "How long will you grieve over Saul, since I have rejected him from being king over Israel? Fill your horn with oil, and go. I will send you to Jesse the Bethlehemite, for I have provided for myself a king among his sons," (1 Samuel 16:1). Samuel goes to the house of Jesse and when he comes in he sees Eliab who was a very impressive young man. Samuel thought:

> "Surely the Lord's anointed is before him." But the Lord said to Samuel, "Do not look on his appearance or on the height of his stature, because I have rejected him. For the Lord sees not as man sees: man looks on the outward

appearance, but the LORD looks on the heart" (1 Samuel 16:6-7).

There is the principle. God looks at the heart. He sees and knows our hearts. How beautiful and scary is that? Therefore, the Love of Christ cannot be imposed on the human heart; it must be born. We can fool men and women, as Samuel would have been fooled if he followed his own instincts, but God sees through appearances. On the one hand, we long for this same use of judgment. Remember the revered words of the Rev. Martin Luther King, Jr. (1929-1968)? He said, "I have a dream that my four little children will one day live in a nation where they will not be judged by the color of their skin but by the content of their character."[68] These are words that we celebrate with immense pride, yet we fail miserably to live up to its calling. Even beyond the color of our skin, we look down on those who are disabled or overweight or don't have enough money for the latest fashions. Not so with God. There is simply no use on imposing my values on you, as they say. God will see right through that.

What we do seek is to persuade others that God's values are true and good. For, of that, there is no doubt. God's ways are real and best for all, the Christian and the non-Christian alike. We are confident that our experiences and all scientific evidence will always affirm that universal truth that God's ways are above any other. Therefore, we welcome policy debates and the respectful exchange of ideas. We are confident that truth will always be exposed whether immediately or in the long run. And, let me stress, that I am talking about a true exchange of ideas. We want to consider other people's views. We approach the Word of God and His principles with extreme humility, knowing that we do not know it all and still have much to discover. We are not always right on everything. God tells us in Isaiah 55:8, "For my thoughts are not your thoughts, neither are your ways my ways, declares the LORD." So we know that God's ways are even higher than we can attain. But we seek to discover them. The modern secularist has abandoned that pursuit, even when the Bible tells us that God will reveal His ways to us. Listen to the words of Jesus: "No longer do I call you servants, for the servant does not know what his master is doing; but I have called you friends, for all that I have heard

---

68   Martin Luther King, Jr., *I Have a Dream* speech, March on Washington, DC, August 28, 1963.

from my Father I have made known to you," (John 15:15).

The search for that truth is part of that "pursuit of happiness" mentioned in our Declaration of Independence.[69] I conducted an informal study of the word "happiness" going as far back as the early 1700s and a curious shift is seen in the definitions. Happiness was usually tied to "blessedness." In 1725, for example, Nathan Bailey's *An Universal Etymological Dictionary* did not have a definition of "happiness," but defined "happy" as, "Prosperous, felicitous, blessedness."[70] In 1755, "Happiness is defined as "felicity, blessedness."[71] This concept of "blessedness" remains associated with happiness for some time, but then an interesting change is easily seen in the late 1700s, early 1800s. The idea of "luck" starts to creep in to replace "blessedness." I found it first in Francis Allen's *A Complete English Dictionary* (1765), which defined "happiness" as "a state wherein a person is happy; good luck or fortune."[72] Thomas Sheridan's *A Complete Dictionary of the English Language* in 1789 has, "Felicity, state in which the desires are satisfied; good luck, good fortune."[73] To stress the transition, in 1806, William Perry's *The Royal Standard English Dictionary* defines "happiness" as both "good-luck, blessedness."[74] You see "blessedness" used a few times after that, but we clearly moved past that vision for the most part. Today, the *Merriam-Webster* dictionary defines happiness as "the state of being happy," and happy as "feeling pleasure and enjoyment because of your life, situation, etc.;"[75] also, "favored by luck or fortune."[76] "Blessedness" is nowhere to be found. I mentioned this simple observation because it illustrates

---

69   The Declaration of Independence para. 2 (U.S. 1776).

70   Nathan Bailey, *An Universal Etymological Dictionary*. (3rd ed. printed for J. Darby. A. Bettesworth, F. Fayram, J. Pemberton, J. Hooke, C. Rivington, F. Clay, J. Batley, and E. Symon [etc.], 1726).

71   Nathan Bailey, *The New Universal English Dictionary* (4th ed. Printed for James Rivington and James Fletcher, 1759).

72   Francis Allen, *A Complete English Dictionary* (printed for J. Wilson and J. Fell, 1765).

73   Thomas Sheridan, *A Complete Dictionary of the English Language* (C. Dilly, 1789).

74   William Perry, *The Royal Standard English Dictionary* (3rd ed. Merriam, 1806).

75   Merriam-Webster.com, *Merriam-Webster, n.d.* Web., available at http://www.merriam-webster.com/dictionary/happiness (accessed Sept. 9, 2014).

76   *Id.* available at http://www.merriam-webster.com/dictionary/happy (accessed Sept. 9, 2014).

two different worldviews. "Blessedness" implies that we have received something from someone. It implies order and purpose. "Luck," on the other hand, implies randomness and chaos. It suggests a lack of purpose and unreason.

Depending which of the two paths you take (the "blessedness" path or the "luck" path) in order to define that "pursuit of happiness," it will have a great influence on whether you seek after that purpose for your life. Whether you think it is attainable in the first place. If you tend to think that everything is random and there is no real purpose to your life, it would be hard for you to seek after purpose, to seek after truth. When we are just the product of "time plus matter plus chance" hopelessness can set in very easily.

The Christian citizen seeks after Truth, as we have already discussed, he or she takes the "blessedness path." And we are confident enough to submit to that path (to God's truth), even when it shatters our most deeply held earthly convictions—even human religious convictions. The standard is the important thing. We do not move based on the flimsy whim of our feelings and emotions. That is the spirit of this age, and one that we reject completely. Let us summarize by quoting Ephesians 2:1-10:

> And you were dead in the trespasses and sins in which you once walked, following the course of this world, following the prince of the power of the air, the spirit that is now at work in the sons of disobedience— among whom we all once lived in the passions of our flesh, carrying out the desires of the body and the mind, and were by nature children of wrath, like the rest of mankind. But God, being rich in mercy, because of the great love with which he loved us, even when we were dead in our trespasses, made us alive together with Christ—by grace you have been saved— and raised us up with him and seated us with him in the heavenly places in Christ Jesus, so that in the coming ages he might show the immeasurable riches of his grace in kindness toward us in Christ Jesus. For by grace you have been saved through faith. And this is not your own doing; it is the gift of God, not a result of works,

so that no one may boast. For we are his workmanship, created in Christ Jesus for good works, which God prepared beforehand, that we should walk in them.

We were created for good works –to "be spent" for God and our neighbors— to the glory of He Who created us. We display His love not by imposing our will, but by living out His. By showing that this way of living is superior – more beautiful, pleasurable, deeper and meaningful than any other way to live.

Part Two
GOVERNING PRINCIPLES

CHAPTER FOUR
GOD'S ESTABLISHED AUTHORITY

What is the relationship between the Christian citizen and governmental authorities? In the next two chapters we will explore this relationship more fully, establishing some principles that will help us guide our influence in society. We aim to strike that critical balance we see in Scripture. We will try to avoid focusing too much on one particular verse of Scripture as such an approach tends to give us a distorted view of the principles, which usually lead to excesses. We will try to take a view of the whole of Scripture, hoping we can land exactly within God's vision for us.

Are Christians above government authority?

The question of our relationship to governmental authority surfaces naturally after our discussion of "Kingdom Focus" in chapter two. If we are citizens of heaven then we owe nothing to earthly authority, goes the thinking. We have a different allegiance. It is one of the reasons dictators usually despise Christianity. It will defy the state authority by claiming it has a higher authority to follow. That thought process, though logical, shows no real understanding of Christianity. It would be like saying that because Christians are to love God above all, they are not able to love others. This God we are to love tells us one way to show our love for Him is to show love for our neighbors. In the same way, Romans 13 gives us guidance on the topic of our relationship to governmental authority:

> Let every person be subject to the governing authorities. For there is no authority except from God, and those that exist have been instituted by God. Therefore whoever resists the authorities resists what God has appointed, and those who resist will incur judgment. For rulers are not a terror to good conduct, but to bad. Would you have no fear of the one who is in authority? Then do what is good, and you will receive his approval, for he is God's servant for your good. But if you do wrong, be afraid, for he does not bear the sword in vain. For he is the servant of God, an avenger who carries out God's wrath on the wrongdoer. Therefore one must be in subjection, not only to avoid God's wrath but also for the sake of conscience. For because of this you also pay taxes, for the authorities are ministers of God, attending to this very thing. Pay to all what is owed to them: taxes to whom taxes are owed, revenue to whom revenue is owed, respect to whom respect is owed, honor to whom honor is owed (Romans 13:1-7).

We start by noting that the passage applies to "every person." No one, in this sense is above the law, religious or not. Our Supreme Authority, which is ultimately God, requires that we be subjected to governmental authorities. The reason the text gives us for this is mind-blowing. "For there is no authority except from God, and those that exist have been instituted by God." This is such an explosive text, you probably figured, because it makes no qualification for the statement. In fact, it is unequivocal in asserting that God has established all who are in authority. Yes, even the worst rulers in history. This much is clear from all of Scripture.

We have already mentioned Nebuchadnezzar, the evil Babylonian king who orchestrated the siege of Jerusalem and the looting and destruction of the temple, and who threw God's servants Shadrach, Meshach, and Abednego into the fiery furnace for failing to bow down to his golden image. In chapter 27 of the Book of Jeremiah, God speaks to Jeremiah.

Listen to how God describes Nebuchadnezzar: "Now I have given all these lands into the hand of Nebuchadnezzar, the king of Babylon, my servant, and I have given him also the beasts of the field to serve him," (Jeremiah 27:6 emphasis mine). That is exactly the way Paul describes government authorities in Romans, "he is God's servant," (Romans 13:4). Daniel recognized that when he spoke after receiving the interpretation of Nebuchadnezzar's dream in Daniel 2:21 saying, "[God] removes kings and sets up kings." King Solomon in Proverbs also recognized God's hand over rulers saying, "The king's heart is a stream of water in the hand of the LORD; he turns it wherever he will," (Proverbs 21:1). This is revealed to us also with King Jeroboam in 1 Kings 12:15 where "the king did not listen to the people, for it was a turn of affairs brought about by the LORD that he might fulfill his word." The king did not listen because, "God." According to Scripture, it is undisputed that God's Providence is at work in the establishing of governmental authorities.

The God-given authority of earthly rulers does not mean that God always endorses or supports their rule. We have already mentioned the most poignant example of this principle in our discussion of the time the Israelites asked God for a king. As we discussed, the prophet Samuel was devastated by it and when he went to God for guidance, God said:

> Obey the voice of the people in all that they say to you, for they have not rejected you, but they have rejected me from being king over them. According to all the deeds that they have done, from the day I brought them up out of Egypt even to this day, forsaking me and serving other gods, so they are also doing to you. Now then, obey their voice; only you shall solemnly warn them and show them the ways of the king who shall reign over them (1 Samuel 8:7-9).

It was not a pretty picture. Samuel told them of the many perils of having a king, but the people still wanted to have a king, like other nations.[77] God allowed them to have a king and suffer the consequences. Much like the terrible choices we have made in America over the years.

The passage in Romans then tells us that, "whoever resists the authori-

---

77   "[T]hat we also may be like all the nations, and that our king may judge us and go out before us and fight our battles," (1 Samuel 8:20).

ties resists what God has appointed, and those who resist will incur judgment" (Romans 13:2). A casual reading of the passage might lead you to resist any opposition to government at all, but the text is not conveying that. The fact that when you stand up against authority you are standing up against the authority God has established does not mean that we are never to do it. Only that we are to be very cautious that when we do it we are standing on the side of justice and righteousness, for we "will incur judgment." Sometimes resistance to oppressive rulers, that as we have seen now have been established by God, is exactly what God wills for us to do. Take the Israelites' exodus from Egypt. Pharaoh was that authority established by God, yet the same God called Moses to stand up to Pharaoh and demand to let His people go.

> [T]he LORD said to Moses, "See, I have made you like God to Pharaoh, and your brother Aaron shall be your prophet. You shall speak all that I command you, and your brother Aaron shall tell Pharaoh to let the people of Israel go out of his land. But I will harden Pharaoh's heart, and though I multiply my signs and wonders in the land of Egypt, Pharaoh will not listen to you. Then I will lay my hand on Egypt and bring my hosts, my people the children of Israel, out of the land of Egypt by great acts of judgment. The Egyptians shall know that I am the LORD, when I stretch out my hand against Egypt and bring out the people of Israel from among them" (Exodus 7:1-5).

We will flesh out this concept in more depth in the next chapter, *Against God's Established Authority*, but for now, suffice it to say that there are indeed various instances when we are required to stand up to earthly authorities in true obedience to God. This is in no way incompatible with the fact that all earthly authorities are set up by God and we are generally to submit to it.

One of the most powerful examples of the earthly authorities established by God comes to us from that story we've already visited of our Lord and Savior Jesus Christ standing before Pilate. In chapter two, we left that compelling encounter when Pilate asked Jesus, "What is truth?" But what followed is just as important to our discussion. Pilate goes before the crowd that accused Jesus and said he found "no guilt in him."[78] Still, having found no guilt in him, Pilate is too much of a coward to stand up to the mob and release Jesus. So he offers to release "one man" for them according to their Passover tradition. The crowd choses a convicted robber named Barabbas instead of Jesus their Messiah.[79]

> Then Pilate took Jesus and flogged him. And the soldiers twisted together a crown of thorns and put it on his head and arrayed him in a purple robe. They came up to him, saying, "Hail, King of the Jews!" and struck him with their hands. Pilate went out again and said to them, "See, I am bringing him out to you that you may know that I find no guilt in him." So Jesus came out, wearing the crown of thorns and the purple robe. Pilate said to them, "Behold the man!" When the chief priests and the officers saw him, they cried out, "Crucify him, crucify him!" Pilate said to them, "Take him yourselves and crucify him, for I find no guilt in him." The Jews answered him, "We have a law, and according to that law he ought to die because he has made himself the Son of God." When Pilate heard this statement, he was even more afraid (John 19:1-8).

Pilate does not know what to do. He fears the mob, but he has stood before the Christ and knows He is innocent. He had even been warned by his wife who sent him a message before he was to meet Jesus saying, "Have nothing to do with that righteous man, for I have suffered much because of him today in a dream," (Matthew 27:19). He knows there is something about this Man. So he goes back to question Jesus, "Where are You from?" he asks (John 19:9, NKJV), but Jesus does not answers him. And listen to what Pilate asks Him next: "Are You not speaking to me? Do You not know that I have power to crucify You, and power to release You?" (John 19:10, NKJV). Well, does he? Jesus answers with one of the most powerful statements in all of history: "You would have no authority over me at all unless it had been given you from above," (John 19:11). Please stop and consider this carefully. Jesus, the Son of the Living God, recognizes the authority given to Pilate over Him, to the Glory of God the Father. We could write an entire volume on that profound

---

78   John 18:38.

79   *Id.* at 18:39-40.

statement. It is a statement of full submission to the will of God and His glory, above and beyond self-preservation. It is an act of Love[80] that will pave the way for us to be in communion with a Holy God.[81] He who knew no sin was crucified as the worst of sinners, for our sake.[82] Everything about this scene calls out for someone to stand up and shout, "No!" But it happened, as it must have, to fulfill God's eternal plan.

Moral law

The Romans 13 passage we started the chapter with then goes into a matter that can also be puzzling. It says:

> For rulers are not a terror to good works, but to evil. Do you want to be unafraid of the authority? Do what is good, and you will have praise from the same. For he is God's minister to you for good. But if you do evil, be afraid; for he does not bear the sword in vain; for he is God's minister, an avenger to execute wrath on him who practices evil (Romans 13:3-4, NKJV).

The passage is troubling because it deals with the issue in terms of "right and wrong." If rulers are not a terror to good conduct, but to bad, then where do Nebuchadnezzar, and Pharaoh and Jeroboam, and Hitler, and the many other oppressors of history fit? They were indeed a terror to good conduct, morally speaking. We can unlock the mystery in Paul's statement by thinking of the way I am writing to you in these pages. I have been talking about what Christian citizens do. I say they are peacemakers and love their neighbors and are good workers, even while we know this is not always the case. We all fail this standard. We are talking about the standard we are called to live by. We are focusing on a calling to what we "ought" to be. That is the same figure of speech Paul seems to use here. Not a rationalization or excuse for immoral behavior, but a call to a higher standard. The Bible often speaks in these terms. The

---

80   "For God so loved the world that He gave His only begotten Son, that whoever believes in Him should not perish but have everlasting life," (John 3:16).

81   "For our sake he made him to be sin who knew no sin, so that in him we might become the righteousness of God," (2 Corinthians 5:21).

82   "Surely he has borne our griefs and carried our sorrows; yet we esteemed him stricken, smitten by God, and afflicted. But he was pierced for our transgressions; he was crushed for our iniquities; upon him was the chastisement that brought us peace, and with his wounds we are healed," (Isaiah 53:4-5).

statement we are dealing with here actually servers as an indictment for those in authority. It lets them know what it is they ought to do. It helps us correct the abuses by applying the standard. I once heard Pastor John Piper use the example of his children to explain the point. In the same manner a father tells a child, "That is not the way we speak in this family," when the child has just used unacceptable language, so Paul indicts rulers who abuse their God-given authority to do something other than rewarding good conduct and punishing wrong conduct. Paul is talking about the way governments and rulers ought to behave. And if they deviate from that standard, they will be dealt with, as every single one of our examples illustrates. This, again, does not call into question the fact that God still gives them the authority over the people for a period of time, even when they fail the standard completely.

The passage also stands in judgment of what *we* ought to do. Paul continues, "Therefore one must be in subjection, not only to avoid God's wrath but also for the sake of conscience," (Romans 13:5). It is our conscience that helps us decide between right and wrong. This is that moral law that brought C.S. Lewis to a belief in the existence of God. Listen to his words in *Mere Christianity*:

> My argument against God was that the universe seemed so cruel and unjust. But how had I gotten this idea of *just* and *unjust*? A man does not call a line crooked unless he has some idea of a straight line. What was I comparing this universe with when I called it unjust? If the whole show was bad and senseless from A to Z, so to speak, why did I, who was supposed to be part of the show, find myself in such violent reaction against it? A man feels wet when he falls into water, because man is not a water animal: a fish would not feel wet. Of course I could have given up my idea of justice by saying it was nothing but a private idea of my own. But if I did that, then my argument against God collapsed too — for the argument depended on saying that the world was really unjust, not simply that it did not happen to please my private fancies. Thus in the very act of trying to prove that God did not exist — in other words, that the whole of reality was senseless — I found I was forced to assume that one

part of reality — namely my idea of justice — was full of sense. Consequently, atheism turns out to be too simple. If the whole universe has no meaning, we should never have found out that it has no meaning: just as, if there were no light in the universe and therefore no creatures with eyes, we should never know it was dark. *Dark* would be without meaning.[83]

As you can see, one need not be a Christian to see this. The philosopher Immanuel Kant (1724-1804) tried to get a hold of these truths on his book *The Critique of Practical Reason*, ultimately concluding:

Two things fill the mind with ever new and increasing admiration and awe, the oftener and the more steadily we reflect on them: the starry heavens above and the moral law within. I have not to search for them and conjecture them as though they were veiled in darkness or were in the transcendent region beyond my horizon; I see them before me and connect them directly with the consciousness of my existence. The former begins from the place I occupy in the external world of sense, and enlarges my connection therein to an unbounded extent with worlds upon worlds and systems of systems, and moreover into limitless times of their periodic motion, its beginning and continuance. The second begins from my invisible self, my personality, and exhibits me in a world which has true infinity, but which is traceable only by the understanding, and with which I discern that I am not in a merely contingent but in a universal and necessary connection, as I am also thereby with all those visible worlds. The former view of a countless multitude of worlds annihilates as it were my importance as an animal creature, which after it has been for a short time provided with vital power, one knows not how, must again give back the matter of which it was formed to the planet it inhabits (a mere speck in the universe). The second, on the contrary, infinitely elevates my worth as an intelligence by my personality, in which the moral law reveals to me a

---

83   C.S. Lewis, *Mere Christianity* 38-39 (Harper 2009 (1952)).

life independent of animality and even of the whole sensible world, at least so far as may be inferred from the destination assigned to my existence by this law, a destination not restricted to conditions and limits of this life, but reaching into the infinite.

But though admiration and respect may excite to inquiry, they cannot supply the want of it.[84]

"[T]he starry heavens above and the moral law within"— creation and conscience, beauty and reason. These are inescapable, universal truths that transcend cultural norms and personal preferences. They are truths that every human being lives under, whatever their religion. However difficult the task of understanding these proves to be, abandoning the quest or denying them will not help in any way. We must deal with them in an honest, humble, sincere way.

The plight of conscience

Note that this Moral Law cries out incessantly within. It is an improper, inopportune, undisciplined companion, always meddling on our every affair— calling us to be better continually. Sometimes quite reasonably, like when it calls us to give respect to our mother. But oh, sometimes it cries out for the most irrational of things, the illogical really, like putting ourselves in harm's way, even at the risk of our own lives, to save the life of a stranger in peril. It demands the unpopular and elusive "good." The objective good that many even refuse to acknowledge today. Sadly, they become the protagonists on that tragic tale of the man who refused to believe in the law of gravity, launching himself of a balcony to prove he was right. He was not.

This "good," this that we "ought to be," comes from our Creator. It is the basis of reality, of the Christian faith and of the American ideal that we are "endowed by our Creator."[85] Christians believe we were made to respond positively to this Moral Law for it points us to that Eternal Moral Law Giver. We were made for God. It is that beautiful sentence

---

84   Immanuel Kant, *The Critique of Practical Reason* 163 (CreateSpace 2010 (1788)).

85   The Declaration of Independence para. 2 (U.S. 1776).

that, "Man's chief end is to glorify God, and to enjoy him forever."[86] We were made for this purpose and we won't be at ease within our own soul if we do not recognize that and live accordingly. If you use a hammer to brush your teeth, it won't be very effective. It was not made for that purpose. But when you use it for its intended purpose, to hammer in nails, it fits perfectly. It was made for that. We fit perfectly in God's hands. We are His instruments. It's Ephesians 2:10, "For we are His workmanship, created in Christ Jesus for good works, which God prepared beforehand that we should walk in them," (NKJV). And further, 1 Corinthians 3:9-11:

> For we are God's fellow workers. You are God's field, God's building. According to the grace of God given to me, like a skilled master builder I laid a foundation, and someone else is building upon it. Let each one take care how he builds upon it. For no one can lay a foundation other than that which is laid, which is Jesus Christ.

We simply cannot change who we are by wishing we were something else; nor by acting as if we were something else.

Paul's admonition in Romans 13 appeals to that conscience, telling us it will also stand in judgment of our actions, when we stand in defiance of the authority God has established on earth. Again, it does not follow that we are never to stand against that authority, but only that God and even our consciences will direct us and judge our actions in this regard. We must proceed with extreme caution and humility. The principle demands complete alertness on the part of the Christian citizen to ensure He is acting in accordance with God's justice and righteousness. If we do, as with Daniel and, Shadrach, Meshach, and Abednego, God will bless our efforts in victory or defeat, as He has done all throughout history. His name will be glorified regardless.

To bring this down to the practical reality of nations, here are some excerpts from the public address of U.S. General Omar N. Bradley (1893-1981) on Memorial Day, November 10, 1948, commemorating the agreement between the Allies and Germany for the cessation of hostilities on the west front in World War I (1914-1918), which was combined with

---

86   Westminster Assembly, *Westminster Shorter Catechism*, Question 1, (1647).

Veterans Day and Remembrance Day after World War II (1939-1945):

> Tomorrow is our day of conscience. For although it is a monument to victory, it is also a symbol of failure. Just as it honors the dead, so must it humble the living. Armistice Day is a constant reminder that we won a war and lost a peace.
>
> It is both a tribute and an indictment: A tribute to the men who died that their neighbors might live without fear of aggression. An indictment of those who lived and forfeited their chance for peace.
>
> Therefore, while Armistice Day is a day for pride, it is for pride in the achievements of others—humility in our own.
>
> Neither remorse nor logic can hide the fact that our armistice ended in failure. Not until the armistice myth exploded in the blast of a Stuka bomb did we learn that the winning of wars does not in itself make peace. And not until Pearl Harbor did we learn that non-involvement in peace means certain involvement in war. We paid grievously for those faults of the past in deaths, disaster, and dollars. It was a penalty we knowingly chose to risk. We made the choice when we defaulted on our task in creating and safeguarding a peace.
>
> It is no longer possible to shield ourselves with arms alone against the ordeal of attack. For modern war visits destruction on the victor and the vanquished alike. Our only complete assurance of surviving World War III is to halt it before it starts.
>
> For that reason we clearly have no choice but to face the challenge of these strained times. To ignore the danger of aggression is simply to invite it. It must never again be said of the American people: Once more we won a war; once more we lost a peace. If we do we shall doom our children to a struggle that may take their lives.

Armed forces can wage wars but they cannot make peace. For there is a wide chasm between war and peace—a chasm that can only be bridged by good will, discussion, compromise, and agreement. ...

Time can be for or against us. It can be for us if diligence in our search for agreement equals the vigilance with which we prepare for a storm. It can be against us if disillusionment weakens our faith in discussion—or if our vigilance corrodes while we wait. Disillusionment is always the enemy of peace...

There can be no compromise with aggression anywhere in the world. For aggression multiplies—in rapid succession—disregard for the rights of man. Freedom when threatened anywhere is at once threatened everywhere.

With the monstrous weapons man already has, humanity is in danger of being trapped in this world by its moral adolescents. Our knowledge of science has clearly outstripped our capacity to control it. We have many men of science; too few men of God. We have grasped the mystery of the atom and rejected the Sermon on the Mount. Man is stumbling blindly through a spiritual darkness while toying with the precarious secrets of life and death. The world has achieved brilliance without wisdom, power without conscience. Ours is a world of nuclear giants and ethical infants...[87]

The appeal to conscience is easily felt in the words of the General. Man's solutions are not enough, not only for spiritual matters, but also for prosperity, joy, peace, respect and freedom on earth. It is important for us to see and feel how hopeless we are without this appeal in every area of our lives.

---

87   General Omar N. Bradley, "An Armistice Day Address," *The Collected Writings Of General Omar N. Bradley*. Vol. 1. 584-589 (1967), available at: http://www.opinionbug.com/2109/armistice-day-1948-address-general-omar-n-bradley/ (accessed Sept. 9, 2014).

We must preserve the standard

Moral relativism is a hopeless, dark, empty, enslaving, unreal, unworkable, incoherent philosophy that provides no answers, no structure and no help for life whatsoever. It was the ultimate discovery of that highly esteemed philosopher Friedrich Nietzsche (1844-1900) on his "Parable of a Mad Man," where it is said "god was killed." Listen to this revealing passage:

> THE MADMAN----Have you not heard of that madman who lit a lantern in the bright morning hours, ran to the market place, and cried incessantly: "I seek God! I seek God!"---As many of those who did not believe in God were standing around just then, he provoked much laughter. Has he got lost? asked one. Did he lose his way like a child? asked another. Or is he hiding? Is he afraid of us? Has he gone on a voyage? emigrated?—Thus they yelled and laughed.
>
> The madman jumped into their midst and pierced them with his eyes. "Whither is God?" he cried; "I will tell you. We have killed him---you and I. All of us are his murderers. But how did we do this? How could we drink up the sea? Who gave us the sponge to wipe away the entire horizon? What were we doing when we unchained this earth from its sun? Whither is it moving now? Whither are we moving? Away from all suns? Are we not plunging continually? Backward, sideward, forward, in all directions? Is there still any up or down? Are we not straying, as through an infinite nothing? Do we not feel the breath of empty space? Has it not become colder? Is not night continually closing in on us? Do we not need to light lanterns in the morning? Do we hear nothing as yet of the noise of the gravediggers who are burying God? Do we smell nothing as yet of the divine decomposition? Gods, too, decompose. God is dead. God remains dead. And we have killed him.
>
> "How shall we comfort ourselves, the murderers of all

murderers? What was holiest and mightiest of all that the world has yet owned has bled to death under our knives: who will wipe this blood off us? What water is there for us to clean ourselves? What festivals of atonement, what sacred games shall we have to invent? Is not the greatness of this deed too great for us? Must we ourselves not become gods simply to appear worthy of it? There has never been a greater deed; and whoever is born after us---for the sake of this deed he will belong to a higher history than all history hitherto."

Here the madman fell silent and looked again at his listeners; and they, too, were silent and stared at him in astonishment. At last he threw his lantern on the ground, and it broke into pieces and went out. "I have come too early," he said then; "my time is not yet. This tremendous event is still on its way, still wandering; it has not yet reached the ears of men. Lightning and thunder require time; the light of the stars requires time; deeds, though done, still require time to be seen and heard. This deed is still more distant from them than most distant stars--- and yet they have done it themselves.

It has been related further that on the same day the madman forced his way into several churches and there struck up his requiem *aeternam deo*. Led out and called to account, he is said always to have replied nothing but: "What after all are these churches now if they are not the tombs and sepulchers of God?"[88]

The account has captivated the imagination of many, seduced by the possibility of a world without moral objectivity. But the implications are also palpable, even if merely imaginary. Without a Moral Law Giver, there is no Moral Law and we have no point of reference. There is no up or down. We are falling backwards and forwards through an infinite nothing. It becomes darker, colder, denser... If that were true. Many have tried and some continue to try to live as if this were true, only to

---

88   Friedrich Nietzsche, *The Gay Science* (1882, 1887) para. 125; Walter Kaufmann ed. (New York: Vintage, 1974), 181-82, available at http://www.fordham.edu/halsall/mod/nietzsche-madman.asp (accessed Sept. 9, 2014).

find that ever-present conscience bother assailing their every thought. It is why many of them do not end well psychologically. Nietzsche himself paid a heavy price for the assault on his own conscience and his unbelief. It cost him his sanity. Here is the way Alan Ryan describes Nietzsche's last days in a revealing book review in the *New York Times*:

> [A]t 44 he was stricken with a dementia caused by syphilis, was rescued from a dingy boardinghouse in Turin by his devoted friend Franz Overbeck, taken to asylums in Switzerland and Germany, and later incarcerated in a red-brick villa in Weimar. There his sister, Elisabeth Forster-Nietzsche, received her anti-Semitic friends and allowed them to view the dying sage, a fate from which death released him in August 1900. Thirty years after, the most repulsive of Nietzsche's many dubious admirers visited; Herr Hitler was given one of Elisabeth's husband's anti-Semitic treatises and her brother's sword stick.[89]

So is the fate of man's every effort to live apart from objective truth. Many talk about a post-Christian America, or post-modern world were morality is as subjective as your favorite cup of tea. But, though the terminology can be useful as an intellectual discussion, the truth is there is no post-Christian nothing. Nothing is post-God. Everything exists because He exists and apart from Him there is nothing. Our wishful rejection of God does not change reality, because we did not create reality. Our fantasies will be awakened by reality sooner or later. We did not create ourselves, "It is He who has made us, and not we ourselves..." (Psalm 100:3, NKJV). "For of Him and through Him and to Him *are* all things, to whom *be* glory forever. Amen," (Romans 11:36, NKJV). Our insolence to disregard and even question God is met with something like the way God responded to Job's questioning. Here is a small sample:

> "Who is this that darkens counsel by words without knowledge?
> Dress for action like a man;
> I will question you, and you make it known to me.
> "Where were you when I laid the foundation of the

---

89   Alan Ryan, *The Will to Madness*, N.Y. Times, January 24, 1999, available at http://www.nytimes.com/1999/01/24/books/the-will-to-madness.html?src=pm&pagewanted=1

earth?
Tell me, if you have understanding.
Who determined its measurements—surely you know!
Or who stretched the line upon it?
On what were its bases sunk,
or who laid its cornerstone,
when the morning stars sang together
and all the sons of God shouted for joy?
"Or who shut in the sea with doors
when it burst out from the womb,
when I made clouds its garment
and thick darkness its swaddling band,
and prescribed limits for it
and set bars and doors,
and said, 'Thus far shall you come, and no farther,
and here shall your proud waves be stayed'?
"Have you commanded the morning since your days
began,
and caused the dawn to know its place,
that it might take hold of the skirts of the earth,
and the wicked be shaken out of it?
It is changed like clay under the seal,
and its features stand out like a garment.
From the wicked their light is withheld,
and their uplifted arm is broken.

"Have you entered into the springs of the sea,
or walked in the recesses of the deep?
Have the gates of death been revealed to you,
or have you seen the gates of deep darkness?
Have you comprehended the expanse of the earth?
Declare, if you know all this.
"Where is the way to the dwelling of light,
and where is the place of darkness,
that you may take it to its territory
and that you may discern the paths to its home?
You know, for you were born then,
and the number of your days is great!

"Have you entered the storehouses of the snow,
or have you seen the storehouses of the hail,
which I have reserved for the time of trouble,
for the day of battle and war?
What is the way to the place where the light is distrib-
uted,
or where the east wind is scattered upon the earth?
"Who has cleft a channel for the torrents of rain
and a way for the thunderbolt,
to bring rain on a land where no man is,
on the desert in which there is no man,
to satisfy the waste and desolate land,
and to make the ground sprout with grass?
"Has the rain a father,
or who has begotten the drops of dew?
From whose womb did the ice come forth,
and who has given birth to the frost of heaven?
The waters become hard like stone,
and the face of the deep is frozen.
"Can you bind the chains of the Pleiades
or loose the cords of Orion?
Can you lead forth the Mazzaroth in their season,
or can you guide the Bear with its children?
Do you know the ordinances of the heavens?
Can you establish their rule on the earth?
"Can you lift up your voice to the clouds,
that a flood of waters may cover you?
Can you send forth lightnings, that they may go
and say to you, 'Here we are'?
Who has put wisdom in the inward parts
or given understanding to the mind?
Who can number the clouds by wisdom?
Or who can tilt the waterskins of the heavens,
when the dust runs into a mass
and the clods stick fast together?
"Can you hunt the prey for the lion,
or satisfy the appetite of the young lions,
when they crouch in their dens

or lie in wait in their thicket?
Who provides for the raven its prey,
when its young ones cry to God for help,
and wander about for lack of food? (Job 38:2-41).

That is just a taste, God continues for a few more chapters.

Our conclusion must be that we are simply not gods and we act like fools when we try to put ourselves on par with the Almighty. That we must listen to our consciences and hasten to obey God above all and the authorities he has setup generally. The Christian citizen must approach the world as it is. Reality as it is. We submit to authority as it is established; and objective moral truth in the same manner. For we all experienced it within ourselves and are in no need that anyone tell us what we already know deep inside. If we accept that truth, we would be able to thrive in this world of turmoil.

CHAPTER FIVE

AGAINST GOD'S ESTABLISHED AUTHORITY

We left further discussion of Moses' stand against Pharaoh to free the Israelites from oppression to this chapter so that we could focus on the times we are called by God to stand up to the authorities He has established on earth, having cemented, through Romans 13, the general principle that Christians are to subject themselves to earthly authorities. We know of several instances where God called men to stand up to government rulers. So there is some tension between these principles, but let us explore if they are in any way incompatible.

God and Caesar

The principles are best explained with the passage that many use, erroneously, to encourage Christian citizens to stay out of "dirty politics." It is the famous passage where Jesus is asked about paying taxes to Caesar:

> Then the Pharisees went and plotted how they might entangle Him in His talk. And they sent to Him their disciples with the Herodians, saying, "Teacher, we know that You are true, and teach the way of God in truth; nor do You care about anyone, for You do not regard the person

of men. Tell us, therefore, what do You think? Is it lawful to pay taxes to Caesar, or not?"

But Jesus perceived their wickedness, and said, "Why do you test Me, you hypocrites? Show Me the tax money."

So they brought Him a denarius.

And He said to them, "Whose image and inscription is this?"

They said to Him, "Caesar's."

And He said to them, "Render therefore to Caesar the things that are Caesar's, and to God the things that are God's." When they had heard these words, they marveled, and left Him and went their way (Matthew 22:15-22).[90]

Before we even get into the principles, notice the motivation behind the whole exchange. The Pharisees were seeking to confuse Jesus and entangle Him with His own words. This is important because it is exactly what will happen to you today. There are those whose motivation is never the search for truth but personal pride. Others, not fully aware of Scripture's handling of the issue, can serve as stumbling block to you without even realizing it. Be wise as a serpent[91] and let the Word of God be your guide. It is true that Christian citizens know, as we have already established, that their hope and help ultimately comes from God and God alone. "I lift up my eyes to the hills. From where does my help come? My help comes from the LORD, who made heaven and earth," says the Psalmist (Psalms 121:1-2). But it does not follow that our efforts to affect change in culture and policy, through government engagement, are unnecessary and futile. It does not follow that civic engagement is not part of God's plan for our lives here on earth. Indeed, we have already seen how the Scriptures are full of Christian affecting change in government and policy, in full obedience to God. From Moses before

---

90   *See also* Mark 12:13-17, Luke 20:20-26.

91   Matthew 10:16.

Pharaoh[92] to Esther before King Ahasuerus[93] to Jesus before Pilate[94] to Paul before Festus,[95] there have been many called by God to affect government and policy. This is to be expected, since government affects us all in the way we relate to one another and to earthly authorities. The truth is we are all to be engaged in "politics" in one way or another. In fact, we are all involved whether we recognize it or not. Non-involvement is involvement. There is no escaping this reality. Therefore the only question for us is whether we will be involved in a way that brings glory to God or not; whether we will shine the light of the Gospel in this area of our lives, or not.

The Christian citizen follows Jesus' admonition faithfully. We give to Caesar what is Caesar's and to God what is God's. The question we must often face though (and the one we are almost certain to face if we are detached from involvement in policy making) is, what happens when "Caesar" demands that which only belongs to God? The Christian citizen then must be sensitive to the voice of God in those instances because it may require an immediate clash with civil authority. There are several clear examples. In the book of Daniel, we have already referenced the wonderful story of Daniel's friends: Shadrach, Meshach, and Abed-Nego. King Nebuchadnezzar had built an image of gold and required everyone in Babylon to bow down to it when certain music was played.[96] That was the "law of the land," established by the man God had given earthly authority. Yet Shadrach, Meshach, and Abed-Nego, as believers in God, could not obey it.[97]

---

92   Exodus 7-12.

93   Esther 7.

94   Matthew 27, Mark 15, Luke 23, John 18.

95   Acts 25.

96   Daniel 3:4-5.

97   "And God spoke all these words, saying,
'I am the Lord your God, who brought you out of the land of Egypt, out of the house of slavery.
'You shall have no other gods before me.
'You shall not make for yourself a carved image, or any likeness of anything that is in heaven above, or that is in the earth beneath, or that is in the water under the earth. You shall not bow down to them or serve them, for I the LORD your God am a jealous God, visiting the iniquity of the fathers on the children to the third and the fourth generation of those who hate me, but showing steadfast love to thousands of those who love me and keep my commandments,'" (Exodus 20:1-4).

The king was enraged and threatened to throw them into a burning fiery furnace. Yet here is their eye-opening response:

> O Nebuchadnezzar, we have no need to answer you in this matter. If that is the case, our God whom we serve is able to deliver us from the burning fiery furnace, and He will deliver us from your hand, O king. But if not, let it be known to you, O king, that we do not serve your gods, nor will we worship the gold image which you have set up (Daniel 3:16-18, NKJV).

A Law above the law

Shadrach, Meshach, and Abed-Nego could have bowed down, even as they prayed in their heads that God would destroy the image somehow. I'm an attorney by trade so I know there is always an argument to be made. How many of us if presented with the same situation today would rationalize our actions saying, "I'm only bowing down physically but my heart belongs to God." I'm sure we can convince many of our friends and even be held as heroes for enduring all the pain of bowing down when you don't really want to. But you can't play those games with God. He sees right through our petty arguments and straight into our hearts, revealing all our insecurities and lack of faith, especially when we act contrary to his explicit command and against His expressed will for our lives. Not only can God see, even clearer than we can, what is really motivating us to act in a certain way, but His Word is truth and does not change with the times. He has also given us His Spirit to guide us.[98] And for as much as we are always seeking to know what God wants us to do, He has been surprisingly clear in what He demands of us through His Word. Shadrach, Meshach, and Abed-Nego knew what God demanded of them and would not betray God's commandments, even at the cost of their lives. Notice they did not know if God would save them, but weather in death or life, they knew they would glorify God. This is immensely important for us. We are not seeking specific outcomes; we are seeking to do God's will. We pursue Truth, whatever the outcome. My pastor Keiffer Bent says it this way, "It is always best to have the Provider, rather than the provisions." Remember that Shadrach, Me-

---

98   "[T]hese things God has revealed to us through the Spirit. For the Spirit searches everything, even the depths of God," (1 Corinthians 2:10).

shach, and Abed-Nego were indeed thrown into the fiery furnace. And God honored them by delivering them from the burning flames and the hands of Nebuchadnezzar:

> Then King Nebuchadnezzar was astonished; and he rose in haste and spoke, saying to his counselors, "Did we not cast three men bound into the midst of the fire?"
>
> They answered and said to the king, "True, O king."
>
> "Look!" he answered, "I see four men loose, walking in the midst of the fire; and they are not hurt, and the form of the fourth is like the Son of God."
>
> Then Nebuchadnezzar went near the mouth of the burning fiery furnace and spoke, saying, "Shadrach, Meshach, and Abed-Nego, servants of the Most High God, come out, and come here." Then Shadrach, Meshach, and Abed-Nego came from the midst of the fire. And the satraps, administrators, governors, and the king's counselors gathered together, and they saw these men on whose bodies the fire had no power; the hair of their head was not singed nor were their garments affected, and the smell of fire was not on them.
>
> Nebuchadnezzar spoke, saying, "Blessed be the God of Shadrach, Meshach, and Abed-Nego, who sent His Angel and delivered His servants who trusted in Him, and they have frustrated the king's word, and yielded their bodies, that they should not serve nor worship any god except their own God! (Daniel 3:24-28, NKJV).

The answer is clear for us then when it comes to earthly authorities and ultimate Authority. Peter and the apostles best articulated the concept when they were before the high priest who demanded that they stop preaching the Gospel of Christ. The high priest told them, "'We strictly charged you not to teach in [Jesus'] name, yet here you have filled Jerusalem with your teaching, and you intend to bring this man's blood upon us.' But Peter and the apostles answered, 'We must obey God rather than men,'" (Acts 5:28–29). And so must we; both in our submission to earthly authority: "Be subject for the Lord's sake to every human institution, whether it be to the emperor as supreme, or to governors as sent by him to punish those who do evil and to praise those who do good. For this is the will of God, that by doing good you should put to silence the ignorance of foolish people," (1 Peter 2:13–15), and in standing up for justice and righteousness, even when we are to clash with earthly authorities capable of causing great harm to our physical body, as was the case with Shadrach, Meshach, and Abed-Nego, and Peter. Such was also the case with the death of John the Baptist whose beheading was one of the most shameful acts of the abuse of government authority in history. Here is the account from the Gospel according to Mark:

> For it was Herod who had sent and seized John and bound him in prison for the sake of Herodias, his brother Philip's wife, because he had married her. For John had been saying to Herod, "It is not lawful for you to have your brother's wife." And Herodias had a grudge against him and wanted to put him to death. But she could not, for Herod feared John, knowing that he was a righteous and holy man, and he kept him safe. When he heard him, he was greatly perplexed, and yet he heard him gladly.
>
> But an opportunity came when Herod on his birthday gave a banquet for his nobles and military commanders and the leading men of Galilee. For when Herodias's daughter came in and danced, she pleased Herod and his guests. And the king said to the girl, "Ask me for whatever you wish, and I will give it to you." And he vowed to her, "Whatever you ask me, I will give you, up to half of my kingdom." And she went out and said to her mother, "For what should I ask?" And she said, "The head of John the Baptist." And she came in immediately with haste to the king and asked, saying, "I want you to give me at once the head of John the Baptist on a platter." And the king was exceedingly sorry, but because of his oaths and his guests he did not want to break his word to her. And immediately the king sent an executioner with orders to bring John's head. He went and beheaded him in the prison and brought his head on a platter and gave it to the

girl, and the girl gave it to her mother. When his disciples heard of it, they came and took his body and laid it in a tomb (Mark 6:17–29).

John was killed for "speaking truth to power," as the expression is commonly used today. So it is not only about being required by law to violate God's Law, but about righteousness and God's will for our lives. John was not being required to violate his conscience, yet he was called to speak truth. True truth, the kind that may get you killed in this world.

Think of Queen Esther. She seemingly had it all as Queen, yet she risked it all to save her people. Here is what happened. Haman was promoted to be the highest official in King Ahasuerus court and everyone bowed down to him except one man: Mordechai. He (Mordechai) had brought up Esther, the daughter of his uncle, when her parents died. Mordechai did not bow down to Haman for he was a Jew who would only bow down to God. Haman was enraged at this "insolence" and plotted to kill all Jews, through a decree that he coned the king into signing.[99] Mordechai is devastated for his people's sake and he appeals to Esther to intervene. But Esther replied with what the king's law said:

> All the king's servants and the people of the king's provinces know that if any man or woman goes to the king inside the inner court without being called, there is but one law—to be put to death, except the one to whom the king holds out the golden scepter so that he may live. But as for me, I have not been called to come in to the king these thirty days. (Esther 4:11)

Esther had done nothing wrong and she was not being required to do anything wrong, but a great injustice was about to be committed. Esther's mention of the law is particularly urgent in the story because she became queen when the previous queen (Vashti) refused to come when summoned by the king and was dethroned.[100] If Esther were to show up when she had not been summoned, it is reasonable to think that she may suffer the same fate. Especially in light of the specific law we have already referenced. No doubt Esther would be gambling with her throne

---

99   Esther 3.

100   *Id.* at 1:10-22.

and perhaps her life, if she were to go before the king without being summoned. But Mordechai's response laid the call of God for her life:

> Do not think to yourself that in the king's palace you will escape any more than all the other Jews. For if you keep silent at this time, relief and deliverance will rise for the Jews from another place, but you and your father's house will perish. And who knows whether you have not come to the kingdom for such a time as this? (Esther 4:13-14).

This call has reverberated throughout history: "For such a time as this…" God has a specific call for each one of us and He is never early or late, but just precise in His timing. Esther's time had come; ours will too. "How will we respond to that call?" is one of the most important questions we can ponder. Here is Queen Esther's response:

> Go, gather all the Jews to be found in Susa, and hold a fast on my behalf, and do not eat or drink for three days, night or day. I and my young women will also fast as you do. Then I will go to the king, though it is against the law, and if I perish, I perish (Esther 4:16).

Courage

May we respond with such boldness and trust in the Almighty when our time is called. "If I perish, I perish." So is the mindset of He who trusts in a God that is bigger than any single moment; bigger than any single life. An Eternal God who had allowed these events to unfold and who would use Queen Ether to save the Jewish people. She was indeed not only spared, but she found favor before the king who ended up turning on Haman and hanging him from the very gallows he had prepared for Mordechai. But she needed to act in faith against an unjust law, an unjust ruler, and before an unrighteous king who had been given authority to rule by Almighty God.

Daniel is another example of someone who was not required to break a precise commandment but that felt the will of God for his life was to stand up against injustice and what is done against the people of God. God blessed Daniel above any other of King Darius' officials. So they became envious and plotted against him. They went to the king and said:

> O King Darius, live forever! All the high officials of the
> kingdom, the prefects and the satraps, the counselors and
> the governors are agreed that the king should establish
> an ordinance and enforce an injunction, that whoever
> makes petition to any god or man for thirty days, except
> to you, O king, shall be cast into the den of lions. Now,
> O king, establish the injunction and sign the document,
> so that it cannot be changed, according to the law of the
> Medes and the Persians, which cannot be revoked (Dan-
> iel 6:6–8).

The last part, referring to "the law of the Medes and the Persians, which
cannot be revoked" would put enormous pressure on the king to keep
his word, once he realized the consequences of his decree on his most
loyal servant Daniel. They did that, of course, because they know how
devoted Daniel was to his God. So, did Daniel adjust his Christian beliefs to accommodate for what "the law of the land" said? Let's see:

> When Daniel knew that the document had been signed,
> he went to his house where he had windows in his up-
> per chamber open toward Jerusalem. He got down on
> his knees three times a day and prayed and gave thanks
> before his God, as he had done previously (Daniel 6:10).

"As he had done previously" is key, because Daniel was not trying to
show off. He was not merely starting to do something to prove a point.
He was doing what he had felt God calling him to do all along. Notice
there is no commandment in the Bible that he is to pray in this manner. He could have gone in a secret room and prayed. But he did "as he
had done previously." The text tells us that he knew the document was
signed, so he knew he was breaking the law. Yet he also knew that he
was to obey God, rather than man. What followed is to be expected. The
officials accused Daniel and he was ultimately put in the lion's den, even
after the king struggle to find a "legal" way to get him out. But God's
angel miraculously saved Daniel, as we have already discussed. God was
faithful to Daniel's faithfulness. Daniel gave his life to the Glory of God
because this is good and proper. It was what he was created to do, just as
we are created to bring glory to God. I hope you feel the weight of God's
call in your life. If God is God, He is worthy. That is why it is not "crazy"

to do such things. Not surprisingly, God's name was also glorified in the case of Daniel.

> Then King Darius wrote to all the peoples, nations, and languages that dwell in all the earth: "Peace be multiplied to you. I make a decree, that in all my royal dominion people are to tremble and fear before the God of Daniel, for he is the living God, enduring forever; his kingdom shall never be destroyed, and his dominion shall be to the end. He delivers and rescues; he works signs and wonders in heaven and on earth, he who has saved Daniel from the power of the lions."

> So this Daniel prospered during the reign of Darius and the reign of Cyrus the Persian (Daniel 6:25–28).

Are we then to sacrifice the spiritual to preserve the material; the soul for the body; truth for convenience; eternity for immediate pleasure? Are we to remain passive spectators to government affairs and the effect of the laws signed in our state, in Washington, D.C. and indeed the world for fear of personal retribution? Are we to be concerned only with our own wellbeing and that of our immediate family to the detriment of our neighbors? Are we to accept the injustices we see around us because "that is just the way things are" and besides "God is in control?" The answer we get from Scripture is, "Absolutely not." We are to be discerning and alert to God's work in our country and our lives, for we might be called "for such a time as this." To lift our voice, lead a people, write a book, run for office, spend our wealth, suffer in body, mind, or spirit, or even give our very lives for righteousness sake and to the glory of God. If we really believe God's Word, then we cannot turn away from his commandments, no matter the cost.

Growing hostility

Hostility toward God and His principles grows every day in our country, and the world. As Christian citizens, we cannot continue to be disengaged and apathetic. We must bow down in humility hoping for deliverance, but we must also work towards that deliverance in accordance to God's will. For it has pleased Him time after time to work through the faithfulness and sacrifices of his servant's obedience to deliver His people. I suspect He will do so again. And who knows if you might be the one called for the task this time. Sometimes we must be thrown into the fiery furnace first, but other times we can prevent the fiery furnace by being engaged in lawmaking before an unjust decree is established. Sometimes we can be that prophetic voice that exposes the plot of injustice well ahead of its execution. Sometimes we are called to expose a well-intentioned law with disastrous unintended consequences.

Let us remain alert, engaged and open to the will of God for our lives. Let us remain engaged as Christian citizens at every level of government, shining the light of truth wherever we go. Let us be agents of change for the glory of God and the good of the people.

To what end?

There are two more points to be made as we close this chapter. First and foremost I want to stress that the purpose of the principles we have discussed is always the glory of God. In the case of Shadrach, Meshach, and Abed-Nego, the people ended up praising God for His amazing protection of His servants. "Blessed be the God of Shadrach, Meshach, and Abed-Nego, who sent His Angel and delivered His servants who trusted in Him…" (Daniel 3:28, NKJV). In the case of Daniel, King Darius ended up fearing and trembling before God. Do you think the Jews that were saved by Queen Ester's bravery had something to glorify God about? Not to mention the most glorious event we discussed, the death of Christ on the Cross. By that one act, all of humanity is blessed and God is most glorified.

The principle then is that though the Christian citizen presents revolutionary ideas, because such is the amazing effect of God's Word, we are not revolutionaries for revolution's sake. There are plenty of people in the world who dedicate their lives to that. They rebel against all authority for its own sake. The total opposite is true of the Christian citizen. We submit completely and willfully to authority and that submission will demand a careful consideration of the hierarchy and purposes established by God. His glory stands above all. At the end of His ministry, Jesus stressed the Father's glory was His aim: "I have glorified You on the earth. I have finished the work which You have given Me to do," (John 17:4, NKJV). So we, also, as Christ, aim to bring glory to God through all of life's travails. As Paul explained to the church in Corinth:

> [W]e have this treasure in jars of clay, to show that the surpassing power belongs to God and not to us. We are afflicted in every way, but not crushed; perplexed, but not driven to despair; persecuted, but not forsaken; struck down, but not destroyed; always carrying in the body the death of Jesus, so that the life of Jesus may also be manifested in our bodies. For we who live are always being given over to death for Jesus' sake, so that the life of Jesus also may be manifested in our mortal flesh... knowing that he who raised the Lord Jesus will raise us also with Jesus and bring us with you into his presence. For it is all for your sake, so that as grace extends to more and more people it may increase thanksgiving, to the glory of God (2 Corinthians 4:7-11, 14-15).

Let us, therefore, keep the glory of God always before us as a banner of both our brokenness and His power. It will be immeasurably helpful for every aspect of our lives, including civic engagement.

The second principle I want to stress is that we do not look to governmental authorities for hope. I am afraid we can fall into that type of mentality easier than many of us would think at first glance. If we are merely looking at the next election continually for things to "get better," we will be greatly disappointed. The Christian citizen lives under no such delusion. In fact, the Christian citizen already has an eternal hope! We are in need of nothing. Everything we need we get from our Lord and Savior Jesus Christ. Therefore, we engage in civil society and government, not to look for hope, but to bring hope! We have the hope that this hurting world needs. We seek to serve and show the love, peace, joy and contentment that only come from having a relationship with our Creator. We testify of His goodness and mercy. We testify of His awesome power to save and transform, not only individual, but also nations. We call our nation to a high standard; to a love of God above all and our neighbors as ourselves. We call our nation to repentance and submission. We call it to acknowledge reality and truth. We work and give in love, till we are spent for the cause of Christ.

The blessings of responding positively to that call are innumerable. Remember that famous passage from 2 Chronicles 7:14:

> [I]f my people who are called by my name humble them-
> selves, and pray and seek my face and turn from their
> wicked ways, then I will hear from heaven and will for-
> give their sin and heal their land.

May we heed that invitation and take a hold of that promise, for it can truly be ours. No matter how far we have fallen, God will not reject a contrite heart.[101] Our obedience will never go unnoticed. God is "slow to anger and abounding in steadfast love," (Psalm 145:8). He is just and trustworthy; He stands ready to receive us. "For everyone who asks receives, and the one who seeks finds, and to the one who knocks it will be opened," (Matthew 7:8). The question is, are we willing to humble ourselves and repent from our wicked ways.

---

101   Psalm 51:17.

CHAPTER SIX

THE DESPERATE CONDITION OF MAN

We have envisioned so far a very unique role for men and women in history, according to the Christian worldview shared by our forefathers. This is no accident. When they wrote that we are "endowed by [our] Creator with certain unalienable rights," they knew the massive implications they invoked. We are not just born, but created. This powerful truth denotes first and foremost the existence of a Creator. The Christian citizen knows this by faith: "By faith we understand that the universe was created by the word of God, so that what is seen was not made out of things that are visible," (Hebrews 11:3). That is the ultimate explanation of our beginnings, even for those who want to believe in the Big Bang Theory and the Evolutional Theory. For something to explode, it must *be something* first. The atheist scientist and the post-modern secular philosopher offer nothing to alleviate this obvious existential problem. How can something be created out of nothing? It is simply not possible. Unless one dares consider God. In the God of the Bible, more specifically, we find His Word in complete harmony with reality. He is eternal. He has no beginning and no end, but has always been. Not only that, His creation came to be by His Word, "so that what is seen was not made out of things that are visible." That is much different than saying

He took something out of Himself and created with that. This is simply an extraordinary claim that fits perfectly with our universe. He spoke and *it was*. Talk about a big bang.

The Word made flesh

"The word" is one of the most glorious mysteries of our existence. How can something intangible be so powerful? Words are just that, words. But oh how potent they can be! We shouldn't be that surprised for words continue to shape our world today. It is a simple, yet amazing reality. No wonder the Gospel according to John commences with those precious words, "In the beginning was the Word, and the Word was with God, and the Word was God," (John 1:1). Our ability to reason is the evolutionists' worst nightmare. They have no way of accounting for it. The great Roman philosopher Cicero (106 BC-43 BC) wrote, "[T]he first common possession of man and God is reason."[102] This is a profound mystery that fits perfectly with what we see around us and with the Word of God. Indeed it cannot be separated from the idea of our Creator—of meaning and purpose. It is self-evident. None of us were there with God in the beginning. Therefore, all theories about the beginning of the universe, including the Big Bang and Evolution, must be taken with some measure of faith by looking at the evidence we have available to us today. The Bible is realistic and surprisingly open in that sense, unlike the modern sophists who present their theories as "facts."

One last word on this matter —which is really not at the center of our topic in this chapter,— some modern believers have tried to reconcile the Biblical account of creation with the Big Bang and Evolutional theories. I find this a curious attempt in futility. What are they trying to accomplish? Why call into question the Biblical account to accommodate the unproven theories of mere men? If one dares consider an all-powerful God, that can create a universe out of nothing, He could create a new universe, or a very old one. In other words, in a second He can make a universe that looks as if it has been there for millions of years or one that looks completely new, just like a painter can paint a picture that looks very modern or one that looks very old. If you are starting from a belief in an all-powerful God, Who spoke and it was done, it is a curious endeavor then to feel the need to accommodate His Word to the

---

102   Marcus Tullius Cicero, *De Legibus*, (Clinton Walker Keyes trans., 1928).

speculative theories of men that are here today but will be gone tomorrow. I suspect these efforts might have something to do with our own insecurities, rather than with the Word of God. The acceptance of these theories has become a pre-requisite in some communities (especially in certain professional and academic circles), so it is understandable that some of us feel enormous pressure to adapt. As is always the case, God will look at our hearts.

In His image

But let us get back to human nature. The Founders asserted not only that we were created, but that we were created in a certain way: endowed with certain unalienable rights. Why would they say that? Could it be that this vision of the reality between men and women and God is indispensable to freedom? Since government does not give us these unalienable rights, it cannot take them away. It is a decidedly Christian worldview, and more importantly, it is true. It fits with reality. We all know there is a law written in the human heart that transcends our familial and cultural development. Cicero talked about it in terms of reason, saying it "exist[s], derived from the nature of the universe, urging men to right conduct and diverting them from wrongdoing, and this reason did not first become Law when it was written down, but when it first came into existence; and it came into existence simultaneously with the divine mind."[103] The Christian citizen agrees. We are more than a collection of cells that developed through "time plus matter plus chance." Here is the Genesis account of the creation of man and woman:

> Then God said, "Let Us make man in Our image, according to Our likeness; let them have dominion over the fish of the sea, over the birds of the air, and over the cattle, over all the earth and over every creeping thing that creeps on the earth." So God created man in His own image; in the image of God He created him; male and female He created them. Then God blessed them, and God said to them, "Be fruitful and multiply; fill the earth and subdue it; have dominion over the fish of the sea, over the birds of the air, and over every living thing that

---

103   Marcus Tullius Cicero, *The Great Legal Philosophers: Selected Readings in Jurisprudence* 51 (Clarence Morris ed., University of Pennsylvania Press 1971).

moves on the earth."

And God said, "See, I have given you every herb that yields seed which is on the face of all the earth, and every tree whose fruit yields seed; to you it shall be for food. Also, to every beast of the earth, to every bird of the air, and to everything that creeps on the earth, in which there is life, I have given every green herb for food"; and it was so. Then God saw everything that He had made, and indeed it was very good. So the evening and the morning were the sixth day. (Genesis 1:26–31)

The Biblical account is explained further in Genesis 2 where the Bible tells us, "[T]hen the LORD God formed the man of dust from the ground and breathed into his nostrils the breath of life, and the man became a living creature," (Genesis 2:7). Once again, this helps explain what we know to be true, that men and women are more than their bodies, we have souls. We have reason, the breath of life; we were created in His image. Ever wonder why we are such creative beings? We resemble the original "Creator." We bear our Maker's stamp. It fits perfectly.

No other creature was created in that way. We are not animals. That is why it is self-evident that modern efforts to treat animals equally (sometimes protected even more than we protect people) are deeply misguided. Sure, we are to be good stewards of God's creation, but to equate man with an animal is to devalue God whose image we bear. Men and women are rational beings and, as such, we are especially capable of taking care of animals and the rest of creation. In fact, this is what God desires us to do. He takes care of us; we are to take care of each other and creation. We were made that way. Notice, we did not have any say in the way we were created. "Will what is molded say to its molder, 'Why have you made me like this?'" (Romans 9:20). Therefore, we do not give ourselves value, we have it intrinsically. Our responsibility as to creation, as to each other and as to God is self-evident. Not to mention the responsibility we owe to ourselves. This is the genesis of the Founders' profession that we are "all created equal." Listen to the appeal of that great statesman Frederik Douglas (c.1818-1895) as he denounced the slave trade:

You profess to believe "that, of one blood, God made all

nations of men to dwell on the face of all the earth," and hath commanded all men, everywhere to love one another; yet you notoriously hate, (and glory in your hatred,) all men whose skins are not colored like your own.[104]

More on the Christian citizen's response to the injustice of slavery will come in Chapter eight, *Out of Biblical Soil*, where we will focus on religious freedom. The point here is that the nature of man and woman and the principles we are discussing are true, even when we don't follow them. It is a fact that we don't follow them. Those who wish to call our founding principles into question frequently point to our failures as if they were disproving the principles themselves, but the logic does not follow. The man who destroys his marriage by engaging in an adulterous relationship does not disprove the wisdom of marriage because he used to preach of faithfulness. He proves it. He too will see the consequences of failing to abide by his own advice — by God's law.

The way we were created has innumerable consequences to the way we live; very important practical consequences. Listen to the psalmist:

> For you formed my inward parts;
> you knitted me together in my mother's womb.
> I praise you, for I am fearfully and wonderfully made.
> Wonderful are your works;
> my soul knows it very well.
> My frame was not hidden from you,
> when I was being made in secret,
> intricately woven in the depths of the earth (Psalm 139:13-15).

If God formed us in our mother's womb, how are we then to justify abortion, for example? Who are we to interfere with God's grand design by calling it "a woman's right to choose?" To rebuke our Maker in such a way is beyond arrogant, it is suicidal. I am reminded of the powerful words of Supreme Court Justice Anthony Kennedy in *Gonzalez v. Carhart*, the famous partial-birth abortion case, where many were justifying the killing of a child while he or she was fully formed, with only his or her head remaining inside the womb. Justice Kennedy wrote:

---

104   Frederick Douglas, *Oration*, Delivered in Corinthian Hall, July 5, 1852, available at https://www.lib.rochester.edu/index.cfm?PAGE=2945, (accessed Sept. 11, 2014).

It is self-evident that a mother who comes to regret her choice to abort must struggle with grief more anguished and sorrow more profound when she learns, only after the event, what she once did not know: that she allowed a doctor to pierce the skull and vacuum the fast-developing brain of her unborn child.[105]

It pains me to read that paragraph. Abortion is one of the great tragedies (one of the great sins) of our age. President Ronald Reagan (1911-2004) articulated well the challenge before us:

This nation fought a terrible war so that black Americans would be guaranteed their God-given rights. Abraham Lincoln recognized that we could not survive as a free land when some could decide whether others should be free or slaves. Well, today another question begs to be asked: How can we survive as a free nation when some decide that others are not fit to live and should be done away with?

I believe no challenge is more important to the character of America than restoring the right to life to all human beings. Without that right, no other rights have meaning.[106]

The Christian citizen should stand boldly against this horrible violation of God's design, even as we care for the millions of women who have been duped into thinking what they have inside of their bodies is nothing but "a clump of cells."[107] The Biblical view of new life is much different than the world's: "Behold, children are a heritage from the LORD, the fruit of the womb a reward," (Psalm 127:3). Children are a blessing, not a curse. Our policies must reflect that.

---

105   *Gonzales v. Carhart*, 550 U.S. 124, 159-60, 127 S. Ct. 1610, 1634, 167 L. Ed. 2d 480 (2007).

106   Ronald Reagan, Remarks at the Annual Convention of the National Religious Broadcasters, January 30, 1984, available at http://www.presidency.ucsb.edu/ws/?pid=40394, (accessed Sept. 14, 2014).

107   Susan Michelle Tyrell, "Pro-life teen attacked on street by foul-mouthed abortion supporter," *LifeSiteNews*, July 10, 2014, available at http://www.lifesitenews.com/pulse/pro-life-teen-attacked-on-street-by-foul-mouthed-abortion-supporter, (accessed Sept. 11, 2014).

The call of the prophet Jeremiah takes us one step further: "[T]he word of the LORD came to me, saying, 'Before I formed you in the womb I knew you, and before you were born I consecrated you; I appointed you a prophet to the nations,'" (Jeremiah 1:4-5). Not only does God created us in our mother's womb, but He also has an eternal plan for us. We are created with a purpose. And this is exactly what our human experiences reveal. It is that indescribable feeling inside you that tells you that you were made for something bigger than yourself. You feel that way because you were indeed made for something more. Don't buy the lies of the modern-day serpents that tell you everything happens by accident. Remember the words of Paul to the Ephesians: [W]e are His workmanship, created in Christ Jesus for good works, which God prepared beforehand that we should walk in them," (Ephesians 2:10, NKJV). We were created for good works to the glory of God.

The Christian citizen must stand against any exploitation or devaluing of God's created beings for any reason, because of disability or old age, or race, or gender, or nationality or socioeconomic background, or any specific sin. Every man, woman and child is valuable. Yes, including those who consider themselves homosexual or transgender, and who choose to live in plain rebellion of God's admonition. I single the topic out given the urgency for wisdom and direction in this specific area for our culture at this point in history, not because homosexual conduct is any more problematic than any other sexual struggle in our lives. The man who continues to be unfaithful to his wife, finds himself in the same position before God, unable to see the infinitely more precious pleasures God has to offer that make the need to act on our internal appetites unprofitable and indeed undesirable. The Christian citizen must stand against the practice of homosexuality, but we must also stand against any attempt to mistreat those who identify as homosexual, treating them as less valuable than any other human created in the image of God. Our call is to repentance, never oppression. This is an important distinction to keep in today's day and age because anything less than the celebration of homosexuality is treated as bigotry. The truth is the Christian citizen has no choice in the matter. We follow God, He doesn't follow us. It is truly impossible to read the Word of God as a whole and conclude that Jesus Christ approves of the practice of homosexuality or any other sexual immorality for that matter. If we must suffer for standing on God's principles, then suffer we must. More on this in Chapter 12, *Joy Through*

Adversity. The bottom line is that we do not get to choose which parts of God's principles we wish to follow. We follow Him, the Person, Jesus Christ. He is our Maker and He loves us. We trust Him in every area of our lives, including with our sexuality. His love for us is most visible in the price He paid for our salvation: "For God so loved the world that He gave His only begotten Son, that whoever believes in Him should not perish but have everlasting life. For God did not send His Son into the world to condemn the world, but that the world through Him might be saved," (John 3:16-17, NKJV).

God's loving care for us should never cease to amaze us. It should make us stop and consider His ways. Listen to the way Jesus spoke about it:

> What do you think? If a man has a hundred sheep, and one of them goes astray, does he not leave the ninety-nine and go to the mountains to seek the one that is straying? And if he should find it, assuredly, I say to you, he rejoices more over that sheep than over the ninety-nine that did not go astray. Even so it is not the will of your Father who is in heaven that one of these little ones should perish (Matthew 18:12-14, NKJV).

Thanksgiving should be our response to this kind of God—thanksgiving, honor, fear and obedience. It is through Him that we look at all of creation and even ourselves.

Fallen

When I was growing up, many times I would go on the car with my dad I would ask, "Dad, where are we going?" and he would jokingly reply, "Pa' Viejo," in Spanish, roughly translated, "We're going to get old." His way, of course, of bringing a smile to my face and tell me "don't worry about it, what's the hurry?" For we are all going to die in the physical sense one day. It was a humorous way to express a massive reality; one that should not be overlooked because it serves as a great motivator for us, especially for the Christian citizen who knows "we will all stand before the judgment seat of God," (Romans 14:10). Second Corinthians 5:10 tells us why: "[W]e must all appear before the judgment seat of Christ, so that each one may receive what is due for what he has done in the body, whether good or evil." The words of Christ are even more chilling: "I tell you, on the day of judgment people will give account for every careless word they speak, for by your words you will be justified, and by your words you will be condemned," (Matthew 12:36–37). This concept is not popular today but that does not make it any less real. The reality has enormous implications for us personally and also for society. A citizenry who believes this truth has a big incentive, no doubt, to behave in a way that will be more beneficial to their standing before God and therefore, for the community at large. Whether in public or private, the Christian citizen knows God, who sees everything, will be his final judge. In fact, to God, who we are and how we behave in private is perhaps more important than who we are when others are present. In the next chapter we will discuss further how this is especially important when doing charitable work, but we see the same principle in many other areas. Take prayer, for example:

> [W]hen you pray, you must not be like the hypocrites. For they love to stand and pray in the synagogues and at the street corners, that they may be seen by others. Truly, I say to you, they have received their reward. But when you pray, go into your room and shut the door and pray to your Father who is in secret. And your Father who sees in secret will reward you (Matthew 6:5–6).

In this sense, God's command for us is to be good citizens, not merely to act like one. It is a profound distinction, and one that benefits society in many ways.

Jesus' main concern is with our spiritual death, not our physical one. We are all likely to experience a physical death and there is not much to it. But the astoundingly delicate condition of man is that he is born to a physical life but is spiritually dead. It is this death, the spiritual one, which has eternal implications. In other words, we are all sinners in need of redemption. "[F]or all have sinned and fall short of the glory of God," writes Paul in Romans 3:23. He also quoted the Psalms in that chapter:

> "None is righteous, no, not one;
> no one understands;
> no one seeks for God.

> All have turned aside; together they have become
> worthless;
> no one does good,
> not even one."
>
> "Their throat is an open grave;
> they use their tongues to deceive."
> "The venom of asps is under their lips."
> "Their mouth is full of curses and bitterness."
> "Their feet are swift to shed blood;
> in their paths are ruin and misery,
> and the way of peace they have not known."
> "There is no fear of God before their eyes" (Romans
> 3:10–18).

This is true equality; we are all sinners in need of redemption. That understanding of the desperate condition of man is also foundational to the form of government the founders envisioned. The genius of the separation of powers found in our Constitution lies on this basic truth: men, left to their own devices, are prone to evil—to give into their selfish ambitions. If men were to pursue their own desires, without regard to outside forces, it would be disastrous for society. We need "checks and balances," personally and corporately. The words of John Adams we referenced earlier allude to this reality, "[W]e have no government armed with power capable of contending with human passions unbridled by morality and religion..."[108] But as related to our form of government, the words of James Madison (1751-1836) in the Federalist No. 51 on the structure of government are very helpful:

> Ambition must be made to counteract ambition. The interest of the man must be connected with the constitutional rights of the place. It may be a reflection on human nature, that such devices should be necessary to control the abuses of government. But what is government itself, but the greatest of all reflections on human nature? If

---

108   John Adams, *The Works of John Adams, Second President of the United States: with a Life of the Author, Notes and Illustrations* Vol. 9. July 31, 2014 (Charles Francis Adams ed., Little, Brown and Co., 1856), available at http://oll.libertyfund.org/titles/2107#lf1431-09_head_222.

men were angels, no government would be necessary. If angels were to govern men, neither external nor internal controls on government would be necessary. In framing a government which is to be administered by men over men, the great difficulty lies in this: you must first enable the government to control the governed; and in the next place oblige it to control itself. A dependence on the people is, no doubt, the primary control on the government; but experience has taught mankind the necessity of auxiliary precautions.[109]

There is much wisdom in Madison's words. Our country has seen the blessings of the separation of powers, but we are experiencing a crisis at the moment that will test our character as it relates to this principle. Those checks and balances are being eroded in many different ways and we must get back to a place where we can embrace those checks even when they are a considerable inconvenience to our personal desires, because they serve as a check on our own selfish, sinful propensities. To accept that is both humble and wise.

Our humanity

Both the Christian worldview and American founding principles take men and women as they are and not as they wish they would be. Listen to the words of Paul describing his own sinful nature:

> For we know that the law is spiritual, but I am of the flesh, sold under sin. For I do not understand my own actions. For I do not do what I want, but I do the very thing I hate. Now if I do what I do not want, I agree with the law, that it is good. So now it is no longer I who do it, but sin that dwells within me. For I know that nothing good dwells in me, that is, in my flesh. For I have the desire to do what is right, but not the ability to carry it out. For I do not do the good I want, but the evil I do not want is what I keep on doing (Romans 7:14–19).

---

109   James Madison, *Federalist #51*, Independent Journal, Wednesday, February 6, 1788, available at http://www.constitution.org/fed/federa51.htm (accessed Sept. 11, 2014).

This wise, realistic understanding of human nature tells us we are to guard against ourselves, even as we strive to do what is good. I always remember that no one can hurt me more than I can hurt myself. Dietrich Bonhoeffer (1906-1945) said it this way in *The Cost of Discipleship*, "When all is said and done, the life of faith is nothing if not an unending struggle of the spirit with every available weapon against the flesh."[110] It is the cry of Robert Robinson (1735 – 1790) on his great hymn, *Come, Thou Fount of Every Blessing*:

> Prone to wander, Lord, I feel it,
> Prone to leave the God I love;
> Here's my heart, O take and seal it,
> Seal it for Thy courts above.[111]

Every man knows this to be true in his own life. The Christian citizen especially feels the great weight of his sin and the Lord's unmerited grace towards us, that "while we were still sinners, Christ died for us," (Romans 5:8). The result of such a belief is humility before God and empathy toward others. The great Charles Spurgeon (1834-1892), that incredible English preacher of the Word of God said, "The nearer a man lives to God, the more intensely has he to mourn over his own evil heart."[112]

We are wise then to acknowledge this truth in the way we govern. We must guard against human nature with a de-concentration of power that makes us rely on each other, enabling true accountability and inciting us to do better and more importantly to be better. If we fail to do this, we will only increase our sufferings, for we would be lying to ourselves about our true nature. And this in turn will bring great implications. Listen to the words of Fyodor Dostoyevsky (1821-1881) in *The Brothers Karamazov*:

> A man who lies to himself and listens to his own lie comes to a point where he does not discern any truth

---

110   Dietrich Bonhoeffer, *The Cost of Discipleship* 171 (Touchstone 1995 (1937)).

111   "Come, Thou Fount of Every Blessing," words by Robert Robinson (1758), music by John Wyeth (1813), available at http://cyberhymnal.org/htm/c/o/comethou.htm (accessed Sept. 11, 2014).

112   Rev. C. H. Spurgeon, "The Fainting Warrior," a sermon delivered on January 23rd, 1859 at the Music Hall, Royal Surrey Gardens, London, available at http://www.spurgeon.org/sermons/0235.htm (accessed Sept. 14, 2014).

either in himself or anywhere around him, and thus falls into disrespect towards himself and others. Not respecting anyone, he ceases to love, and having no love, he gives himself up to passions and coarse pleasures, in order to occupy and amuse himself, and in his vices reaches complete bestiality, and it all comes from lying continually to others and to himself. A man who lies to himself is often the first to take offense. It sometimes feels very good to take offense, doesn't it? And surely he knows that no one has offended him, and that he himself has invented the offense and told lies just for the beauty of it, that he has exaggerated for the sake of effect, that he has picked on a word and made a mountain out of a pea—he knows all of that, and still he is the first to take offense, he likes feeling offended, it gives him great pleasure and thus he reaches the point of real hostility…[113]

We would be blind not to recognize modern-day America in that passage. What ails us is more than a mere economic malaise. Sir Arthur Conan Doyle (1859-1930) put it on the lips of his most celebrated character, Sherlock Holmes this way: "It is my belief, Watson, founded upon my experience, that the lowest and vilest alleys in London do not present a more dreadful record of sin than does the smiling and beautiful countryside."[114] Sin knows no economic class, age, race, gender or nationality. A proper view of human nature gives us the proper foundation to guard against it on its application to government work and society in general. Even as applied to religion itself. It was the insight expressed by James Fenimore Cooper (1789-1851) on his socio-political novel *The Heidenmauer*:

> However pure may be a social system, or a religion, in the commencement of its power, the possession of an undisputed ascendency lures all alike into excesses fatal to consistency, to justice, and to truth. This is a consequence of the independent exercise of human volition, that seems

---

113   Fyodor Dostoevsky, *The Brothers Karamazov* 38 (Richard Pevear and Larrissa Volokhonsky trans., Farrar, Straus and Giroux, 12th edition 2002 (1880)).

114   Sir Arthur Conan Doyle, *Sherlock Holmes: The Complete Novels and Stories, Volume I,* 502 (Bantman Classic 1986 (1891)).

nearly inseparable from human frailty. We gradually come to substitute inclination and interest for right, until the moral foundation of the mind are sapped by indulgence, and what was once regarded with the aversion that wrong excites in the innocent, gets to be not only familiar, but justifiable by expediency and use.[115]

Such is the desperate condition of man that we must accept and deal with, while at the same time recognizing the incredible grace of God that always leaves us with hope instead of despair. It is a great mystery and something that makes the Christian citizen live in thanksgiving. The Psalmist wrote:

What is man that You are mindful of him,

And the son of man that You visit him?

For You have made him a little lower than the angels,

And You have crowned him with glory and honor.

You have made him to have dominion over the works of Your hands;

You have put all things under his feet... (Psalm 8:4-6, NKJV).[116]

We must strive to strike that balance. It is the balance of freedom. It makes us both wise as to each other and respectful towards God "who gives life to all things," (1 Timothy 6:13).

The good news

I am compelled to include one more reality here — the remedy for this desperate condition of man. It is, of course, the Gospel of Jesus Christ. The Scriptures tell us that we are all sinners and fall short of the glory of God.[117] God is holy and just. We, as sinners, not only cannot be in communion with this holy God, but His Justice condemns us as sinners.

---

115   James Fenimore Cooper, *The Heidenmauer* 98 (Wildside Press 2011 (1859)).

116   Also quoted by Paul in Hebrews 2:6-8.

117   Romans 3:23.

Remember that, "[T]he wages of sin is death," (Romans6:23). That is the just punishment for our sin. As a just god, God cannot just let us go, for that would be unjust. Therefore God sent his only Son Jesus Christ, who knew no sin, to bare our sins upon Him, that the justice of God might be satisfied. Jesus paid for our transgressions. As Isaiah 53:5 puts it: "[H]e was pierced for our transgressions; he was crushed for our iniquities; upon him was the chastisement that brought us peace, and with his wounds we are healed."

This is why I always tell my students to be careful about thinking that God "forgives" our sins, because although true, this idea tends to give us the picture that they have simply gone away, when in reality Jesus bore it all on the cross. He paid for the sins we have and will commit. That is the good news of the Gospel, that through His sacrifice on the cross we can be healed. Remember those magnificent words in John 3:16? "For God so loved the world, that he gave his only Son, that whoever believes in him should not perish but have eternal life." And 1 Corinthians 15:3-4: "For I delivered to you as of first importance what I also received: that Christ died for our sins in accordance with the Scriptures, that he was buried, that he was raised on the third day in accordance with the Scriptures."

Not only does God, through Jesus, forgive our sins but He also gives us His righteousness, so that His perfection is now attributed to us. What a wonderful thought! We are co-heirs with Christ, the Bible tells us.[118] That sinful, human nature that we have been discussing can be transformed and we can become new creatures in Christ.[119] We do this by repenting of our sins and turning our lives to God. We surrender our nature to Christ. We believe. "Believe in the Lord Jesus, and you will be saved," Acts 16:31tells us.

I invite you to do that right this minute. Put your trust in Christ. Believe, and you too will be saved.

---

118   *Id.* at 8:17.

119   "Truly, truly, I say to you, unless one is born of water and the Spirit, he cannot enter the kingdom of God. That which is born of the flesh is flesh, and that which is born of the Spirit is spirit," (John 3:5-6).

CHAPTER SEVEN
A PEOPLE

I find it extremely encouraging and intriguing that God deals with us at such a personal level (where He cares for every detail of our lives) while at the same time He keeps dealing with us as peoples and nations, and dealing with us in those terms, as He works all things for His purposes at the macro, eternal-perspective. Our personal actions have consequences beyond ourselves.

Establishing nations

We hear of God's dealings with nations all over Scripture. "Righteousness exalts a nation," says Proverbs 14:34, "but sin is a reproach to any people." Therefore, David would say things like, "Blessed is the nation whose God is the LORD, the people He has chosen as His own inheritance," (Psalm 33:12, NKJV). And, "The wicked shall be turned into hell, and all the nations that forget God," (Psalm 9:17, NKJV). This is so, of course, because God is the One who established us as nations in the first place. Acts 17:26-27 says, "And he made from one man every nation of mankind to live on all the face of the earth, having determined allotted periods and the boundaries of their dwelling place, that they should seek God, in the hope that they might feel their way toward him and find him." We, as Americans, are a people that God has established.

The examples are numerous. Psalm 22:28: "For kingship belongs to the Lord, and he rules over the nations." Isaiah 60:12: "For the nation and kingdom that will not serve you shall perish; those nations shall be utterly laid waste." Jesus spoke of nations at the final judgment, "When the Son of Man comes in his glory, and all the angels with him, then he will sit on his glorious throne. Before him will be gathered all the nations, and he will separate people one from another as a shepherd separates the sheep from the goats," (Matthew 25:31–32). And even in the New Earth, God speaks of nations:

> And the city has no need of sun or moon to shine on it, for the glory of God gives it light, and its lamp is the Lamb. By its light will the nations walk, and the kings of the earth will bring their glory into it, and its gates will never be shut by day—and there will be no night there. They will bring into it the glory and the honor of the nations. But nothing unclean will ever enter it, nor anyone who does what is detestable or false, but only those who are written in the Lamb's book of life (Revelations 21:23–27).

So, not only the way we behave as individuals matter, but the way we behave as peoples, as nations also matter. Listen to the way God spoke to Israel in Jeremiah 18:

> If at any time I declare concerning a nation or a kingdom, that I will pluck up and break down and destroy it, and if that nation, concerning which I have spoken, turns from its evil, I will relent of the disaster that I intended to do to it. And if at any time I declare concerning a nation or a kingdom that I will build and plant it, and if it does evil in my sight, not listening to my voice, then I will relent of the good that I had intended to do to it (Jeremiah 18:7–10).

Note then that a people's actions in relation to reality, in relation to the truth, mattered. The Bible speaks in terms of good and evil nations. The character of nations matter to the Lord and He responds to them according to righteousness. That is the point of that beautiful passage we mentioned earlier: "If My people who are called by My name will humble themselves, and pray and seek My face, and turn from their wicked ways, then I will hear from heaven, and will forgive their sin and heal their land," (2 Chronicles 7:14 NKJV). The call is to *His* people. It is the Christian citizens, those who believe and trust in Him, who must turn to Him in complete trust, His people on every nation on earth. It is not enough to identify ourselves with God and continue to behave as the world behaves. No, we have an eternal hope that changes everything, and the primary thing it should change is us. We must turn away from the sin that enslaves us and embrace His freedom. We must thirst for righteousness. We must get serious about God. But, again it is the people of God who have this burden. The world is under no such obligation. It falls on us. We are to influence our culture and government through the way we live—through the way we speak and act.

So strong is this call to the people of God that one man from among us can have a significant impact on the entire group. The story of Joshua helps us illustrate the point. After that incredible victory over Jericho we have already discussed where the walls came miraculously tumbling down, Israel had a major defeat at Ai. Joshua is devastated and takes his frustration to the Lord:

> Then Joshua tore his clothes and fell to the earth on his face before the ark of the Lord until the evening, he and the elders of Israel. And they put dust on their heads. And Joshua said, "Alas, O Lord God, why have you brought this people over the Jordan at all, to give us into the hands of the Amorites, to destroy us? Would that we had been content to dwell beyond the Jordan! O Lord, what can I say, when Israel has turned their backs before their enemies! For the Canaanites and all the inhabitants of the land will hear of it and will surround us and cut off our name from the earth. And what will you do for your great name?" (Joshua 7:6-9).

But the Lord's response came swiftly, demanding Joshua account for his people:

> The Lord said to Joshua, "Get up! Why have you fallen on

your face? Israel has sinned; they have transgressed my covenant that I commanded them; they have taken some of the devoted things; they have stolen and lied and put them among their own belongings. Therefore the people of Israel cannot stand before their enemies (Joshua 7:10-12a).

Here is what happened. Joshua had commanded his people in this as they were about to take Jericho: "But you, keep yourselves from the things devoted to destruction, lest when you have devoted them you take any of the devoted things and make the camp of Israel a thing for destruction and bring trouble upon it," (Joshua 6:18). They did not listen; at least not all of them. One man, "Achan the son of Carmi, son of Zabdi, son of Zerah, of the tribe of Judah, took some of the devoted things. And the anger of the Lord burned against the people of Israel," (Joshua 7:1). One man caused a national defeat. We, the people of God, bear an enormous responsibility and we must take God's commandment seriously. We have a duty unto God, ourselves and each other.

Listen to 1 Peter 2:5, "you yourselves like living stones are being built up as a spiritual house, to be a holy priesthood..." We as individuals are being built up as families to be a people that can offer hope and healing to whole nations, which is part of what a priest does wherever he operates. That is the role of Christian citizens within the bigger American family. There is no question we are built in and for community. Communion with God first and foremost, as Paul reminds us in the book or Romans: "For none of us lives to himself, and none of us dies to himself. For if we live, we live to the Lord, and if we die, we die to the Lord," (Romans 14:7-8). But going deeper, this is a God who continually commands us to "feed His sheep."[120] We have a call to serve our neighbors, to live outwardly. We certainly serve in different ways, for we all have different talents and gifts, but we all serve one God, who calls us to love and serve our neighbors as ourselves.[121] Here is Paul again:

---

120   "Jesus said to Simon Peter, 'Simon, son of John, do you love me more than these?' He said to him, 'Yes, Lord; you know that I love you.' He said to him, 'Feed my lambs.' He said to him a second time, 'Simon, son of John, do you love me?' He said to him, 'Yes, Lord; you know that I love you.' He said to him, 'Tend my sheep.' He said to him the third time, 'Simon, son of John, do you love me?' Peter was grieved because he said to him the third time, 'Do you love me?' and he said to him, 'Lord, you know everything; you know that I love you.' Jesus said to him, 'Feed my sheep,'" (John 21:17).

121   Mark 12:31.

Now there are varieties of gifts, but the same Spirit; and there are varieties of service, but the same Lord; and there are varieties of activities, but it is the same God who empowers them all in everyone. To each is given the manifestation of the Spirit for the common good (1 Corinthians 12:4-7).

Unity in diversity

Wherever we serve, whatever we have, it is not for ourselves but for the glory of God and, through Him, for the common good (for others). Paul explains this further with his magnificent analogy of the body:

> For just as the body is one and has many members, and all the members of the body, though many, are one body, so it is with Christ. For in one Spirit we were all baptized into one body—Jews or Greeks, slaves or free—and all were made to drink of one Spirit.

> For the body does not consist of one member but of many. If the foot should say, "Because I am not a hand, I do not belong to the body," that would not make it any less a part of the body. And if the ear should say, "Because I am not an eye, I do not belong to the body," that would not make it any less a part of the body. If the whole body were an eye, where would be the sense of hearing? If the whole body were an ear, where would be the sense of smell? But as it is, God arranged the members in the body, each one of them, as he chose. If all were a single member, where would the body be? As it is, there are many parts, yet one body.

> The eye cannot say to the hand, "I have no need of you," nor again the head to the feet, "I have no need of you." On the contrary, the parts of the body that seem to be weaker are indispensable, and on those parts of the body that we think less honorable we bestow the greater honor, and our unpresentable parts are treated with greater modesty, which our more presentable parts do not require. But God has so composed the body, giving greater honor to the part that lacked it, that there may be no division

in the body, but that the members may have the same care for one another. If one member suffers, all suffer together; if one member is honored, all rejoice together.

Now you are the body of Christ and individually members of it (1 Corinthians 12:12-27).

It would be hard for us to overstate how important this is to God. Paul encourages us to be of "one mind striving side by side for the faith of the gospel…" (Philippians 1:27). When Jesus took the time to pray of us (for future believers) He prayed for this one thing: unity. He prayed to the Father:

I do not ask for [the apostles] only, but also for those who will believe in me through their word, that they may all be one, just as you, Father, are in me, and I in you, that they also may be in us, so that the world may believe that you have sent me (John 17:20-21).

It is therefore in our unity that our best testimony is conveyed to the world. God deals with us as a body (His body), as a people. Just think of the wonderful examples of how God dealt with the people of Israel. It is extremely insightful for us to realize that under the new covenant, after the coming of Christ, God continues to deal with us as a people, as Christian citizens. There are no Christian "Lone Rangers" out there. If you feel yourself increasingly isolated as a Christian, it would be wise for you to seek out after other brothers and sisters around you. It is part of God's plan for His people. Later in that second chapter of 1 Peter, the Apostle says we have become a people precisely through Jesus Christ, that is, because of Him:

But you are a chosen generation, a royal priesthood, a holy nation, His own special people, that you may proclaim the praises of Him who called you out of darkness into His marvelous light; who once were not a people but are now the people of God, who had not obtained mercy but now have obtained mercy (1 Peter 2:9–10, NKJV).

Therefore, we are citizens of heaven, as we have discussed, with only One King, placed here in America for such a time as this and we submit to authorities and engage our culture and government to the glory of God the Father and through the power of His Son Jesus Christ. Peter continued:

> Beloved, I urge you as sojourners and exiles to abstain from the passions of the flesh, which wage war against your soul. Keep your conduct among the Gentiles honorable, so that when they speak against you as evildoers, they may see your good deeds and glorify God on the day of visitation (1 Peter 2:11–12).

Servants of the living God

As you can see we are indeed a people, sojourners and exiles, meaning we should behave not according to the standards of this age, but according to the standard of Him who put us right where we are, abstaining from conduct detrimental to our own bodies and soul, and serving others through good conduct. Notice Peter mentions our good deeds. This is appropriate, for the Christian citizen is a doer. We not only stand up against immoral conduct that falls short of the glory of God, but we, perhaps more importantly, do the deeds of God. We serve God and our fellow men and women, giving of ourselves till we are poured out for our neighbors. That is the hidden power of the verse that has directed my life and ministry and that gives title to this book, "And I will very gladly spend and be spent for your souls; though the more abundantly I love you, the less I am loved," (2 Corinthians 12:15 NKJV). It is one of the most difficult things to accept and to learn to live out. To reject our own tendency to live selfishly, for what we want and for the way we feel, and instead learn to give ourselves joyfully for the sake of others. Paul was so radical in this belief, he even said he would give his very soul for his brethren: "For I could wish that I myself were accursed and cut off from Christ for the sake of my brothers, my kinsmen according to the flesh," (Romans 9:3).

Take a look at Philippians 2:3-8:

> Do nothing from selfish ambition or conceit, but in humility count others more significant than yourselves. Let each of you look not only to his own interests, but also to the interests of others. Have this mind among yourselves,

which is yours in Christ Jesus, who, though he was in the form of God, did not count equality with God a thing to be grasped, but emptied himself, by taking the form of a servant, being born in the likeness of men. And being found in human form, he humbled himself by becoming obedient to the point of death, even death on a cross.

To take the principle even further, we seek to serve unselfishly, expecting nothing in return. In fact, we look to serve those who cannot repay us. This was Jesus' illustration with the Parable of the Great Banquet:

When you give a dinner or a banquet, do not invite your friends or your brothers or your relatives or rich neighbors, lest they also invite you in return and you be repaid. But when you give a feast, invite the poor, the crippled, the lame, the blind, and you will be blessed, because they cannot repay you. For you will be repaid at the resurrection of the just (Luke 14:12–14).

This can only be accomplished by being free from the slavery of our "wants," to give without expectancy. Sure, we can be charitable when we are celebrated for our charity. The world is full of such people, famous for their philanthropic work. I assure you, they have their reward. But ours is eternal reward, not an earthly one; a reward that comes when we do not seek our own benefit, but the glory of Him from whom all blessings come. We gain nothing by the praises of men. In fact, we must be weary of it. For while our flesh is eager to receive worldly praise, its taste, though sweet at the moment, turns bitter in a flash; it can be deadly. The praise of man actually hinders our work. Our joy is to please our Maker. He sees all and is most pleased when we do things, receiving nothing in return. It is what Jesus' admonition at the Sermon of the Mount was all about:

Beware of practicing your righteousness before other people in order to be seen by them, for then you will have no reward from your Father who is in heaven.

Thus, when you give to the needy, sound no trumpet before you, as the hypocrites do in the synagogues and in the streets, that they may be praised by others. Truly, I say to you, they have received their reward. But when you give to the needy, do not let your left hand know what your right hand is doing, so that your giving may be in secret. And your Father who sees in secret will reward you (Matthew 6:1–4).

You can see this is not a small, superficial principle. But a deep call to a way of living that can have an immense impact in our culture and in government. This should be our *modus operandi.*

Free in Christ

If we go back to that passage in 1 Peter 2, the Apostle Peter said we are his people "that [we] may proclaim the excellencies of him who called [us] out of darkness into his marvelous light," (v. 9) and we do what we do in order that people might "glorify God." Further down the chapter he calls us to, "Live as people who are free, not using your freedom as a cover-up for evil, but living as servants of God. Honor everyone. Love the brotherhood. Fear God. Honor the emperor," (v. 16–17). Again, that is a beautiful picture of our calling as Christian citizens. We even honor the "emperor," the authority set up by God for our good. We are to simply love God above all and our neighbor as ourselves. We are to be joyful servants. We reject the modern philosophy that "if it feels good, it must be right." We reject the culture's call to "believe in ourselves." The modern motivational speaker who gives this junk is setting us up for failure and disappointment. Oh, what peril there is in trusting what the Bible calls "deceitful above all things." For that is what Jeremiah 17:9 tells us about the human heart: "The heart is deceitful above all things, and desperately sick; who can understand it?" The answer comes swiftly in the next verse, only through Christ can we overcome our wickedness: "I the LORD search the heart and test the mind, to give every man according to his ways, according to the fruit of his deeds," (Jeremiah 17:10). Do not trust in yourself. Trust in God and repent. He knows you better than you know yourself. The Christian citizen is completely free and in his freedom he chooses to be a servant of the living God, serving his fellow countrymen in the fear of God and submitting to governmental authorities. Our times may be obscure, but our call is clear and it is an eternal call. It is unchanging. It does not evolve in relation to the obstacles before us. Our God is always bigger than the flimsy wants of men. He is always with us. "Just as I was with Moses," He promises Joshua, "so I will be with you. I will not leave you or forsake you," (Joshua 1:5).

So what then if we are repaid evil for good, as often happens in this world? What if the men and women for whom we give our lives reject us? What if our call to repentance and joyful living goes unanswered? Peter again:

> [H]ave unity of mind, sympathy, brotherly love, a tender heart, and a humble mind. Do not repay evil for evil or reviling for reviling, but on the contrary, bless, for to this you were called, that you may obtain a blessing. For
>
>> "Whoever desires to love life
>> and see good days,
>> let him keep his tongue from evil
>> and his lips from speaking deceit;
>> let him turn away from evil and do good;
>> let him seek peace and pursue it.
>> For the eyes of the Lord are on the righteous,
>> and his ears are open to their prayer.
>> But the face of the Lord is against those who do evil."
>
> Now who is there to harm you if you are zealous for what is good? But even if you should suffer for righteousness' sake, you will be blessed. Have no fear of them, nor be troubled, but in your hearts honor Christ the Lord as holy, always being prepared to make a defense to anyone who asks you for a reason for the hope that is in you; yet do it with gentleness and respect, having a good conscience, so that, when you are slandered, those who revile your good behavior in Christ may be put to shame. For it is better to suffer for doing good, if that should be God's will, than for doing evil (1 Peter 3:8–17).

A charitable people

The Christian concept of charity also presents to us a very different concept than the world presents us. It is amazing to see how easily it can be misconstrued. Take for example the never-ending discussions about the redistribution of wealth. To hear some, it seems we must rebel against the rich because all they want is to get richer, while the poor get poorer. Therefore, they would sanction the government taking from one group of people by force to give to those who don't have as much. Others, seeing the concept for what it is (thievery) rebel against the whole idea and show little regard for the poor. This is also a foolish mistake. The idea of giving to the poor is a Christian principle. Some, as they so often do, have distorted that principle to use it for political reasons, but we must resist the temptation to respond in like manner. It's the distortion we must fight, not the principle.

Jesus was approached by a rich young ruler who asked what he had to do to inherit eternal life. "[K]eep the commandments," Jesus answered, "You shall not murder, You shall not commit adultery, You shall not steal, You shall not bear false witness, Honor your father and mother, and, You shall love your neighbor as yourself," (Matthew 19:17-19). The young man responded, "'All these things I have kept from my youth. What do I still lack?' Jesus said to him, 'If you want to be perfect, go, sell what you have and give to the poor, and you will have treasure in heaven; and come, follow Me,'" (Matthew 19:20-21, NKJV).[122] Notice that Christian charity is about giving. The world's concept focuses on receiving, or in the case of government, on taking. The Messiah wants us to discover the joy of giving to the poor. The modern plan is different. They want the government to take what you have and they will make sure the poor get it, robing you of the liberating experience of willful giving. The Christian principle not only helps the person receiving the blessing but will, perhaps more importantly, make a better person of the giver. The world's concept deprives people of the redemptive quality of giving and actually makes it harder to be charitable.

That brings us to the next point: we are all required to give, no matter how little we have. Jesus' call is a radical departure from our human per-

---

122   *See also* Mark 10:17-22, Luke 18:18-23.

ceptions. Jesus said: "Whoever has two tunics is to share with him who has none, and whoever has food is to do likewise," (Luke 3:11). And: "[W]hen you give a feast, invite the poor, the crippled, the lame, the blind, and you will be blessed, because they cannot repay you. For you will be repaid at the resurrection of the just," (Luke 14:13-14). Many feel the call to charity is for the wealthy; they don't believe they have much, so that they are excused. But remember the widow who gave all she had?

> Jesus looked up and saw the rich putting their gifts into the offering box, and he saw a poor widow put in two small copper coins. And he said, "Truly, I tell you, this poor widow has put in more than all of them. For they all contributed out of their abundance, but she out of her poverty put in all she had to live on" (Luke 21:1-4).

Some may say the widow gives the money to the church and that's different. But listen to Jesus' illustration of the Day of Judgment, where He envisions all nations gathered before him as He "separate people one from another as a shepherd separates the sheep from the goats," (Matthew 25:32). To the "sheep" he says:

> Come, you who are blessed by my Father, inherit the kingdom prepared for you from the foundation of the world. For I was hungry and you gave me food, I was thirsty and you gave me drink, I was a stranger and you welcomed me, I was naked and you clothed me, I was sick and you visited me, I was in prison and you came to me (Matthew 25:34-36).

When those listening ask in astonishment, "When did we do that," He answers: "Truly, I say to you, as you did it to one of the least of these my brothers, you did it to me," (Matthew 25:40).

That's the principle: if you we love God, we will love those created in His image too. That means that giving comes naturally through the Spirit and it will have an everlasting impact on us and on society at large. Jesus modeled this perfectly for us. Time and again, the Bible tells us He was moved with compassion[123] for the people he saw and provided for those in need. Upon his touch, the blind could see,[124] the mute spoke,[125] the paralytic walked,[126] lepers were healed,[127] and the hungry were fed,[128] among other things. The Christian citizen, as follower of Christ, aims to do the same.

Lastly, the world's idea of "redistribution" through government is laughable on the practical side because the government does not really give to the poor. We all know how the government spends *the people's* money; billions go to bureaucratic commissions, taskforces and departments. They even use it to support organizations like Planned Parenthood, the number one abortion provider in the country (who profits not only from abortion but from the sale of baby organs as a result of abortions[129]), to the tune of over $500 million a year.[130] Government does many things, caring for the poor is not one of them. That's because caring for the poor is about relationships. It goes beyond money and, most certainly, beyond governments; it's about you and me. It is about the church, the body of Christ. This vision will strengthen individuals, families, communities, cities, states and our country.

If we really want to help the needy, let's promote that old Christian spirit of loving our neighbors as ourselves, instead of counting on the government to "spread the wealth around." Because they'll spread it around alright, around their political coffers, that is, while the poor get many things, except the care they desperately seek.

---

123 Matthew 9:36, 14:14, 15:32, 18:27, 20:34; Mark 1:41, 5:19, 6:34, 8:2; Luke 7:13.

124 *Id.* at 9:27-30.

125 *Id.* at 9:32-34.

126 *Id.* at 9:1-8, Mark 2:1-12, Luke 5:18-26.

127 *Id.* at 8:1-3, Mark 1:40-42, Luke 17:11-19.

128 Matthew 14:16-21, 15:29-39; Mark 6:35-44, 8:1-10; Luke 9:12-17; John 6:5-14.

129 Austin Ruse, "Planned Parenthood Investigation Reportedly Shows Doctors Discussing How to Maximize Revenue from Sale of Fetal Tissue," *Breitbart* (July 28, 2015), available at http://www.breitbart.com/big-government/2015/07/28/planned-parenthood-investigation-reportedly-shows-doctors-discussing-how-to-maximize-revenue-from-sale-of-fetal-tissue-graphic-footage/ (accessed July 28, 2015).

130 "Planned Parenthood receives record amount of taxpayer support," *Fox News* (January 08, 2013), available at http://www.foxnews.com/politics/2013/01/08/planned-parenthood-receives-record-amount-taxpayer-support/ (accessed Sept. 14, 2014).

United in prayer

We take it upon ourselves then. We serve, not only through service but also through prayer for those in need at home and abroad. As His righteous body, God hears our prayers and we must, in and through love, plead for the church and our nation. The prayer of Daniel for his people comes to mind:

> Then I turned my face to the Lord God, seeking him by prayer and pleas for mercy with fasting and sackcloth and ashes. I prayed to the Lord my God and made confession, saying, "O Lord, the great and awesome God, who keeps covenant and steadfast love with those who love him and keep his commandments, we have sinned and done wrong and acted wickedly and rebelled, turning aside from your commandments and rules. We have not listened to your servants the prophets, who spoke in your name to our kings, our princes, and our fathers, and to all the people of the land. To you, O Lord, belongs righteousness, but to us open shame, as at this day, to the men of Judah, to the inhabitants of Jerusalem, and to all Israel, those who are near and those who are far away, in all the lands to which you have driven them, because of the treachery that they have committed against you. To us, O LORD, belongs open shame, to our kings, to our princes, and to our fathers, because we have sinned against you. To the Lord our God belong mercy and forgiveness, for we have rebelled against him and have not obeyed the voice of the LORD our God by walking in his laws, which he set before us by his servants the prophets. All Israel has transgressed your law and turned aside, refusing to obey your voice. And the curse and oath that are written in the Law of Moses the servant of God have been poured out upon us, because we have sinned against him. He has confirmed his words, which he spoke against us and against our rulers who ruled us, by bringing upon us a great calamity. For under the whole heaven there has not been done anything like what has been done against Jerusalem. As it is written in the Law of Moses, all this

calamity has come upon us; yet we have not entreated the favor of the LORD our God, turning from our iniquities and gaining insight by your truth. Therefore the LORD has kept ready the calamity and has brought it upon us, for the LORD our God is righteous in all the works that he has done, and we have not obeyed his voice. And now, O Lord our God, who brought your people out of the land of Egypt with a mighty hand, and have made a name for yourself, as at this day, we have sinned, we have done wickedly.

"O Lord, according to all your righteous acts, let your anger and your wrath turn away from your city Jerusalem, your holy hill, because for our sins, and for the iniquities of our fathers, Jerusalem and your people have become a byword among all who are around us. Now therefore, O our God, listen to the prayer of your servant and to his pleas for mercy, and for your own sake, O Lord, make your face to shine upon your sanctuary, which is desolate. O my God, incline your ear and hear. Open your eyes and see our desolations, and the city that is called by your name. For we do not present our pleas before you because of our righteousness, but because of your great mercy. O Lord, hear; O Lord, forgive. O Lord, pay attention and act. Delay not, for your own sake, O my God, because your city and your people are called by your name" (Daniel 9:3–19).

The passion and compassion of Daniel for his misguided brethren is evident. So we too must have the same heart. Our God is real. He hears our prayers and he answers. Nehemiah prayed in a similar way:

"O LORD God of heaven, the great and awesome God who keeps covenant and steadfast love with those who love him and keep his commandments, let your ear be attentive and your eyes open, to hear the prayer of your servant that I now pray before you day and night for the people of Israel your servants, confessing the sins of the people of Israel, which we have sinned against you. Even

I and my father's house have sinned. We have acted very corruptly against you and have not kept the commandments, the statutes, and the rules that you commanded your servant Moses. Remember the word that you commanded your servant Moses, saying, 'If you are unfaithful, I will scatter you among the peoples, but if you return to me and keep my commandments and do them, though your outcasts are in the uttermost parts of heaven, from there I will gather them and bring them to the place that I have chosen, to make my name dwell there.' They are your servants and your people, whom you have redeemed by your great power and by your strong hand. O LORD, let your ear be attentive to the prayer of your servant, and to the prayer of your servants who delight to fear your name, and give success to your servant today, and grant him mercy in the sight of this man" (Nehemiah 1:5–11).

This attitude of the Christian citizen is not just real and a very good thing with infinite benefits to the nation, but it is solidly cemented as a foundational command from our Lord. Listen to the call of Paul in 1 Timothy 2:1-6:

First of all, then, I urge that supplications, prayers, intercessions, and thanksgivings be made for all people, for kings and all who are in high positions, that we may lead a peaceful and quiet life, godly and dignified in every way. This is good, and it is pleasing in the sight of God our Savior, who desires all people to be saved and to come to the knowledge of the truth. For there is one God, and there is one mediator between God and men, the man Christ Jesus, who gave himself as a ransom for all, which is the testimony given at the proper time.

There is simply no better blessing to a nation than a praying citizenry. This starts with a praying church. Jesus envisioned the church as a "House of Prayer,"[131] a church that answers this specific call to pray for all men, including our governmental authorities. Notice it is not just

---

131   "Is it not written, 'My house shall be called a house of prayer for all the nations'?" (Mark 11:17), quoting Isaiah 56:7; (see also Matthew 21:13).

for those who are Christians but for our worst enemies too; and also for those in power at every level. For all. The Christian citizen knows this is not a futile exercise. We are not just "meditating." We know God hears our prayers and He will answer in His love, mercy and righteousness.

Our country has seen the many benefits of this holy discipline. This Senate Resolution requesting the president to proclaim a day for "national prayer and humiliation" was introduced by Senator James Harlan on March 2, and adopted on March 3, 1863:

March 30, 1863

By the President of the United States of America.

A Proclamation.

Whereas, the Senate of the United States, devoutly recognizing the Supreme Authority and just Government of Almighty God, in all the affairs of men and of nations, has, by a resolution, requested the President to designate and set apart a day for National prayer and humiliation:

And whereas it is the duty of nations as well as of men, to own their dependence upon the overruling power of God, to confess their sins and transgressions, in humble sorrow, yet with assured hope that genuine repentance will lead to mercy and pardon; and to recognize the sublime truth, announced in the Holy Scriptures and proven by all history, that those nations only are blessed whose God is the Lord: And, insomuch as we know that, by His divine law, nations like individuals are subjected to punishments and chastisements in this world, may we not justly fear that the awful calamity of civil war, which now desolates the land, may be but a punishment, inflicted upon us, for our presumptuous sins, to the needful end of our national reformation as a whole People? We have been the recipients of the choicest bounties of Heaven. We have been preserved, these many years, in peace and prosperity. We have grown in numbers, wealth and power, as no other nation has ever grown. But we have forgotten God. We have forgotten the gracious hand which preserved us in peace, and multiplied and enriched and strengthened us; and we have vainly imagined, in the deceitfulness of our hearts, that all these blessings were produced by some superior wisdom and virtue of our own. Intoxicated with unbroken success, we have become too self-sufficient to feel the necessity of redeeming and preserving grace, too proud to pray to the God that made us!

It behooves us then, to humble ourselves before the offended Power, to confess our national sins, and to pray for clemency and forgiveness.

Now, therefore, in compliance with the request, and fully concurring in the views of the Senate, I do, by this my proclamation, designate and set apart Thursday, the 30th. day of April, 1863, as a day of national humiliation, fasting and prayer. And I do hereby request all the People to abstain, on that day, from their ordinary secular pursuits, and to unite, at their several places of public worship and their respective homes, in keeping the day holy to the Lord, and devoted to the humble discharge of the religious duties proper to that solemn occasion.

All this being done, in sincerity and truth, let us then rest humbly in the hope authorized by the Divine teachings, that the united cry of the Nation will be heard on high, and answered with blessings, no less than the pardon of our national sins, and the restoration of our now divided and suffering Country, to its former happy condition of unity and peace.

In witness whereof, I have hereunto set my hand and caused the seal of the United States to be affixed.

[L. S.]

Done at the City of Washington, this thirtieth day of March, in the year of our Lord one thousand eight hundred and sixty-three, and of the Independence of the

United States the eighty seventh.

By the President: ABRAHAM LINCOLN

WILLIAM H. SEWARD, Secretary of State.[132]

In 1952, President Harry S. Truman signed into law Public Law 82-324 establishing a National Day of Prayer after the U.S. Congress passed a Joint Resolution to that effect. President Ronald Reagan then established the first Thursday in May as the National Day of Prayer through Public Law 100-307 on January 25, 1988. And in 1998 President Bill Clinton signed a law that asks the president to issue a proclamation each year for the National Day of Prayer. The blessings we have enjoyed in America are undeniable. Some may dispute if there is any correlation between our national attitude towards prayer and these blessings, but they cannot deny the record. It is a fact that we have exalted prayer and it is a fact that we have been blessed. The Christian citizen knows there is definitely a specific correlation between the two. These blessings cannot exist apart from our humble call to Almighty God.

Unfortunately, many today work tirelessly to eradicate such exercises as a violation of "the separation of church and state." These misguided efforts seek the blessings of America, while failing to recognize the source of every blessing we have. They promote not a historical or factual view of religious freedom, but a distorted one that we must stand squarely against. The U.S. Supreme Court has rejected such efforts based on America's great heritage of reliance in Almighty God through prayer. In the 1983 landmark case of *Marsh v. Chambers*, the Court said unequivocally:

> In light of the unambiguous and unbroken history of more than 200 years, there can be no doubt that the practice of opening legislative sessions with prayer has become part of the fabric of our society. To invoke Divine guidance on a public body entrusted with making the laws is not, in these circumstances, an "establishment" of religion or a step toward establishment; it is simply a tol-

---

132   Abraham Lincoln, "Proclamation Appointing a National Fast Day," *Collected Works of Abraham Lincoln Volume 6* (March 30, 1863), available at http://quod.lib.umich.edu/l/lincoln/lincoln6/1:336.1?rgn=div2;view=fulltext (accessed Sept. 14, 2014).

erable acknowledgment of beliefs widely held among the people of this country. As Justice Douglas observed, "[w]e are a religious people whose institutions presuppose a Supreme Being."[133]

That is who we are as a people — as Americans. May we never forget.

---

133   *Marsh v. Chambers*, 463 U.S. 783, 792, 103 S. Ct. 3330, 3336, 77 L. Ed. 2d 1019 (1983).

Part Three
PRACTICAL APPLICATION

CHAPTER EIGHT
OUT OF BIBLICAL SOIL

The American ideal was born of self-evident truths, as the Declaration of Independence puts it. We value and protect unalienable rights. These are rights given to us by our Creator and which the government cannot take away. Religious freedom is known as America's first freedom because it is the first of the rights protected by the First Amendment to the U.S. Constitution. There is a reason for that distinction; religion deals with the most important questions in life. Without religious freedom, there can be no freedom at all. The Founders knew this from personal experience and because of their love and respect for the Bible. The whole system of government they created was based on the basic principles of the Christian Faith, which is the only fertile soil for the First Amendment to spring out. Not on the principles of any particular denomination, to be sure, but on the principles of a sincere pursuit of God through the Holy Scriptures. Some quotes will help us see this is the case. Here is John Adams, the principal author of the Bill of Rights:

> The general principles on which the fathers achieved independence, were... the general principles of Christianity... Now I will avow, that I then believed, and now

believe that those general principles of Christianity are as eternal and immutable as the existence and attributes of God; and that those principles of liberty are as unalterable as human nature and our terrestrial, mundane system... I believe they would never make discoveries in contradiction to these general principles.[134]

He has been proven right; time has only affirmed each and every principle of the Christian faith. Though we stray away from them time after time, we eventually have to return to the truth after much heartache. We had to fight a civil war to prove what we already knew, that "all men are created equal." Notice John Adams recognizes that the principles are eternal and immutable. This is very important to remember as we seek to withstand today's attacks and the ones we will surely face in the future. The progress we seek cannot come at the expense of the principles or we are bound to fail. We have traveled the road that leads away from these principles already and its end is unspeakable pain.

The Founders also knew the perils of straying away from these basic principles. It is why they linked them so closely to our foundations. John Quincy Adams (1767-1848), the sixth president of the United States, had this to say when he was invited to speak on the Sixty First Anniversary of the Declaration of Independence, July 4th, 1837:

Why is it, Friends and Fellow Citizens, that you are here assembled? ... Why is it that, next to the birthday of the Savior of the World, your most joyous and most venerated festival returns on this day? ... Is it not that, in the chain of human events, the birthday of the nation is indissolubly linked with the birthday of the Savior? That it forms a leading event in the progress of the gospel dispensation? Is it not that the Declaration of Independence first organized the social compact on the foundation of the Redeemer's mission upon earth? That it laid the corner stone of human government upon the first

---

134   Kees de Mooy, *The Wisdom of John Adams* 35-36 (Kensington Publishing Corp. 2003).

precepts of Christianity...[135]

Almost no one would make or even see this connection today, but it is real and there was a time when it was obviously clear, not only to the Founders but to the majority of people in America. One of the Founding Fathers Samuel Adams (1722-1803) argued we could not give up our unalienable rights even if we wanted to. He wrote:

> The right of freedom being the gift of God Almighty, it is not in the power of man to alienate this gift and voluntarily become a slave... These may be best understood by reading and carefully studying the institutes of the great Law-giver and head of the Christian Church, which are to be found clearly written and promulgated in the New Testament.[136]

In other words, it is impossible to understand freedom and liberty, as the Founders developed it through the founding documents, apart from Holy Scripture. It would be like trying to understand Shakespeare without language. Thomas Jefferson (1743-1826), the principal author of the Declaration of Independence, had his famous words on the topic forever carved in the stones at his memorial in Washington, D.C.:

> Almighty God hath created the mind free. All attempts to influence it by temporal punishments or burthens... are a departure from the plan of the Holy Author of our religion...No man shall be compelled to frequent or support any religious worship or ministry or shall otherwise suffer on account of his religious opinions or belief, but all men shall be free to profess and by argument to maintain, their opinions in matters of religion. I know but

---

135   John Quincy Adams, *An Oration Delivered Before the Inhabitants of the Town of Newburyport, at their request, on the Sixty-First Anniversary of the Declaration of Independence*, July 4th, 1837 (Morss and Brewster), available at http://www.wallbuilders.com/libissuesarticles.asp?id=9717 (accessed Sept. 11, 2014).

136   *Harper's Encyclopedia of United States History 458 A.D. to 1905*. New York Tribune Edition 56 (Benson John Lossing, Woodrow Wilson ed., Harper & Brothers 1905), available at http://books.google.com/books?id=igA7AQAAIAAJ&printse c=frontcover&source=gbs_ge_summary_r&cad=0#v=onepage&q&f=false (accessed Sept. 11, 2014).

one code of morality for men whether acting singly or collectively.[137]

The free man

God created man free; He is the author of religious freedom. He could have created a man that could only believe in Him, but He didn't. He gave us logic and reason and has even included us in His plan to make His name known to all mankind. This is incredibly powerful and humbling. Here is another quote inscribed in the Jefferson Memorial:

> God who gave us life gave us liberty. Can the liberties of a nation be secure when we have removed a conviction that these liberties are the gift of God? Indeed I tremble for my country when I reflect that God is just, that his justice cannot sleep forever.[138]

Such was the mindset of those who listed religious freedom at the top of our Bill of Rights. They thought of a God that was always involved in human affairs. Some may find it odd today to say that religious freedom was born out of Biblical soil, but this is a most consistent teaching with Scripture. We have already mentioned numerous Christians throughout Scriptures who not only survived but thrived under the rule of hostile governmental authorities and cultures, who glorified God in word and deed, among other religious practices. It is interesting, in the case of Daniel, the Bible tells us that, after Daniel was able to interpret the king's dream when all other "magicians, enchanters and sorcerers" failed,[139] "Then the king gave Daniel high honors and many great gifts, and made him ruler over the whole province of Babylon and chief prefect over all the wise men of Babylon."[140] So here is Daniel, the servant of the Living God, and not only must he serve Nebuchadnezzar (which would be bad

---

137   Thomas Jefferson Memorial, Panel II, Washington, D.C., text available at http://www.monticello.org/site/jefferson/quotations-jefferson-memorial   (accessed Sept. 11, 2014).

138   Thomas Jefferson Memorial, Panel III, Washington, D.C., text available at http://www.monticello.org/site/jefferson/quotations-jefferson-memorial   (accessed Sept. 11, 2014).

139   Daniel 2:2.

140   *Id.* at 2:48.

enough), but he is now to be in charge of "the magicians, the enchanters and the sorcerers," etc. It must not have been easy. Yet Daniel did everything in that position to the glory of God. We know already that this did not meant that he would do everything that was commanded of him, that he would stand up to Nebuchadnezzar when and if his religious freedom was violated, but he had enough confidence in the God he served that he did not feel threatened in any way by these pagan magicians and sorcerers. The Christian faith does not shy away among other faiths, it is the true faith and we believe it will stand up to the most rigorous scrutiny and evaluation, among all others, for those who humbly seek after truth. It will be proven true in due course.

This was the confidence of Elijah before the prophets of Baal who tested God and saw Him respond right before their eyes. Here is the scene: At the time when Elijah was the principal prophet of Israel, Ahab reigned as the seventh king of Israel in Samaria. The Bible tells us that "Ahab did more to provoke the LORD, the God of Israel, to anger than all the kings of Israel who were before him," (1 Kings 16:33). He had taken for his wife Jezebel, the daughter Ethbaal king of the Sidonians and he went and served Baal and worshiped him. Not surprisingly, he also created other idols also.[141] Elijah, prompted by the Lord, predicts a drought, which of course comes to pass.[142] He is then called into hiding.[143] Though at first we don't know why, the story soon tells us that Ahab becomes so evil that he allows Jezebel to kill all of the prophets of the Lord; only Elijah and a hundred others hidden in caves by Obadiah, a believer who oversaw Ahab's household, survived.[144] But God soon calls Elijah to go back and confront Ahab. He gets Ahab to gather all the people of Israel and the 450 prophets of Baal at Mount Carmel and he makes an incredible proposal. He says:

> I alone am left a prophet of the Lord; but Baal's prophets
> are four hundred and fifty men. Therefore let them give
> us two bulls; and let them choose one bull for themselves,
> cut it in pieces, and lay it on the wood, but put no fire un-

---

141   1 Kings 16:33.

142   *Id.* at 17:1.

143   *Id.* at 17:3.

144   *Id.* at 18:4.

der it; and I will prepare the other bull, and lay it on the wood, but put no fire under it. Then you call on the name of your gods, and I will call on the name of the Lord; and the God who answers by fire, He is God (1 Kings 18:22-24, NKJV).

Can you imagine such boldness? The people were pleased with his proposal. The prophets of Baal went first, but they failed, as we might expect. They cried out for hours, danced and did everything they could to try to get their god to respond. But no response came, of course.

Elijah mocked them and said, "Cry aloud, for he is a god; either he is meditating, or he is busy, or he is on a journey, or perhaps he is sleeping and must be awakened." So they cried aloud, and cut themselves, as was their custom, with knives and lances, until the blood gushed out on them. And when midday was past, they prophesied until the time of the offering of the evening sacrifice. But there was no voice; no one answered, no one paid attention (1 Kings 18:27-29).

It was time for Elijah to call on Yahweh, the One true God, and nobody could have predicted what he did next.

[H]e said, "Fill four jars with water and pour it on the burnt offering and on the wood." And he said, "Do it a second time." And they did it a second time. And he said, "Do it a third time." And they did it a third time. And the water ran around the altar and filled the trench also with water (1 Kings 18:33-35).

Such is the confidence we can have on God. He is real. He hears our prayers. And He answers our prayers. Elijah prayed. "Then the fire of the Lord fell and consumed the burnt offering and the wood and the stones and the dust, and licked up the water that was in the trench," (1 Kings 18:38). No need for the Christian citizen to fear the contradictory ideas of different belief systems. Our God is true. The prophets of Baal lost their lives that day, not because of their religious beliefs, but because of the heinous acts they had committed in the name of religion. Evil acts committed under any religious name, including Christianity, are nevertheless evil. Dressing evil up in a "goodness" or "religious" costume does not sanctify it.

Equality and truth

Religious freedom by no means is synonymous with saying that all religions are equal. All men are equal, not all ideas. That all religions are equal is a common fallacy, but one that is easily disproven. Religious equality is in no way necessary for religious freedom. In fact, as I will expand on later, it is precisely because there is one objective truth that is ascertainable to us all, that we should all be free to pursue that truth. For the Christian citizen, the need for religious freedom is most easily seen in the charge that our Lord and Savior Jesus Christ gave us before he went to be with the Father. Namely, the Great Commission:

> Now the eleven disciples went to Galilee, to the mountain to which Jesus had directed them. And when they saw him they worshiped him, but some doubted. And Jesus came and said to them, "All authority in heaven and on earth has been given to me. Go therefore and make disciples of all nations, baptizing them in the name of the Father and of the Son and of the Holy Spirit, teaching them to observe all that I have commanded you. And behold, I am with you always, to the end of the age" (Matthew 28:16–20).

It is a curious thing to think of our Lord's command. We know that the work of someone believing and accept Him is a work of the Holy Spirit, not ours. John 3:3 says, "Truly, truly, I say to you, unless one is born again he cannot see the kingdom of God." And John 6:63, "It is the Spirit who gives life; the flesh is no help at all." Yet most times God chooses to use His people to convey the life-giving message of the Gospel. "Faith comes by hearing," says Paul in Romans 10:17. "[H]ow are they to believe in him of whom they have never heard? And how are they to hear without someone preaching?" (Romans 10:14). Again, God need not do it this way, but He chooses to do it this way in His eternal wisdom.

Therefore, we must be free to preach the good news of the Gospel and the Christian citizen must do so whether he is free to do so or not, in human terms. We have religious liberty; it is an unalienable right. We only seek government's respect of that right, as our forefathers recognized it must happen at the start of the great American experiment, so that it may not interfere with it in an abusive way. Again, we do not look to government for hope. We have hope and we want to be free to share that hope with others, as we are commanded.

The constitutional text

A proper understanding of the text of the First Amendment is essential for an accurate interpretation of these ideas in America. The religious freedom clauses of the First Amendment have been interpreted or misinterpreted to mean the exact opposite of what the writers intended in some cases. So it is helpful for us to go back to the text and highlight some important parts. Here is the full text of the First Amendment:

> Congress shall make no law respecting an establishment of religion, or prohibiting the free exercise thereof; or abridging the freedom of speech, or of the press; or the right of the people peaceably to assemble, and to petition the Government for a redress of grievances.[145]

The first two clauses deal with religion, "Congress shall make no law respecting an establishment of religion, or prohibiting the free exercise thereof." The first clause is known as the Establishment Clause: "Congress shall make no law respecting an establishment of religion." The second is known as the Free Exercise Clause: "or prohibiting the free exercise thereof." The Free Exercise Clause is perhaps easier to understand this way: Congress shall make no law... prohibiting the free exercise of religion. Notice the first word for the two clauses is "Congress." These are clauses that limit Congress' actions, not the actions of individuals. I know you hear these clauses used to limit the actions of individuals time and again, but that is not the original meaning of the text. Over and over, Government has tried to dictate and manipulate the receipt of government benefits on conditions of the surrender of certain unpopu-

---

145   U.S. Const. amend. I.

lar religious beliefs, but that runs totally contrary to what the Founders sought to protect. It is precisely the type of manipulation they wanted to prevent and it is a clear violation of our unalienable right to religious liberty.

Let's move to the next part of the religion clauses in the First Amendment, "shall make no law." These clauses limit Congress, and Congress alone, in the making of laws, not in any other way. Today, Congress wants to limit who it contracts with to those who are willing to surrender certain religious beliefs, for example. It wants to control what teachers say in their History classes, because they might be "Establishing a religion" by citing the Pledge of Allegiance or reading the Bible. All nonsense. They are the deeply misguided efforts of a few radicals to secularize our nation and transform it forever. The only way for government to fulfill the vision of the Free Exercise Clause is to be impartial as to the individual pursuit of religion. It should only concern itself with the actions and character of individuals and not with their faiths.

The Establishment Clause

"Establishing a religion" is heavy language. It is not prohibiting mere involvement in religious things. If I tell you I am establishing a charity, you do not suppose me merely being involved with a charity, but with the forming, the setting up of that charity. So too it is with the establishment of a religion, it is very clear that the language goes beyond mere participation in religious practices. In fact, the examples are endless of the many things the Founders did that seemingly run afoul of today's distorted understanding of the Establishment Clause. They established paid chaplains,[146] they had services at the capitol,[147] and they proclaim days of prayer and thanksgiving, as we have seen. The examples are overwhelming. Today's poor understanding of the Establishment clause has been of no help to freedom. It has not alleviated disputes or cleared our understanding of these issues, in fact it has worsened them. Today,

---

146   David Barton, "Congressional Records on Chaplains" (*WallBuilders*), available at http://www.wallbuilders.com/LIBissuesArticles.asp?id=171919 (accessed July 28, 2015).

147   David Barton, "Church in the U.S. Capitol" (*WallBuilders* November 10, 2005), available at http://www.wallbuilders.com/libissuesarticles.asp?id=90 (accessed July 28, 2015).

those who claim tolerance are the most intolerant of all and that is to be expected when you ignore the clear principles of our founding, which have their root in the Word of God.

A great example is the display of the Ten Commandments in public property. As we will discuss in the upcoming chapters these laws serve as the basis of much of American jurisprudence and our adherence to them have blessed our nation beyond measure. They are as historically engrained on our laws as the Constitution itself. But in a series of cases the Supreme Court of the United States has now decided it will judge the display of the Ten Commandments based on the motives of those who enacted them.[148] The result is not clarity in jurisprudence, but a mudding of the waters that serves no real purpose but to encourage the fake outrage of secularists to challenge every display and question the motives of those who support them.

The Free Exercise Clause

The modern dangers in the area of the Free Exercise Clause come from a novel approach that seeks to limit the free exercise of religion to a selected few areas. The issue was discussed prominently in the Supreme Court of the United States' case that created a constitutional right to same-sex "marriage" (*Obergefell v. Hodges)*. The creation of this new constitutional right to same-sex "marriage" creates an inevitable conflict with the religious liberties protected in the First Amendment. Many, in fact most, people of faith believe that, as Scripture says, marriage was created by God as the union between one man and one woman for life, reflecting the relationship of Christ and the Church. Trying to assure Americans of their religious liberty, Justice Anthony Kennedy writing for the Court said:

> Finally, it must be emphasized that religions, and those who adhere to religious doctrines, may continue to advocate with utmost, sincere conviction that, by divine precepts, same-sex marriage should not be condoned. The First Amendment ensures that religious organizations and persons are given proper protection as they seek to

---

148   *See Van Orden v. Perry*, 545 U.S. 677 (2005) upholding the display and *McCreary County v. ACLU*, 545 U.S. 844 (2005) declaring it unconstitutional.

teach the principles that are so fulfilling and so central to their lives and faiths, and to their own deep aspirations to continue the family structure they have long revered.[149]

Did you notice the limitation on the exercise of religion? The First Amendment guarantees much more than just the teaching and advocacy of our religious beliefs. The Chief Justice of the Supreme Court John Roberts identified the Court's sleight of hand:

> The majority graciously suggests that religious believers may continue to "advocate" and "teach" their views of marriage. The First Amendment guarantees, however, the freedom to "exercise" religion. Ominously, that is not a word the majority uses. Hard questions arise when people of faith exercise religion in ways that may be seen to conflict with the new right to same-sex marriage—when, for example, a religious college provides married student housing only to opposite-sex married couples, or a religious adoption agency declines to place children with same-sex married couples. Indeed, the Solicitor General candidly acknowledged that the tax exemptions of some religious institutions would be in question if they opposed same-sex marriage. There is little doubt that these and similar questions will soon be before this Court. Unfortunately, people of faith can take no comfort in the treatment they receive from the majority today. (Internal citations omitted)[150]

Others want to limit our First Amendment religious liberty protections to the freedom of worship. But again, that is not what the Constitution protects. It is a complete distortion of the text and of the basic concept of freedom of religion. We usually do not run into trouble with the way we worship God because it is usually an extremely personal thing. The issues arise when we want to live out our lives in a manner that reflect the teachings of our faiths. The "exercise" of religion implies action, movement, doing, service. That's the freedom that must be recognized

---

149   *Obergefell v. Hodges*, 576 U.S. ___, 27 (2015).

150   *Obergefell v. Hodges*, 576 U.S. ___, 28 (2015) (Roberts, J. dissenting).

and protected, the whole movement and service of religion. How many cases we see today of Christian ministries having to close or move due to the heavy hand of government forcing them to betray their religious beliefs if they want to continue to operate in the "stream of commerce"?[151]

The Little Sisters of the Poor case can help us illustrate. The Sisters run 30 health care facilities for the elderly poor in the United States — from nursing homes, to intermediate care to residential or assisted living and other independent-living facilities. These devoted Sisters disregarded worldly comforts, taking vows of poverty, chastity, obedience and hospitality, in order to serve their Lord and their neighbors. The Little Sisters of the Poor actually maintain a tradition of begging, demonstrating a life of true dependence on faith. For many on the outside looking in, the Sister's devotion is unparalleled, even compared to many churches and pastors. But the government maintains that the Sisters and their fellow laborers are not religious enough to deserve a "religious exemption" from a mandate, imposed by law, that they must offer contraceptives and abortifacients through their health insurance, in violation of their deeply held religious beliefs. Churches and other religious organizations are exempted, but not the Little Sisters of the Poor.[152]

This is a most insidious violation of the First Amendment and one that has significant consequences for individuals and families. The government's solution to their violation of the *exercise* of religion is to "exempt churches and pastors" from their oppressive policies. But, do you remember reading the words "church" or "pastor" in the text of the first amendment? No. Religious freedom belongs to the individual, not just to churches and pastors. We all should enjoy full religious freedom. It is preposterous to say that our religious liberties are attached to a seminary degree. We must be on guard that we do not buy a government selling us laws that limit our individual religious freedom, while allowing churches and pastors to be "free" or limiting what we do to what is done within the four walls of a church. That is a form of imprisonment that is contrary to our founding principles. These are oppressive laws, despite their benevolent appearance. Part of that promise to be free to

---

151   Laurie Goodstein, "Bishops Say Rules on Gay Parents Limit Freedom of Religion," *N.Y. Times*, December 29, 2011 at A16.

152   *Little Sisters of the Poor v. Burwell,* The Becket Fund for Religious Liberty, available at http://www.becketfund.org/littlesisters/ (accessed July 29, 2015).

"pursue happiness" is the ability to seek and obey God in all that we do, including the way we run businesses, have friends and marriages, play sports, establish schools, practice medicine or law, etc., in a way that is in complete harmony with our deeply held religious beliefs. Government should be supportive of those efforts, for it benefits enormously from a free people that are content and productive in their endeavors. Oppression is never prosperous in the long run.

The separation of church and state

You might have noticed that the text of the First Amendment lacked today's most popular phrase when talking about this topic: "the wall of separation between church and state." That is because the phrase is not in the text of the Constitution. The phrase was adopted by the U.S. Supreme Court from a letter by Thomas Jefferson when interpreting the First Amendment, which is not wrong in and of itself, but the substitution of the language out of context certainly is. That is what we have today, a complete substitution of the language that has had disastrous consequences and has opened us up to the abuses and exploitations of those in power and a few militant secularists. This is especially true when one realizes the phrase itself has acquired the exact opposite meaning given by Jefferson. The phrase as Jefferson used it was in line with the Biblical concept of religious freedom. Let's take a look.

Jefferson received a letter from the Danbury Baptists on October 7, 1801, expressing their concerns that the new federal government would intervene with their religious liberty:

> Our sentiments are uniformly on the side of religious liberty: that religion is at all times and places a matter between God and individuals, that no man ought to suffer in name, person, or effects on account of his religious opinions, [and] that the legitimate power of civil government extends no further than to punish the man who works ill to his neighbor.[153]

---

153   Thomas Jefferson, *Letter From the Danbury Baptist Association*, October 7, 1801, available at https://jeffersonpapers.princeton.edu/selected-documents/danbury-baptist-association (accessed Sept. 17, 2014).

Jefferson, in turn, replies in full agreement, assuring them that this "wall of separation between church and state," recognized by the First Amendment, would prevent the federal government from interfering with the religious liberties of the states. Here is the text of his letter of reply:

> Believing with you that religion is a matter which lies solely between man and his God; that he owes account to none other for his faith or his worship; that the legislative powers of government reach actions only and not opinions, I contemplate with sovereign reverence that act of the whole American people which declared that their legislature should "make no law respecting an establishment of religion or prohibiting the free exercise thereof," thus building a wall of separation between Church and State.
>
> Adhering to this expression of the supreme will of the nation in behalf of the rights of conscience, I shall see with sincere satisfaction the progress of those sentiments...[154]

It is preposterous, therefore, to read this language, as some courts have interpreted, to prohibit a state government from allowing religious monuments for our veterans on government land[155] or allowing voluntary prayer in public schools.[156] Americans should be free to express their faith and worship, even their religiosity, without government interference. Unfortunately, as judges have appropriated themselves of the legislative role, they have become increasingly the ones infringing on our religious freedoms.

More religious freedom, not less

The Biblical view of religious freedom actually supports the "separation of church and state" on its face. It does not run contrary to it in any way. That is why the more application of Biblical truth we have, the

---

154   Thomas Jefferson, *Final Letter to the Danbury Baptists*, January 1, 1802, available at: http://www.loc.gov/loc/lcib/9806/danpre.html (accessed Sept. 17, 2014).

155   Tony Perry, "U.S. Supreme Court declines to take up Mt. Soledad cross case," *L.A. Times*, available at: http://www.latimes.com/local/lanow/la-me-ln-court-mt-soledad-cross-20140630-story.html (accessed Sept. 17, 2014).

156   *Engel v. Vitale*, 370 U.S. 421, 82 S. Ct. 1261, 8 L. Ed. 2d 601 (1962).

more religious freedom we will have for all. U.S. Supreme Court Justice Louis Brandeis famously wrote that the answer to objectionable speech "is more speech, not enforced silence."[157] This seems a most reasonable proposition. If you are offended by someone's position, you can counter it with your own arguments and expose their error for the world to see and reject. It is a concept that has served our Republic well in the fight for liberty and freedom. The concept applies to all areas of the First Amendment, not just free speech. Freedom of the press demands it. We always hear complaints about a biased media, but the answer to such complaints is more media. We do not want the government policing newsrooms, like dictators do. What we want are more voices in media, so that people are free to listen and make up their own minds about any particular story. Lest we think this is all a theoretical exercise with little practical application, the Federal Communications Commission (FCC) recently, after immense criticism, backed away from its "Multi-Market Study of Critical Information Needs," where it intended to examine "the process by which stories are selected." According to FCC Commissioner Ajit Pai, the FCC wanted to have government officers in TV and radio newsrooms "to grill reporters, editors and station owners about how they decide which stories to run."[158] The proposal was tabled, but the idea lives, as it always has. Americans are wise to continue to reject such efforts.

Freedom of assembly is guarded by the principle as well. If an assembly of people is particularly offensive, it is the right of the people to assemble in opposition. Except in very rare circumstances, this will preserve freedom for everyone. That is also the case with religious freedom. The answer to a particularly offensive religion or religious practice is more religion. Expose the error.

Correcting the abuses of religion

A particularly offensive part of our history was the fact that, despite our Judeo-Christian foundations as a nation, we allowed slavery to continue within our midst for far too long. Many even used the Bible to justify the

---

157   *Whitney v. California*, 274 U.S. 357, 377 (1927).

158   Ajit Pai, "The FCC Wades Into the Newsroom," *The Wall Street Journal*, February 10, 2014, available at: http://online.wsj.com/news/articles/SB1000142405270230 4680904579366903828260732 (accessed Sept. 17, 2014).

heinous acts committed against African-Americans. But notice the answer to this clear violation of the Biblical principle, Natural Law, and our Constitution was to appeal to religion itself. Abraham Lincoln certainly appealed to it. He said, "I know there is a God and that He hates injustice and slavery. I see the storm coming and I know that His hand is in it. If He has a place for me, and I think He has, I believe I am ready."[159] And again, "The battle for freedom is to be fought on principle. Slavery is a violation of eternal right. We have temporized with it from the necessities of our condition, but as surely as God reigns and school children read, that black foul lie can never be consecrated into God's hallowed truth."[160] While some today would blame religion for the troubles we faced and, therefore, cry out for government hostility towards religion, which they see as a great evil, Lincoln fought the distortion of religion with more religion— with truth.

Martin Luther King, Jr., did the same thing. Let us never forget that he was a Christian minister. Therefore, he did not want to abolish our form of government, our Constitution, or our Judeo-Christian foundations. He actually sought for the country to live up to those ideals. He called us back to the Christian principles that demanded freedom for all Americas. His "Letter from a Birmingham Jail" is a most powerful document — a passionate appeal to a higher law. He cried out for those "God-given rights" acknowledged in our Declaration of Independence and guaranteed by our Constitution. Listen to his explanation of a just law:

> A just law is a man-made code that squares with the moral law or the law of God. An unjust law is a code that is out of harmony with the moral law. To put it in the terms of St. Thomas Aquinas: An unjust law is a human law that is not rooted in eternal law and natural law.[161]

He appeals to Jesus, Amos, Paul, Martin Luther, and Lincoln. He even indicts the church's inaction on this matter: "The judgment of God is

---

159   Joe Wheeler, *Abraham Lincoln A Man of Faith and Courage* 120 (Howard Books 2008).

160   *Id.* at 187.

161   Martin Luther King, Jr., *Letter from a Birmingham Jail*, April 16, 1963, available at: http://www.africa.upenn.edu/Articles_Gen/Letter_Birmingham.html (accessed Sept. 17, 2014).

upon the church as never before. If today's church does not recapture the sacrificial spirit of the early church, it will lose its authenticity, forfeit the loyalty of millions, and be dismissed as an irrelevant social club with no meaning for the twentieth century."[162] He understood that the answer to objectionable religious practices, and even apathy, is more religion, not enforced atheism in the public square. We have already alluded at Frederick Douglas' use of the same principle on his appeal to end slavery. Here is more of what he said:

> You profess to believe "that, of one blood, God made all nations of men to dwell on the face of all the earth," and hath commanded all men, everywhere to love one another; yet you notoriously hate, (and glory in your hatred,) all men whose skins are not colored like your own. You declare, before the world, and are understood by the world to declare, that you "hold these truths to be self-evident, that all men are created equal; and are endowed by their Creator with certain, unalienable rights; and that, among these are, life, liberty, and the pursuit of happiness;" and yet, you hold securely, in a bondage, which according to your own Thomas Jefferson, "is worse than ages of that which your fathers rose in rebellion to oppose," a seventh part of the inhabitants of your country.[163]

He also appealed to our original founding texts as written:

> Now, take the constitution according to its plain reading, and I defy the presentation of a single pro slavery clause in it. On the other hand it will be found to contain principles and purposes, entirely hostile to the existence of slavery.[164]

He was confident that God would bring about the end of slavery, one way or another, saying:

---

162   *Id.*

163   Frederick Douglas, *Oration, Delivered in Corinthian Hall*, July 5, 1852, available at https://www.lib.rochester.edu/index.cfm?PAGE=2945 (accessed Sept. 17, 2014).

164   *Id.*

> Allow me to say, in conclusion, notwithstanding the dark
> picture I have this day presented, of the state of the na-
> tion, I do not despair of this country. There are forces in
> operation, which must inevitably, work the downfall of
> slavery. "The arm of the Lord is not shortened," and the
> doom of slavery is certain.[165]

Even Thomas Jefferson, who owned slaves, knew he was in violation of God's Law, saying: "Commerce between master and slave is despotism. Nothing is more certainly written in the book of fate than that these people are to be free."[166] That is precisely where the strength to fight for what is right comes from. It does not happen in a vacuum. It comes from a pursuit of Truth. That standard itself provides the anchor for our complaints.

Today's America is in danger of losing that standard, instead suppressing it and opting to silence dissenting views, especially religious views in the name of "separation of church and state" or equality or reproductive rights or human rights or any number of things. We are already seeing the targeting of Christians in public service, including former Fire Chief Kelvin Cochran, who was fired for his faith and his beliefs regarding God's model for marriage and sexuality. Although a formal investigation found "no indication that Chief Cochran allowed his religious beliefs to compromise his disciplinary decisions,"[167] he was still fired for expressing his beliefs in public. The silencing of unpopular religious beliefs seems to be the ultimate aim. There are numerous examples. Christian ministries, such as Catholic Charities, have been forced out of providing much-needed services for children because of the government's insistence that they violate their conscience and their deeply-held

---

165   *Id.*

166   Thomas Jefferson, Thomas Jefferson Memorial, Panel III, Washington, D.C., text available at http://www.monticello.org/site/jefferson/quotations-jefferson-memorial#Panel_Three (accessed Sept. 17, 2014).

167   Todd Starnes, "Christian ex-fire chief fires back at Atlanta mayor, files discrimination complaint," *Fox News*, January 25, 2015, available at http://www.foxnews.com/opinion/2015/01/26/christian-ex-fire-chief-fires-back-at-atlanta-mayor-files-discrimination/ (last accessed April 29, 2015).

religious beliefs and place children with same-sex parents.[168] We can talk of a number of Christian wedding service providers who are being harassed and forced out of business if they do not participate in same-sex "weddings," no matter the dictates of their conscience. Barronelle Stutzman was the 70-year-old owner of Arlene's Flowers in Washington State where she served all customers, but when one of her regular customers asked that she provided flowers for his same-sex wedding, Ms. Stutzman declined because of her religious beliefs. The customer filed a complaint with the authorities and she was taken to court where she lost and the state went after, not only her business, but her personal assets too.[169] Aaron and Melissa Klein of Sweet Cakes Bakery were similarly sued in Oregon and the judge in that case awarded a $135,000 "emotional damage" award to a lesbian couple, ignoring the Klein's appeal to conscience.[170]

Hostility toward religion is neither required by our Constitution nor desirable in a free and just society. Only those who are insecure of their position seek to impose it by force by silencing their opposition. The Christian citizen must be alert to those who seek to silence religious views and reject their freedom-stifling ideas. As long as we are able and committed to fight the abuse of the First Amendment with the virtues of the First Amendment, we shall preserve liberty and freedom. If we fail, oppression is sure to follow.

Religious freedom, indeed freedom itself, can only be born out of the basic religious principles of Christianity. Secularism promises it, but fails to deliver. Suppressing the principles is suppressing freedom. Our society and form of government depend on them. It is, therefore, vital for us to preserve our ability, not only to live by those principles, but also to be

---

168   Julia Duin, "Catholics end D.C. foster-care program," February 18, 2010, available at http://www.washingtontimes.com/news/2010/feb/18/dc-gay-marriage-law-archdiocese-end-foster-care/?page=all (last accessed April 29, 2015).

169   Samuel Smith, "Christian Florist Can Lose Personal Assets for Declining Gay Wedding Due to 'Relationship With Jesus,' Judge Rules," *Christian Post*, January 13, 2015, available at http://www.christianpost.com/news/christian-florist-can-lose-personal-assets-for-declining-gay-wedding-due-to-relationship-with-jesus-judge-rules-132509/ (last accessed April 29, 2015).

170   Thomas D. Williams, "Lesbian Couple Accuses Christian Bakers of 'Mental Rape,' Awarded $135,000," *Breitbart* (April 26, 2015), available at http://www.breitbart.com/big-government/2015/04/26/lesbian-couple-accuses-christian-bakers-of-mental-rape-awarded-135000/ (last accessed April 29, 2015).

able to pass them to the next generations. We'll take a look at some of the practical benefits of this worldview in the next two chapters.

Chapter Nine
Love God Above All

Self-evident truths are powerful because they are true (we can all recognize them, despite the insistence of some that claim they cannot) and because they are universal (for the benefit of all, even of those who refuse to recognize them). In the United States, there are many who not only refuse to believe in these truths, but who actually despise them, working tirelessly to see them eradicated from public life. And they have been very successful. Their successes come not from effective attacks on the foundations themselves, for these foundations are incorruptible, but from *our unbelief*. The attacks are aimed at us. The assaults have shaken our trust and reliance on what we know to be true. That's the danger. Our forefathers knew how important it was to protect those founding principles. Better stated, how important it was to protect our reliance on those principles. John Adams saw this clearly when he said, "It is Religion and Morality alone, which can establish the Principles upon which Freedom can securely stand."[171] And, "Our Constitution was made only for a religious and moral people. It is wholly inadequate for the govern-

---

171   John Adams, Letter to Zabdiel Adams, June 21, 1776, *The Works of John Adams, Second President of the United States* Vol. IX, 401 (Charles Francis Adams ed., 1854).

ment of any other."[172] So what must we do to ensure this foundation is secure? As Martin Luther King Jr. once said, "If we are to go forward, we must go back and rediscover these precious values: that all reality hinges on moral foundations and that all reality has spiritual control."[173]

In the next two chapters, we will use the Ten Commandments to show how these principles and the self-evident truths they embody sustain our way of life and why we must protect them if freedom and liberty are to flourish in our land once again. In this chapter we will focus on the commandments aimed at God— the first four. The next chapter we will deal with the rest of the commandments, which are aimed at our relationships with one another. This exercise is incredibly profitable for our understanding of freedom's survival because, as Patrick Henry said, "The eternal difference between right and wrong does not fluctuate, it is immutable."[174] Therefore, these principles are just as relevant today as they were at the time of our founding. As relevant as they were from the beginning of time and as they shall be to the end.

I. No other gods

The First Commandment tells us "You shall have no other gods before Me," (Exodus 20:3). This is the first and most basic principle we depend on and one which anchors all others. We are "endowed by our *Creator* with certain unalienable rights."[175] We are "one nation, *under God.*"[176] The principle, of course, presupposes that there is in fact a God. And as a self-evident truth, it suggests that deep inside we all know this to be true. Our belief in a Supreme Being sustains our freedoms because even the skeptic can see that, "All the foundations of the earth are un-stable," (Psalm 82:5, NKJV). In other words, whatever we think of God, we know ourselves, and we know how incredibly flawed we are. Any

---

172   John Adams, Letter to the Officers of the First Brigade of the Third Division of the Militia of Massachusetts, October 11, 1798, *The Works of John Adams, Second President of the United States* Vol. IX, 229 (Charles Francis Adams ed., 1854).

173   Martin Luther King, Jr., *Sermon: Rediscovering the Lost Precious Values*, Detroit, February 28, 1954.

174   Patrick Henry, The Debates in the Several State Conventions: On the Adop-tion of the Federal Constitution, as Recom-mended by the General Convention at Philadelphia, in 1787, Volume 3, 59 (Cornell University Library, 2009).

175   The Declaration of Independence para. 2 (U.S. 1776) (emphasis mine).

176   The Pledge of Allegiance to the Flag, 4 U.S.C. §4 (emphasis mine).

system based on earthly authority (on people) alone is bound to fail as corruption, greed, lust and pride take root. History bears the painful scars of such attempts. Notice the principle refers to one God, a Creator, a God, to the exclusion of all others. There is one true God. This fact, which some attack as "intolerant" and "discriminatory," in fact serves as the foundation for our rich religious liberty tradition, as we discussed in the previous chapter. Since there is a God, all men should be free to pursue Him. We can engage and relate to one another. The principle does not endorse a religion, but merely recognizes man's natural thirst to know his Creator. The concept embraces every sincere attempt to connect with this one God. It does not matter where your search for Him begins — whether in Christianity, Islam, Hinduism, etc. The search for Truth will eventually lead you to the one true God.

As we have already discussed, we do not fear religions that are different from our own. There is no need to "kill infidels" or impose a theocracy. The principle demands freedom. That does not mean all religions are equal, for there is only one God. As Christian citizens, we believe any sincere search for God (for Truth), no matter where it starts, will eventually lead you to the God of the Bible and His Son Jesus Christ. Truth, then, does not require neutrality (as post-modern despots demand), but sincerity and humbleness. Here is a concrete example of how this principle is applied. The *Declaration of Rights of the Maryland Constitution* shows the magnificent balance it brings:

> [I]t is the duty of every man to worship God in such manner as he thinks most acceptable to Him, all persons are equally entitled to protection in their religious liberty; wherefore, no person ought by any law to be molested in his person or estate, on account of his religious persuasion, or profession, or for his religious practice, unless, under the color of religion, he shall disturb the good order, peace or safety of the State, or shall infringe the laws of morality, or injure others in their natural, civil or religious rights ...[177]

Notice how the "duty" of every man to worship God actually demands religious liberty for all, including the non-believer. Still, the existence of

---

177   MD Const. Declaration of Rights, art. 36.

this One who created us demands a response from us. It imparts in us a sense of gratitude and responsibility. It establishes a hierarchy and order. Respect, reverence, worship, goodwill, a desire to do good while realizing how impossible a task that is, all flow from that recognition of our Creator. Here is another practical example, again, from the *Declaration of Rights of the Maryland Constitution,* relating to witnesses and jurors:

> [N]or shall any person, otherwise competent, be deemed incompetent as a witness, or juror, on account of his religious belief; provided, he believes in the existence of God, and that under His dispensation such person will be held morally accountable for his acts, and be rewarded or punished therefore either in this world or in the world to come.[178]

We gain much as a society when we recognize that our actions have eternal consequences. No need for a military state to enforce common laws when everyone in themselves recognizes their duty to behave in a moral way. When someone serving as a juror recognizes he is responsible before God, who sees everything, he will be much more inclined to tell the truth and resist outside influences. He is not just worried about getting caught, he is now worried about doing the right thing. This is, indeed, an amazing, liberating thought. Far from the restraining, claustrophobic impediment the modern cynic portrays a belief in God to be, this belief actually releases us to be free to trust, love, and coexist in community. As Charles Carroll (1737-1832), the Maryland statesman who was the last of the signers of the Declaration of Independence to die in 1792, said,

> Without morals a republic cannot subsist any length of time; they therefore who are decrying the Christian religion, whose morality is so sublime and pure ... are undermining the solid foundation of morals, the best security for the duration of free governments.[179]

---

178   *Id.*

179   Charles Carroll, "Letter to James McHenry," November 4, 1800, *The Life and Correspondence of James McHenry* 475 (Bernard C. Steiner ed., The Burrows Brothers, 1907).

II. No idols of any kind

The Second Commandment tells us we "shall not make for [ourselves] a carved image, or any likeness of anything that is in heaven above, or that is in the earth beneath, or that is in the water under the earth. You shall not bow down to them or serve them ..." (Exodus 20:4-5, NKJV). This commandment flows right from the first. At first glance, it almost seems redundant. But we take them separately for a very specific reason. Notice the prohibition includes an image of God Himself. We are not to "bow down" to *any* image. If you take time to consider this, you will find it to be both reasonable and sensible. An image of something is not the thing itself. You might cherish immensely an image of your mother or father, for they remind you of them, but you would not love that image as if it were actually your mother or father. That would be foolish. An image of an orange may look appealing, but it won't satisfy your hunger. In the same manner, we are to worship God alone and not any representation of God, for He alone can satisfy our thirst for meaning and purpose.

Some might be tempted to argue this is not a problem for us today as it was for the Israelites with the golden calf,[180] for example. But we have just substituted other things for the calf, that's all. C.S. Lewis reflected on this concept by writing:

> The books or the music in which we thought the beauty was located will betray us if we trust to them; it was not in them, it only came through them, and what came through them was longing. These things – the beauty, the memory of our own past – are good images of what we really desire; but if they are mistaken for the thing itself they turn into dumb idols, breaking the hearts of their worshippers. For they are not the thing itself; they are only the scent of a flower we have not found, the echo of a tune we have not heard, news from a country we have never yet visited.[181]

Idolatry goes far beyond simple caricatures. When we attribute the work or characteristics of God to anything else, we create idols for our-

---

180   Exodus 32.

181   C.S. Lewis, *The Weight of Glory*, 30-31 (HarperCollins March 20, 2001 (1949)).

selves. When we look elsewhere for what we know comes only from God, we break this commandment, violating what we know to be true. Think the Founding Fathers overlooked this commandment? Think again. Its violation was one of the most powerful arguments fueling the American Revolution. Consider Thomas Paine (1737-1809), the great political thinker whose momentous work helped spark the Revolution:

> [W]hen a man seriously reflects on the idolatrous homage which is paid to the persons of kings, he need not wonder that the Almighty, ever jealous of his honor, should disapprove a form of government which so impiously invades the prerogative of heaven.[182]

Or, in the words of James Otis (1725-1783), a Massachusetts lawyer, political activist and a prominent leader of the American Revolution:

> It is the greatest idolatry, begotten by flattery, on the body of pride, that could induce one to think that a single mortal should be able to hold so great a power. ... The power of GOD Almighty is the only power that can properly and strictly be called supreme and absolute.[183]

In his famous speech the day before the signing of the Declaration of Independence, Samuel Adams said:

> We have explored the temple of royalty, and found that the idol we have bowed down to has eyes which see not, ears that hear not our prayers, and a heart like the nether millstone. We have this day restored the Sovereign, to Whom alone men ought to be obedient. He reigns in Heaven, and with a propitious eye beholds His subjects assuming that freedom of thought, and dignity of self-direction which He bestowed on them. From the rising to the setting sun, may His kingdom come.[184]

---

182   Thomas Paine, *Common Sense* 13 (Signet Classic July 1, 2003).

183   James Otis, *The Founders' Constitution*, Vol. I, 52 (Philip Kurland and Ralph Lerner ed., Liberty Fund Inc., 2000 (1776)).

184   Samuel Adams, *American Independence Speech*, August 1, 1776, available at http://www.revolutionary-war-and-beyond.com/american-independence-speech-by-samuel-adams-august-1-1776.html (accessed Sept. 17, 2014).

Our failure to live up to this commandment was very much alive at the time of our country's founding, and it is still alive today. Though few would actually admit it in theory, in practice we lift up very definite idols. Many worship at the altar of science, for example, or a distortion of science, really. So they make claims like, "Evolution is the creator of life."[185] Still others idolize money, making it the central pursuit of their lives, foolishly believing it can bring them security or stability and forgetting that we take nothing when we die.[186] Others make pleasures king. This is perhaps the more modern approach, where we make ourselves the idol. "Believe in yourself," we tell one another. *We* decide what is right and what is wrong, and we end up saying inane things like, "Feels so good, it can't be wrong."

In an insightful review of the acclaimed movie *Into the Woods*, Dr. Taylor Marshall traces the roots of this worldview to the old school of philosophical nominalism. Here is what he wrote:

> Ultimately, *Into the Woods is* an apologetic for the philosophical school of nominalism – an error going back before the days of Socrates and Plato. Nominalism holds that there is not real essence or form out there in the world. There is no real substance or nature out there. Instead, we humans create and apply the names (*nomina* in Latin, hence nominalism) to things and actions out there.

> With nominalism, there is ultimately no meaning. There is no purpose. There is only the meaning and purpose that we create in our own hearts. There is no such thing as natural law. We can decide what we want things to be. If we want to change the *nomen* or definition of "marriage" than we can do so. If we want to change the *nomen* or definition of good and evil, we can do that, too.

> Here's the final (nominalist) sermon from *Into the Woods*. I wanted to cover the ears of my dear children

185   Richard Dawkins and Karen Armstrong, "Man vs. God," The *Wall Street Journal,* September 12, 2009, available at http://online.wsj.com/article/SB10001424052970 20344010457440503064355634.html (accessed Sept. 17, 2014).

186   "For what will it profit a man if he gains the whole world and forfeits his soul? Or what shall a man give in return for his soul?" (Matthew 16:26).

when I heard these words sung to a beautiful melody:

"Wrong things, right things …

Who can say what's true? …

Do things, fight things …

You decide, but …

You are not alone …

Witches can be right.

Giants can be good.

You decide what's right. You decide what's good."

This is the final answer to the pain of the characters. "You decide what's good." But that's the problem. All the bad guys are already playing that game. They have decided what is "right for me" and they are hurting you.[187]

So it doesn't really matter what you decide is wrong or right, or what you put your trust in. We all create our own reality; only it is no reality at all, but a fantasy.

Some make a god of government, hoping it will provide for their every need. We talk about government health care, government jobs, and government charity. Every day we move closer and closer to believing the lie that our rights come from government, instead of from God. Our founders recognized the perils of such a state when they wrote that we are "endowed by our Creator with certain unalienable rights." The idea guards us from making an idol of the Constitution itself, as some may also be tempted to do.

Our failure to recognize this is how we have fallen for the lie that the government "gives" tax-exempt status to churches. The reality is that the government does not grant anything to churches. The government is

---

187   Marshall Taylor, PhD, "Into the Woods Movie – A Dad's Critical Review," December 31, 2014 available at http://taylormarshall.com/2014/12/into-the-woods-movie-a-dads-critical-review.html (accessed March 2, 2015).

required by the Constitution to refrain from interfering on the churches' God-given autonomy; to acknowledge our unalienable right to religious freedom.

No matter what the idol is, we will pay a heavy price every time we attribute to earthly things that which belong only to God. It's a shame we sometimes have to endure the pain of self-imposed ignorance before we acknowledge what is plainly true.

III. The Name of the Lord

The Third Commandment tells us, "You shall not take the name of the LORD your God in vain, for the LORD will not hold him guiltless who takes his name in vain," (Exodus 20:7). This commandment flows beautifully from the first two. We have already discussed how the First Commandment gives us a sense of order or hierarchy, a sense that we must give honor where honor is due. We mentioned how the recognition of our Creator provokes in us a response, a sense of gratitude, respect, and reverence. It should come as no surprise then that we are to treat His name in the same light. Since its founding, the United States of America has benefited immeasurably from our dependence on Almighty God. Consider the words of President John F. Kennedy (1917-1963) on February 9, 1961:

> No man who enters upon the office to which I have succeeded can fail to recognize how every President of the United States has placed special reliance upon his faith in God. Every President has taken comfort and courage when told, as we are told today, that the Lord "will be with thee. He will not fail thee nor forsake thee. Fear not - neither be thou dismayed."

> While they came from a wide variety of religious backgrounds and held a wide variety of religious beliefs, each of our Presidents in his own way has placed a special trust in God. Those who were strongest intellectually were also strongest spiritually.

> Today our Nation is passing through another time of trial. In many ways, our dangers and our problems are

far greater - and certainly infinitely more complex. We will need to draw upon the best that this Nation has - often - and draw upon it physically and intellectually and materially.

But we need also to call upon our great reservoir of spiritual resources. We must recognize that human collaboration is not enough, that in times such as these we must reach beyond ourselves if we are to seek ultimate courage and infinite wisdom.[188]

But the power and truth of the Third Commandment goes much deeper. It highlights something that is as important as anything else for our Republic: the power of words. The First and Second Commandments focus on "doing" (actions), the Third on "saying" (words). We must honor God in word and deed. Words have meaning, and weight, if you will. We touched on this reality in chapter six. We mentioned how John 1:1, very interestingly, refers to Jesus as "the Word:" "In the beginning was the Word, and the Word was with God, and the Word was God." Therefore, it makes sense that this is the main way God chose to communicate with us: through words. Words have real, concrete consequences. Think of the trouble we have created just by distorting the definition of marriage.

Those who choose to mock, or take the name of the Lord in vain, are not "just saying stuff." The cost is real. The relationship between speech and reality is self-evident and undeniably powerful. Consider the words of Victor Frankl, a survivor of Auschwitz:

The gas chambers of Auschwitz were the ultimate consequence of the theory that man is nothing but the product of heredity and environment. I am absolutely convinced that the gas chambers of Auschwitz, Treblinka, and Maidanek were ultimately prepared not in some ministry or other in Berlin, but rather at the desks and in lecture halls of nihilistic scientists and philosophers.[189]

---

188   John F. Kennedy, *Remarks at the Dedication Breakfast of International Christian Leadership,* February 9, 1961, available at http://www.jfklink.com/speeches/jfk/publicpapers/1961/jfk26_61.html (accessed Sept. 17, 2014).

189   Viktor E. Frankl, *The Doctor and the Soul: From Psychotherapy to Logotherapy* xxvii (Vintage 1986 (1946)).

There you have the very powerful correlation of "mere words" and reality. Our Founders recognized the power of words. The words of the Declaration of Independence changed the course of history. And their insistence on a written Constitution to guard against tyranny, difficult as that may have seemed at the time, has proven incredibly wise. Thomas Jefferson talked about its importance: "Aware of the tendency of power to degenerate into abuse, the worthies of our country have secured its independence by the establishment of a Constitution and form of government for our nation, calculated to prevent as well as to correct abuse."[190]

As a self-evident truth though, this principle is not exclusive to us, but has been recognized throughout history. The power of the written word was key for the Achaemenid Empire, for example,[191] and on down the line we can go (the Koran is another example). When we honor and respect the Name of our Lord as a nation, we reap the blessings as a nation. Those who ignore this self-evident truth do so at their own peril.

Almost all state constitutions acknowledge and show honor and respect to God. Here is a small sample:

- We, the people of the Commonwealth of Pennsylvania, grateful to Almighty God for the blessings of civil and religious liberty, and humbly invoking His guidance, do ordain and establish this Constitution.[192]

- We, the people of the State of New Jersey, grateful to Almighty God for the civil and religious liberty which He hath so long permitted us to enjoy, and looking to Him for a blessing upon our endeavors to secure and transmit the same unimpaired to succeeding generations, do ordain and establish

---

190   Thomas Jefferson, "To the Tammany Society or Columbian Order of the City of Washington," March 2, 1809, *The writings of Thomas Jefferson*, Volume 16, 346 (The Thomas Jefferson Memorial Association 1904).

191   "Now, O king, establish the decree and sign the writing, so that it cannot be changed, according to the law of the Medes and Persians, which does not alter," (Daniel 6:8, NKJV).

192   PA CONST. pmbl.

this Constitution.[193]

- We, the People of the State of California, grateful to Almighty God for our freedom, in order to secure and perpetuate its blessings, do establish this Constitution.[194]

- We, the People of the State of Illinois – grateful to Almighty God for the civil, political and religious liberty which He has permitted us to enjoy and seeking His blessing upon our endeavors – in order to provide for the health, safety and welfare of the people; maintain a representative and orderly government; eliminate poverty and inequality; assure legal, social and economic justice; provide opportunity for the fullest development of the individual; insure domestic tranquility; provide for the common defense; and secure the blessings of freedom and liberty to ourselves and our posterity – do ordain and establish this Constitution for the State of Illinois.[195]

- We, the people of the State of Washington, grateful to the Supreme Ruler of the Universe for our liberties, do ordain this constitution.[196]

One cannot ignore these, and the many other examples, when considering the blessings we have enjoyed as a nation. And we must wonder what the result would have been if they were not put in place. Even those who express the most vocal opposition to this Commandment (to this worldview) do so by standing on the very freedoms that come as a result of strict adherence to it.

IV. Remember the Sabbath

Jesus summarized all the commandments in two simple statements.

---

193   NJ CONST. pmbl.
194   CA CONST. pmbl.
195   IL CONST. pmbl.
196   WA CONST. pmbl

"You shall love the Lord your God with all your heart and with all your soul and with all your mind," (Matthew 22:37) and, "You shall love your neighbor as yourself," (Matthew 22:39). The Fourth Commandment, "Remember the Sabbath day, to keep it holy," (Exodus 20:8) concludes that first part of the Ten Commandments that relate to loving God. The next chapter will deal with the "loving our neighbors" part. "Six days you shall labor and do all your work, but the seventh day is the Sabbath of the Lord your God," say the next verses (Exodus 20:9-10). The charge of this beautiful commandment, as with every other self-evident truth, accentuates reality (what we experience as human beings), instead of introducing some alien concept, suppressing our experiences, reason, and common sense – which is what some would have us do.

Two things stand out. The first trickles down from that basic recognition of God, that acknowledgement that there is something more than the material. When we recognize that we are more than just a collection of cells, that we also have a spirit, it is only rational and reasonable to conclude that we are to pursue more than the material. "Man shall not live by bread alone," (Matthew 4:4), said Jesus. And we all know that to be true! We have all experienced that spiritual hunger. It is self-evident. Why then should we be surprised that God, in His infinite wisdom, commands us to set aside a specific time to pursue Him above all else? Remember what we have already established: we are to have no other gods before Him, to reject idols of any kind, and we are not to take His name in vain. This Creator is indeed to be respected and honored. We owe everything we have to Him, so it seems reasonable to set aside time to get to know Him. Even in today's materialistic, selfish age we can still recognize that there is more to life than the pursuit of the material. The Founders wrote about "the pursuit of happiness," a phrase that encompasses the whole of life. How many times do we hear of those who spent their entire lives trying to reach the top of the material mountain, just to learn, once they get there, that "the top" is not only just as unfulfilling as the base, but it is also a lot lonelier?

The second part is related to something even more basic: we are cyclical beings. It is the way God designed us and the universe. Rest is part of that design. As King Solomon, known to all for his great wisdom, wrote:

For everything there is a season, and a time for every

matter under heaven:

a time to be born, and a time to die;

a time to plant, and a time to pluck up what is planted;

a time to kill, and a time to heal;

a time to break down, and a time to build up;

a time to weep, and a time to laugh;

a time to mourn, and a time to dance;

a time to cast away stones, and a time to gather stones together;

a time to embrace, and a time to refrain from embracing;

a time to seek, and a time to lose;

a time to keep, and a time to cast away;

a time to tear, and a time to sew;

a time to keep silence, and a time to speak;

a time to love, and a time to hate;

a time for war, and a time for peace. [197]

We know it is not profitable for us to make our work, our hobbies, our favorite sport, the girl or guy of our dreams, or anything else really, the single pursuit of our lives, to the detriment of everything else. A government that recognizes this, proceeding in law and policy within that framework, will inevitably reap the enormous benefits of a more stable and fulfilled citizenry that will, in turn, be a more productive and resilient society. Is there any doubt that we have benefitted from laws requiring employers to accommodate a person's day of worship? Laws against involuntary servitude, stemming from the Thirteenth Amendment, for example, prohibiting a person from employing someone 24/7, even out of an apparent "necessity," have provided great security, order,

---

197   Ecclesiastes 3:1-8.

and stability. Individuals, families, communities, and our entire society are stronger when we follow this self-evident truth. That is especially beneficial when tough times come, as we all know they inevitably will. On November 15, 1862, at the height of the Civil War, President Abraham Lincoln quoted General George Washington in his "General Order Respecting the Observance of the Sabbath Day in the Army and Navy:"

> The President, Commander-in-Chief of the Army and Navy, desires and enjoins the orderly observance of the Sabbath by the officers and men in the military and naval service. The importance for men and beast of the prescribed weekly rest, the sacred rights of Christian soldiers and sailors, a becoming deference to the best sentiment of a Christian people, and a due regard for the divine will demand that Sunday labor in the Army and Navy be reduced to the measure of strict necessity.

> The discipline and character of the national forces should not suffer nor the cause they defend be imperiled by the profanation of the day or name of the Most High. "At this time of public distress," adopting the words of Washington in 1776, "men may find enough to do in the service of God and their country without abandoning themselves to vice and immorality." The first general order issued by the Father of his Country after the Declaration of Independence indicates the spirit in which our institutions were founded and should ever be defended:

> The General hopes and trusts that every officer and man will endeavor to live and act as becomes a Christian soldier defending the dearest rights and liberties of his country.

ABRAHAM LINCOLN[198]

Unfortunately, such a proclamation would be offensive today, but it was crucial to the formation and survival of our republic, and it still lies

---

198   Abraham Lincoln, "General Order Respecting the Observance of the Sabbath Day in the Army and Navy," November 15, 1862, available at http://www.wallbuilders.com/LIBissuesArticles.asp?id=51 (accessed Sept. 17, 2014).

at our foundations, sustaining our very existence. So strong was the Founders' reliance on the importance of remembering the Sabbath that on December 4, 1800, even before Congress met in the Capitol for the first time, the building was approved to be used for church services.[199] Thomas Jefferson himself attended church at the Capitol, even as he wrote those famous words, "separation of church and state" – words that have been distorted today, as we have discussed, in an attempt to eradicate God from the public square. He saw no problem or contradiction between church at the Capitol and religious liberty – because, of course, there is none. Bishop Thomas John Claggett (1743-1816) of Maryland had delivered the sermons at the capitol when he wrote to Dr. Kemp, who was to be his successor, that Jefferson "has very constantly attended prayers every morning, and to a course of sermons which I have delivered on Sundays in the Capitol, on the truth of the Christian system." [200]

The only way to be free is to be truthful. We cannot escape the reality of who we are and how we were created. Like the picture of the man standing before a mirror, rejecting what he sees, so is the modern man who rejects the commandments of the Lord. There is only one fool in that picture.

---

199   Debates and Proceedings in the Congress of the United States, Sixth Congress, December 4, 1800, 797 (Washington: Gales and Seaton, 1853).

200   John Nicholas Norton, *The Life of Bishop Claggett of Maryland* 115 (General Protestant Episcopal S. School Union and Church Book Society 1859).

CHAPTER TEN
LOVE YOUR NEIGHBOR AS YOURSELF

We now turn to those commandments that focus on the second part of Jesus' summary of the law:[201] "lov[ing] your neighbor as yourself," (Matthew 22:39). It is worth pointing out that even though these commandments appropriately follow the ones about loving God above all, in a way they work backwards— our response to our neighbor reveals our attitude towards God. Jesus told us, "If anyone says, 'I love God,' and hates his brother, he is a liar; for he who does not love his brother whom he has seen cannot love God whom he has not seen," (1 John 4:20).

V. Honor your mother and father

The Fifth Commandment tells us, "Honor your father and your mother," (Exodus 20:12). This commandment is as basic as they come, yet immeasurably profound and beneficial to any society that applies it. First, notice that it assumes the basic structure of the family, which has served as the cornerstone of our civilization and our nation's success. Isn't it in-

---

201   "And he said to him, 'You shall love the Lord your God with all your heart and with all your soul and with all your mind. This is the great and first commandment. And a second is like it: You shall love your neighbor as yourself. On these two commandments depend all the Law and the Prophets,'" (Matthew 22:27-40).

teresting that the commandment does not just say "honor your parents," but it delineates the roles specifically as "father and mother?" The stability and security that comes from that strong bond between mother, father and children has sustained our country through our toughest times. And even though a part of today's culture earnestly seeks to dismantle that model, its innumerable benefits are undeniable. Second, this commandment, as the first, follows that sense of hierarchy and order. The great poet William Shakespeare is attributed with giving us this vivid image: "The voice of parents is the voice of gods: for to their children they are heav'n's lieutenants."[202] This relationship between children and parents actually mirrors that of humanity and our Father in heaven. The importance of this order for government has been observed throughout history by numerous religions and philosophies, not just Christianity. Confucius wrote in the Fifth Century: "Honor your parents, simply honor your parents and make your brothers friends—this too is good government."[203]

"Honor your father and mother" is the only commandment accompanied by a specific promise, "that your days may be long in the land that the LORD your God is giving you," (Exodus 20:12). In fact, the next time the Bible refers to this commandment it goes a bit further, "that it may go well with you and that you may live long in the land," (Ephesians 6:3). We have seen this exemplified in the lives of many great men, including our Founders. Here is an example from the life of General Washington:

> His heart was set on going to sea, his trunk was already on board ship; when he bade farewell to his mother he found her in tears.

> "Go and tell them to return my trunk; I will not leave and break my mother's heart" he said to his servant.

> "George, God has promised to bless the children that obey their parents: I believe He will bless you too."[204]

---

202   William Shakespeare, *Double Falsehood, or, The Distressed Lovers*, 289 (Brean Hammond ed., A&C Black Publishers LTD 2010).

203   Confucius, *The Analects*, 2:21, 16 (David Hinton trans. Counterpoint 1998).

204   William Dallman, *Our Father's Faith, Our Children's Language!*, Lutheran Witness, Volume 12 at 12, June 21, 1893.

And it came true. The accounts of God's blessing on George Washington are many, as we have seen. Thomas Jefferson wrote, "The happiest moments of my life have been the few which I have passed at home in the bosom of my family."[205] John Quincy Adams said, "All that I am my mother made me."[206] And Abraham Lincoln said, "All that I am or hope to be, I owe to my angel mother."[207] But more than just a personal blessing, our country has reaped the benefits of such an honorable attitude. It is this family structure that helps us produce virtuous citizens, such as the Founders, who contribute so much to the well-being of our nation. Thus, laws protecting parental rights, supporting the family and marital stability, encouraging parental responsibility and encouraging the care and respect of our elderly are vital to our nation's health. By contrast, modern efforts to redefine marriage and family, to usurp parental rights and to empower children to violate this commandment have had and will continue to have a devastating effect on our future. Many of the problems we face today have been the result of the deteriorating family structure.[208]

Two more ideas are important. One is that there is no statute of limitations on this commandment. Notice we are to honor our father and mother throughout our lives, not theirs. So we honor them, even after they are gone. That brings us to one final point, which is a bit more difficult to grasp, but just as true. The commandment does not ask us to honor only "good" parents. The commandment rests on us and not our parents. Yes, sometimes the best way to honor an abusive parent is to expose him or her so that they are forced to stop the abuse, but the principle still stands. Those who have forgiven a parent for some painful memories will often talk about how they had to do so for their own sake, not the parent's; again highlighting for us at whom the commandment is aimed. We are better persons, a better people and a better nation when we abide by this commandment. Its benefits are not only self-evident but

---

205   Thomas Jefferson, "Letter to Francis Willis," *The Works of Thomas Jefferson*, (G.P. Putnam's Sons, 1904-5). Vol. 6., available at http://oll.libertyfund.org/titles/803#lf0054-06_head_024 (accessed Sept. 17, 2014).

206   Homiletic Review: An International Magazine of Religion, Theology and Philosophy, Volume 69, 420 (The Religious Newspaper Agency, 1915).

207   *Id.*

208   For more on this topic see *Children at Risk* by Janice Shaw Crouse, Ph. D., (Transaction Publishers 2010).

also self-regenerating. There is an old Spanish saying my mother used to tell me growing up that speaks of the profound, enduring nature of this reality. She would always say to me: "Hijo fuiste, padre serás." Which roughly translated means, "A son you have been; a parent you will be." At the time, of course, I had no idea what she meant, but as a father of four today, well, let's just say my mother is a very wise woman.

VI. You shall not murder

We mentioned previously the wonderful words engraved in the Jefferson Memorial in Washington, D.C., where Thomas Jefferson said, "God who gave us life gave us liberty. Can the liberties of a nation be secure when we have removed a conviction that these liberties are the gift of God?"[209] That quote reveals the indispensable worldview that gave birth to the United States of America and that is indispensable for our discussion here. God gave us life! This was not a novel idea. The Psalmist said it this way: "Know that the LORD, He is God; it is He who has made us, and not we ourselves," (Psalm 100:3, NKJV). That reality carries with it an immense sense of wonder and awe. As we discussed, it cries out for a response, a certain attitude from the created towards the Creator. If only God creates life, shouldn't we listen to Him when he sets the parameters for that life? Why do we think it good generally for children to obey their parents? It is with that humbleness that we approach the Sixth Commandment, which tells us, "You shall not murder."[210]

Such a simple and reasonable command from the Creator really needs no explanation. Its truth is self-evident. Yet, as St. Augustine so eloquently put it, "[T]he intelligent are infected by a gross mental disorder which makes them defend the irrational workings of their minds as if they were logic and truth itself, even when the evidence has been put before them as plainly as is humanly possible."[211] I can only agree with his conclusion that, "[W]e are forced very often to give an extended exposition of

209   Thomas Jefferson, Thomas Jefferson Memorial, Panel III, Washington, D.C., text available at http://www.monticello.org/site/jefferson/quotations-jefferson-memorial#Panel_Three (accessed Sept. 17, 2014).

210   Exodus 20:13. Notice the commandment deals with "murder" and not merely "killing," as it is sometimes translated.

211   St. Augustine, *City of God* 48 (Penguin Classics ed., Penguin Books 1984 (1467)).

the obvious, as if we were not presenting it for people to look at, but for them to touch and handle with their eyes shut."[212] We have discussed briefly the most callous violation of this commandment in America today: abortion. When the debate started, abortion supporters argued that what doctors where taking out of a mother's womb was not a person; it was just a "fetus." The words of Supreme Court Justice Harry Blackmun in allowing abortion in the *Roe v. Wade* case should never be too far away from our minds: "If this suggestion of personhood is established, [Roe's] case, of course, collapses, for the fetus' right to life would then be guaranteed specifically by the [Fourteenth] Amendment."[213] Yet today, even after science has opened the window to the womb with technologies like 3D and 4D ultrasound, proving that what we are dealing with here is indeed a baby, the most vulnerable of all human beings, we continue to sanction the practice of abortion to the tune of more than 55 million lives taken since *Roe*.

We saw a great example of our moral schizophrenia in a 2015 article in Cosmopolitan (a radically pro-abortion magazine) with the amazing title, "Disturbing Ultrasounds Show How Unborn Babies React When Their Mothers Smoke."[214] Yes, just as you suspect, Cosmo found incredibly disturbing the ultrasound of unborn babies affected by their mother's smoking, while totally ignoring the horrible pictures of babies dismembered by an abortion doctor. Another example came when undercover videos surfaced of *Planned Parenthood*, the nation's largest abortion provider, bargaining over how much they would get for the hearts, livers, brains, spinal chords and other organs of aborted babies, in violation of at least the spirit of a law passed by Congress that prohibits the sale of human fetal tissue (42 U.S. Code 289g-2).[215] The abortion industry deceives women telling them that what they are aborting is not a baby but just tissue, yet "the tissue's" organs suddenly materialize into hearts and lungs when it comes to making a profit on the discarded baby

---

212   *Id.*

213   *Roe v. Wade*, 410 U.S. 113, 156-57 (1973).

214   Tess Koman, "Disturbing Ultrasounds Show How Unborn Babies React When Their Mothers Smoke," *Cosmopolitan*, March 24, 2015, available at http://www.cosmopolitan.com/health-fitness/news/a38130/ultrasounds-show-how-babies-react-to-smoke/ (last accessed May 5, 2015).

215   Videos and undercover operation by the Center for Medical Progress, available at http://www.centerformedicalprogress.org (last accessed October 5, 2015).

after the procedure.

But we need not go to the extreme example of abortion when exploring the scope of this commandment. Its truth is much more profound. Here is what Jesus said on the subject:

> You have heard that it was said to those of old, "You shall not murder, and whoever murders will be in danger of the judgment." But I say to you that whoever is angry with his brother without a cause shall be in danger of the judgment.[216]

Meditating on this word will open up the horizon of our understanding. We are created in the image of God. Therefore, every human being must be treated with respect and dignity. God created all. Not just those who believe in Him, but all. It should be no surprise, then, that we are commanded to love even our enemies. Jesus said:

> You have heard that it was said, "You shall love your neighbor and hate your enemy." But I say to you, Love your enemies and pray for those who persecute you, so that you may be sons of your Father who is in heaven. For he makes his sun rise on the evil and on the good, and sends rain on the just and on the unjust. For if you love those who love you, what reward do you have? Do not even the tax collectors do the same? (Matthew 5:43-46).

Do you see how powerful this teaching is? How liberating? We need not carry resentment or hold grudges. We need not worry about vengeance for, "Vengeance is mine, I will repay, says the Lord," (Romans 12:19). It was the pursuit of these teachings that permitted this nation to be born, against all odds! It gave us the astonishing power to heal after the horrendous events of the Civil War. That's the miraculous nature of the mere pursuit of these teachings. Our Founders most definitely did not live up to these standards. Neither do we. The problem lies in that we have lost the hunger and will to pursue these self-evident truths. We no longer know, or are interested in knowing, what is right. We create our

---

216   Matthew 5:21-22. Notice again, as with the word "murder," the qualification: "without a cause" here.

own "right." We have lost the thirst to follow God's principles, and we are paying the price. That is also self-evident. We have no excuse. As a nation, we have seen firsthand the blessings that follow a commitment to the principles of our Christian foundations. Peter Bulkley (1583-1659), the Puritan leader who founded the city of Concord, Massachusetts, said:

> We are as a city set upon a hill, in the open view of all the earth; the eyes of the world are upon us because we profess ourselves to be a people in covenant with God, and therefore the Lord our God, with whom we have made covenant, but heaven and earth, angels and men, that are witnesses of our profession, will cry shame upon us, if we walk contrary to the covenant which we have professed and promised to walk in. If we open the mouths of men against our profession by reason of the scandal of our lives, we (of all men) shall have the greater sin.[217]

These are powerful, convicting words. It is scary to consider. But there is still time to turn to God. His mercy and grace have sustained us all throughout many different tumbles. May we turn back to Him once again and repent. May we remember that our Founders pursued His guidance and recognized His unquestionable hand in the events that gave birth to our country. May we do so again. Or, as Benjamin Franklin once asked, "do we imagine that we no longer need his assistance?"[218]

VII. You shall not commit adultery

Those who persist in denying self-evident truths in theory must eventually come face to face with the practical implications of their beliefs. The Seventh Commandment ("You shall not commit adultery," (Exodus 20:14)) gives us a great illustration of this point. Although it is written

---

217   Peter Bulkeley, *Puritans in America* 120 (Harvard University Press 1985).

218   "[H]ave we now forgotten that powerful friend? Or do we imagine that we no longer need his assistance? I have lived, Sir, a long time, and the longer I live, the more convincing proofs I see of this truth-that God governs in the affairs of men. And if a sparrow cannot fall to the Ground without his Notice, is it probable that an Empire can rise without his Aid?" Benjamin Franklin, *The Records of the Federal Convention of 1787*, Farrand's Records, Volume I at 451, July 28, 1787.

from the perspective of the one committing the transgression,[219] consider for a moment the person against whom the transgression has been committed. The popular saying is that "there are no atheists in foxholes," and a similar principle emerges here. When someone's spouse betrays them by breaking this commandment, the person betrayed (skeptic or not) will most likely feel that they have been wronged. This is not because some government law says they have the right to feel that way, or because they were taught that way. It is because this moral law, written on our hearts, will explode like a volcano. Instinctively, we know that this love-bond between spouses, committed to each other for life, should not be dishonored in this way. It is self-evident. If there is no God and no natural law, no right and wrong, then what is the basis for demands of loyalty and honor? Why do we feel betrayed? There is no wrong, we say. Only there is. We can try to explain our feelings away, but we can't deny that they exist.

C.S. Lewis's first step on his journey towards Christianity was the recognition of that undeniable law written on his heart, concluding, "It seems, then, we are forced to believe in a real Right and Wrong. People may be sometimes mistaken about them, just as people sometimes get their sums wrong; but they are not a matter of mere taste and opinion any more than the multiplication table."[220] Although some certainly get it wrong on this commandment, we all know we ought not to violate it.

Notice the commandment presumes the bond of marriage exists in the first place. That sacred union, as established by that Creator from whom our rights come, has been under an intensive attack in America for many years. Though some may single out individual issues (promiscuity, same-sex "marriage," cohabitation, etc.), when talking about these attacks on marriage, the reality is that all of them emanate from one place in particular: our hearts; our prideful, selfish, hardened hearts. When we think of it in those terms, we are able to better understand the words of Jesus, Who spoke about this issue in a most truthful and convicting manner: "You have heard that it was said to those of old, 'You shall not

---

219   "[U]nderstanding this, that the law is not laid down for the just but for the lawless and disobedient, for the ungodly and sinners, for the unholy and profane, for those who strike their fathers and mothers, for murderers, the sexually immoral, men who practice homosexuality, enslavers, liars, perjurers, and whatever else is contrary to sound doctrine," (1 Timothy 1:9-10).

220   C.S. Lewis, *Mere Christianity* 7 (HarperCollins 2001 (1952)).

commit adultery." But I say to you that whoever looks at a woman to lust for her has already committed adultery with her in his heart," (Matthew 5:27-28). It is in our heart that adultery starts, and it is at that level that we must guard against it. That is why we feel the way we feel when we break this commandment. This in no way means that the problem is merely a personal one. A proper understanding of that reality should move us as a society to enact policies that support God's model for marriage and the family. That is what our founders tried to do. They recognized the family as the foundation of a productive society and marriage as that bond that holds that family together. Today, as we move further away from those prosperous policies of the past, we increasingly feel the consequences of the weakening of that foundation.

I serve as legal counsel for the nation's largest public policy women's organization, Concerned Women for America (CWA), which has been fighting for over thirty five years, the lies of a feminist movement that encourages women to treat sex like many men do, as a casual, meaningless, recreational act with no consequences. Much of their abortion theory is born out of that distorted view of equality too. The promotion of these ideas, not only through policy but through the arts, has been intense and consistent for years. That's where we have gotten ideas like the "friends with benefits" lie that has hurt many women (and men too) so deeply, causing incredible harm to our society. The statistics are staggering. More than 40% of marriages end in divorce,[221] and about 41% of children are born out of wedlock.[222] The numbers are absolutely heartbreaking for the African-American community, with more than 70% of children born out of wedlock.[223] A 2012 New York City report by the city's Department of Health and Mental Hygiene found that more black babies were aborted than were born in the city that year.[224] It is

221   National Vital Statistics Report, Volume 58, Number 25, available at http://www.cdc.gov/nchs/fastats/divorce.htm (accessed Sept. 12, 2014).

222   *Id.* at Volume 60, Number 1, available at http://www.cdc.gov/nchs/fastats/unmarry.htm (accessed Sept. 12, 2014).

223   Jesse Washington, "Blacks struggle with 72 percent unwed mothers rate," *Associated Press*, November 7, 2010, available at http://www.msnbc.msn.com/id/39993685/ns/health-womens_health/t/blacks-struggle-percent-unwed-mothers-rate/#.T1jpllGmNMY.

224   Summary of Vital Statistics 2012, The City of New York, Pregnancy Outcomes, available at http://www.cnsnews.com/sites/default/files/documents/Pregnancy%20Outcomes%20%20NYC%20Health%202012.pdf (accessed March 2, 2015).

absolutely heartbreaking. The statistics and the negative consequences associated with them are the direct result of the policies our society has supported for many years. It is estimated that when "no-fault divorce" laws began to be passed in 1969, the divorce rates in the different states went up about 25 percent.[225] We have promoted these policies, despite overwhelming evidence telling us that communities with a higher percent of healthy marriages enjoy more successful, stable lives. Here are some findings from the U.S. Department of Health and Human Services on the benefits of healthy marriages:

For Children and Youth
1. More likely to attend college
2. More likely to succeed academically
3. Physically healthier
4. Emotionally healthier
5. Less likely to attempt or commit suicide
6. Demonstrate less behavioral problems in school
7. Less likely to be a victim of physical or sexual abuse
8. Less likely to abuse drugs or alcohol
9. Less likely to commit delinquent behaviors
10. Have a better relationship with their mothers and fathers
11. Decreases their chances of divorcing when they get married
12. Less likely to become pregnant as a teenager, or impregnate someone.
13. Less likely to be sexually active as teenagers
14. Less likely to contract STD's
15. Less likely to be raised in poverty

For Women
1. More satisfying relationship
2. Emotionally healthier
3. Wealthier
4. Less likely to be victims of domestic violence, sexual assault, or other violent crimes
5. Less likely to attempt or commit suicide
6. Decrease risk of drug and alcohol abuse

---

225   Thomas B. Marvell, "Divorce Rates and the Fault Requirement," *Law & Society Review*, Vol. 23, No. 4 at 543-568, (1989).

7. Less likely to contract STD's
8. Less likely to remain or end up in poverty
9. Have better relationships with their children
10. Physically healthier

For Men
1. Live longer
2. Physically healthier
3. Wealthier
4. Increase in the stability of employment
5. Higher wages
6. Emotionally healthier
7. Decrease risk of drug and alcohol abuse
8. Have better relationships with their children
9. More satisfying sexual relationship
10. Less likely to commit violent crimes
11. Less likely to contract STD's
12. Less likely to attempt or commit suicide

For Communities
1. Higher rates of physically healthy citizens
2. Higher rates of emotionally healthy citizens
3. Higher rates of educated citizens
4. Lower domestic violence rates
5. Lower crime statistics
6. Lower teen age pregnancy rates
7. Lower rates of juvenile delinquency
8. Higher rates of home ownership
9. Lower rates of migration
10. Higher property values
11. Decreased need for social services [226]

As is always the case, our experiences prove God's principles are true and best for all, not just the believer. Our society can either heed that wisdom or continue to suffer the consequences of ignoring reality.

---

226   U.S. Department of Health and Human Services, Administration for Children and Families, Healthy Marriage Initiative, available at http://archive.acf.hhs.gov/healthymarriage/benefits/index.html (accessed Sept. 17, 2014).

VIII. Thou shall not steal

The Eight Commandment, "You shall not steal," (Exodus 20:15), represents a profound reality that is essential to human existence, not to mention America's founding. Its genesis lies at the feet of that Creator who spoke everything into existence and gave us dominion over His creation.[227] Its truth is self-evident, and it assumes an even more basic principle: that of property. The principle's self-evidence was noted by C.S. Lewis, who again is of great help in this area. He was amazed when he heard certain things we say as human beings all the time pointing to some "natural set of rules" by which we all should abide. For example, he talked about those who say, "That's my seat; I was there first."

> Now what interests me about [this remark] is that the man who makes [it] is not merely saying that the other man's behaviour does not happen to please him. He is appealing to some kind of standard of behaviour which he expects the other man to know about. And the other man very seldom replies: "To hell with your standard." Nearly always he tries to make out that what he has been doing does not really go against the standard, or that if it does there is some special excuse. He pretends there is some special reason in this particular case why the person who took the seat first should not keep it. ... It looks, in fact, very much as if both parties had in mind some kind of Law or Rule of fair play or decent behaviour or morality or whatever you like to call it, about which they really agreed.[228]

The principle is not only self-evident; it is also true. That is to say, it conforms perfectly to reality, whatever one may think of the principle. American statesman Daniel Webster (1782-1852) pointed to this when he said, "We have no experience that teaches us that any other rights

---

227   "Then God said, 'Let us make man[h] in our image, after our likeness. And let them have dominion over the fish of the sea and over the birds of the heavens and over the livestock and over all the earth and over every creeping thing that creeps on the earth,'" (Genesis 1:26).

228   C.S. Lewis, *Mere Christianity* 3 (Harper Collins 2001 (1952)).

are safe where property is not safe."[229] Our real life experiences have shown us this principle is so essential that its violation carries all sorts of negative effects for our communities. That is usually the case with all of God's Law – and not only at the personal level where we tend to associate this commandment at first glance, but in public policy perhaps most of all. Thomas Jefferson wrote in an 1816 letter, "The true foundation of republican government is the equal right of every citizen in his person and property and in their management."[230]

The violation of this principle was also a major factor leading to American independence. The principle was being challenged at that time, and it has continued to be challenged throughout our history. The fight against communism during the Cold War is perhaps the most well known example. Even today we hear chants of "redistribution" and the "spreading the wealth." These concepts require the government to steal from one group of people to "do good" to others. And the idea, not matter how well-intentioned, can never be prosperous, as it violates "the Law of Nature and of Nature's God."[231] Here is Jefferson on the issue:

> To take from one because it is thought that his own industry and that of his father's has acquired too much, in order to spare to others, who, or whose fathers have not exercised equal industry and skill, is to violate arbitrarily the first principle of association – the guarantee to every one of a free exercise of his industry and the fruits acquired by it.[232]

Many point to other evils, like greed or the exploitation of the poor, to condemn the principle. But we should never use the exploitation of a principle as condemnation of the principle itself. Here is Abraham Lincoln, who fought so valiantly against forces who wanted to exploit people as property, making sure we did not perceive the property principle

229   Daniel Webster, *The Works of Daniel Webster* Volume III, 15 (Edward Evertt, 15th Ed., Little Brown and Company 1869).

230   Thomas Jefferson, *The Jeffersonian Cyclopedia: A Comprehensive Collection of the Views of Thomas Jefferson* 727 (John P. Foley ed. 1900).

231   Declaration of Independence para. 1 (U.S. 1776).

232   *Thomas Jefferson, The Jeffersonian Cyclopedia: A Comprehensive Collection of the Views of Thomas Jefferson* 424 (John P. Foley ed. 1900).

as the evil itself.

> Property is the fruit of labor – property is desirable – is a positive good in the world. That some should be rich shows that others may become rich, and hence is just encouragement to industry and enterprise. Let not him who is houseless pull down the house of another; but let him labor diligently and build one for himself, thus by example assuring that his own shall be safe from violence when built.[233]

Indeed, some of the problems we experienced in the financial world in our times are a violation of this very commandment. Greed led many of those in power to steal from investors and they cheated the public of millions of dollars. But these events confirm God's Law and should not be used to attack it, as some are trying to do today.

Notice that the commandment does not care about motive. Whether out of greed or necessity, stealing violates God's principles. And the same goes for the nature of the subject or victim; stealing from the rich or the poor makes no difference. The great English jurist Sir William Blackstone (1723-1780) said, "So great moreover is the regard of the law for private property that it will not authorize the least violation of it – no, not even for the general good of the whole community."[234] We stand at a very crucial moment in history when it comes to the philosophical debate behind this commandment. And the consequences of our decisions will decide the future of our country. John Adams sums up the stakes:

> The moment the idea is admitted into society that property is not as sacred as the laws of God, and that there is not a force of law and public justice to protect it, anarchy and tyranny commence. If "Thou shalt not covet" and "Thou shalt not steal" were not commandments of Heaven, they must be made inviolable precepts in every

---

233   Abraham Lincoln, "Reply to New York Workingmen's Democratic Republican Association" (21 March 1864), *Collected Works*, Vol. 7, 259-260 (Moody Bible Institute Monthly, Editorial Notes 6, (1929)).

234   William Blackstone, *Commentaries on the Laws of England* Vol. I, 139 (Philadelphia: Robert Bell, 1771).

society before it can be civilized or made free.[235]

May we listen to the wise counsel of our Founders and, more importantly, our God.

IX. You shall not lie

Isn't it amazing how we do not have to teach children to lie? Human nature is such that at an astonishingly early age we can fully employ deceptive tactics, even though we might not even know what the word "deceptive" means. Yet, something else is self-evident to us, even as children: we ought to do better. We ought to tell the truth. The Ninth Commandment says it this way: "You shall not bear false witness against your neighbor," (Exodus 20:16). Other passages shed light on the Commandment. King David wrote, "He who works deceit shall not dwell within my house; he who tells lies shall not continue in my presence," (Psalm 101:7). In the New Testament, the Apostle Paul pleaded, "Do not lie to one another," (Colossians 3:9). And Jesus admonished us to "let your 'Yes' be 'Yes,' and your 'No,' 'No,'" (Matthew 5:37 NKJV).

As with all of God's truth, the admonition is overwhelmingly profitable for all. We instinctively know it is better to tell the truth rather than lie. Even those who claim that the commandments are just part of our particular culture and morality, so that what is true for us is not true for others, must admit that no culture ever celebrates someone for deceiving those a person loves most. Some may believe that it is better to lie in certain circumstances (to save a life or something of that nature), but no culture ever thought it good, for example, for parents to teach their children the best ways to deceive them. No, every human values truth. It is something that goes beyond "culture" or "morality." It is ingrained in the human spirit.

In America, truth is fundamental to all for which we stand. It is central to the American experiment. The Founders knew that those "Laws of Nature and of Nature's God" on which they based their understand-

---

235   John Adams, *A Defense of the Constitutions of Government of the United States of America*, The Works of John Adams Vol. 6. (Charles Francis Adams, 1856 (1787)), available at http://oll.libertyfund.org/titles/2104#Adams_1431-06_19 (accessed Sept. 17, 2014).

ing were rooted in a truth that was knowable, profitable, and enduring. Thomas Jefferson wrote that, "Honesty is the first chapter of the book of wisdom."[236] And it was based on that wisdom that they sought to establish a government for a free people that would withstand the test of time. It needed to transcend the immediacy of their present circumstances in order to preserve freedom for generations to come. Truth has that enduring quality. That is why the Bible speaks so strongly for truth and honesty. It says that "God is not a man, that he should lie," (Numbers 23:19). It says, "the word of the LORD is right; and all His works are done in truth," (Psalm 33:4, NKJV). It not only says that He is a "God of truth," (Deuteronomy 32:4, NKJV), it testifies that He is Truth: "Jesus said to him, 'I am the way, and the truth, and the life. No one comes to the Father except through me," (John 14:6). And because "His truth endureth to all generations," (Psalms 100:5), Americans should be able to pursue it and cherish it, thereby preserving and continuing through the path of liberty and freedom. "Truthful lips endure forever, but a lying tongue is but for a moment," says Proverbs 12:19.

But, of course, we don't need the Bible in order to know the intrinsic value of truth. Plato (ca. 427-347 BC) said, "[F]alse words are not only evil in themselves, but they infect the soul with evil."[237] Mark Twain valued the commandment's practicality, writing, "When in doubt, tell the truth... If you tell the truth you don't have to remember anything... Truth is the most precious thing we have. Economize it."[238] And perhaps the most famous atheist in history Friedrich Nietzsche is attributed with saying on the topic, "I'm not upset that you lied to me, I'm upset that from now on I can't believe you."[239] And that's the issue, isn't it? The breaking of this commandment has real consequences in the way we see ourselves and the way others see us. That is why we cherish and strive to be men and women of integrity. In public policy, we talk about men and women of "character." We look for it in our leaders and role models.

---

236   Thomas Jefferson, *The Writings of Thomas Jefferson*, January 12, 1819 (Ford, Paul Leicester, ed., G.P. Putnam's Sons, 1892-99. 10 vols.), available at http://www.monticello.org/site/jefferson/honesty-first-chapter-book-wisdom-quotation#_note-0 (accessed Sept. 17, 2014).

237   Plato, *Phaedo* 111 (Benjamin Jowett trans. 2012 (360 BCE).

238   Mark Twain, *Mark Twain's Notebook* 237, 240 (Albert Bigelow Paine ed., Harper Brothers (1935)).

239   Mark Grant, *Out of the Box and Onto Wall Street: Unorthodox Insights on Investments and the Economy,* John Wiley & Sons, (2011).

Samuel Adams said, "The public cannot be too curious concerning the characters of public men,"[240] and "[N]either the wisest constitution nor the wisest laws will secure the liberty and happiness of a people whose manners are universally corrupt."[241] Noah Webster (1758-1843), the Father of American Scholarship and Education, and the creator of the famous Webster's Dictionary said, "The virtues of men are of more consequence to society than their abilities; and for this reason, the heart should be cultivated with more assiduity than the head."[242] And Thomas Jefferson wrote:

He who permits himself to tell a lie once, finds it much easier to do it a second and third time, till at length it becomes habitual; he tells lies without attending to it, and truths without the world's believing him. This falsehood of the tongue leads to that of the heart, and in time depraves all its good dispositions.[243]

There is a reason why our political leaders take an oath of office. We rely on a person's word as they testify in court and as they send in their tax returns. America, from the beginning, was founded on the idea that in order to be free, there must be a sense of self-discipline on the part of our citizens, so that we can trust each other, even with our lives. Our ancestors knew that disregarding this commandment would have dire consequences for our country. Today, we are feeling the painful results of ignoring this principle and their advice. We cannot fight dishonesty with government regulations; it is a matter of the heart. Honesty must be cultivated by attending to the self-evident truths our Creator has placed within us. Because as Benjamin Franklin said, "It's the easiest thing in

---

240   Samuel Adams, letter to James Warren (November 4, 1775), available at http://www.thefederalistpapers.org/founders/samuel-adams/samuel-adams-letter-to-james-warren-11-4-1775 (accessed Sept. 2, 2015).

241   Samuel Adams, essay in *The Public Advertiser* (ca. 1749), available at http://www.thefederalistpapers.org/founders/samuel-adams/political-essay (accessed Sept. 2, 2015).

242   Noah Webster, *On Education of Youth in America*, American educational thought: essays from 1640-1940, 288 (Andrew J. Milson editor (2004 (1790)).

243   Thomas Jefferson, letter to Peter Carr, Aug. 19, 1785, available at http://www.let.rug.nl/usa/presidents/thomas-jefferson/letters-of-thomas-jefferson/jefl32.php (accessed Sept. 2, 2015).

the world for a man to deceive himself."[244] We must turn away from deceit.

X. Thou shall not covet

We finish our look at the self-evident truths embodied on the Ten Commandments with the profound truth encapsulated in the Tenth Commandment: "Thou shall not covet." The full verse reads: "You shall not covet your neighbor's house; you shall not covet your neighbor's wife, or his male servant, or his female servant, or his ox, or his donkey, or anything that is your neighbor's," (Exodus 20:17). The commandment reveals a deep understanding of the human heart, which is simply indispensable to the proper governing of any people, as we saw on chapter six. Left to our own nature, we covet; we envy. We are not content with what we have, no matter how wonderful. All kinds of societal evils flow from the covetous heart. James 4 even attributes wars and fights to our covetousness:

> Where do wars and fights come from among you? Do they not come from your desires for pleasure that war in your members? You lust and do not have. You murder and covet and cannot obtain. You fight and war. Yet you do not have because you do not ask. You ask and do not receive, because you ask amiss, that you may spend it on your pleasures (James 4:1-3).

The first thing to notice is that it is indeed a matter of the heart and not of the ultimate action that comes as the consequence of our covetousness. Most other commandments dealt with those (not stealing, committing adultery, not murdering, etc.). This commandment gets at the root of the issue: our own heart. You cannot legislate that. America's Founders understood this. That is why they constructed a system of government that took into account the reality of man's natural condition and the importance of God as the only One able to affect the change necessary for a truly free society. They envisioned a robust role for the church if the nation was to thrive. A very distinct role from the government, to be sure, but a role so important a free government could not survive without it.

---

244   Benjamin Franklin, *Poor Richard's Almanack* 134 (Barnes & Noble Publishing 2004 (1733-1758)).

This is why John Adams, as we have mentioned, famously said, "Our constitution was made only for a moral and religious people. It is wholly inadequate for the government of any other."[245] In a letter to Benjamin Rush (1745-1813), Adams emphasized the universality of the principle: "Religion and virtue are the only foundations, not only of republicanism and all free government, but of social felicity under all governments and in all the combinations of human society."[246] George Washington expressed this self-evident truth magnificently in his Farewell Address:

> Of all the dispositions and habits which lead to political prosperity, Religion and morality are indispensable supports. In vain would that man claim the tribute of Patriotism, who should labour to subvert these great Pillars of human happiness, these firmest props of the duties of Men & citizens. The mere Politician, equally with the pious man ought to respect & to cherish them. A volume could not trace all their connections with private & public felicity. Let it simply be asked where is the security for property, for reputation, for life, if the sense of religious obligation desert the Oaths, which are the instruments of investigation in Courts of Justice? And let us with caution indulge the supposition, that morality can be maintained without religion. Whatever may be conceded to the influence of refined education on minds of peculiar structure – reason & experience both forbid us to expect that National morality can prevail in exclusion of religious principle.[247]

Notice these are tried and true principles. Washington says he bases it both on reason, by which we are able to study the Scriptures and receive these truths from God, but also by experience, that is by putting

---

245   John Adams, Message to the Officers of the First Brigade of the Third Division of the Militia of Massachusetts (October 11, 1798). *The Works of John Adams*, Vol. 9. of 10 (Charles Francis Adams ed., Little, Brown and Co. 1856), available at http://oll. libertyfund.org/titles/2107#lf1431-09_head_222 (accessed Sept. 8, 2014).

246   John Adams, *Letter to Dr. Benjamin Rush* (August 28, 1811), The Works of John Adams, Second President of the United States. Volume 9, 688, available at https:// books.google.com/books?id=qRLOAwAAQBAJ&printsec=frontcover#v=onepage&q &f=false (accessed Sept. 2, 2015).

247   George Washington, *Farewell Address* (September 19, 1796).

the principles into practice. The Word of God never disappoints. Even the concepts that seem most foreign to us become simple and powerful truths, once they are put to the test. Washington's words reveal that his experience in public service had only strengthened what he knew to be true from the beginning. If you remember, in his *First Inaugural Address*, he had said:

> There exists in the economy and course of nature, an indissoluble union between virtue and happiness; between duty and advantage; between the genuine maxims of an honest and magnanimous policy, and the solid rewards of public prosperity and felicity; since we ought to be no less persuaded that the propitious smiles of Heaven can never be expected on a nation that disregards the eternal rules of order and right, which Heaven itself has ordained.[248]

America simply cannot (and will not) survive as a free nation if it continues down a path that ignores this truth – the reality of the human heart and God's redemptive power. Since its birth, our nation has benefitted from a strong commitment to these principles. But if we continue to draw farther away from them, we will continue to bare the hurtful wounds of our own enslavement until the light of freedom finally extinguishes in our land. It was the point made by Thomas Jefferson, who wondered: "[C]an the liberties of a nation be thought secure when we have removed their only firm basis, a conviction in the minds of the people that these liberties are the gift of God? That they are not to be violated but with his wrath?"[249]

In light of that justice, we should feel the weight of this commandment, "Thou shall not covet." We are better citizens when we obey it. The secularists' response to our unbridled human passions, on the other hand, is an ever-growing police state that has been proven throughout history to have one inevitable end: the oppression of its citizenry.

---

248   George Washington, *First Inaugural Address* (April 30, 1789).
249   Thomas Jefferson, *Notes on the State of Virginia*, Query 18 (1781).

A final word

The self-evident truths we have discussed in these chapters are the fundamental principles of liberty. Daniel Webster said, "Whatever makes men good Christians, makes them good citizens."[250] Value and respect for our neighbors and their possessions is essential to our liberty. Let us reiterate then that Christian morals are good policy for everyone, whatever our religious beliefs. They are the principles of freedom. May we rediscover their true value before it is too late. Those who are interested in ensuring freedom's survival would be wise to preach a return to these essential principles. They truly represent the only way to America's recuperation. It is imperative that we turn now to the preservation of these principles by teaching their truths to the next generations. It is an area where we have failed in the past. One we must rectify before it is too late.

---

250   Daniel Webster, *Speech at Plymouth, Mass.* (Dec. 22, 1820).

Part Four
PRESERVING FREEDOM

Mario Diaz

CHAPTER ELEVEN
SHARING THE BLESSINGS
OF OBEDIENCE

Many of the problems we face as a society stem from the fact that we, as Christian citizens, have failed to communicate the importance of the principles we believe in to the next generations. Indeed, we have forgotten how important they are ourselves. Perhaps more damaging than anything is that we are failing to teach our children not only the truths we believe in, but also *the source* of those truths: the Holy Bible. A 2014 study by Barna Group and American Bible Society titled "The State of the Bible" found that although, "The majority of adults (69%) consider themselves moderately or somewhat knowledgeable about the Bible," only "One in four US adults (43%) can correctly name 'Genesis, Exodus, Leviticus, Numbers, Deuteronomy' as the first five books of the Bible."[251] It found that,

One-fourth of adults (26%) say they never read the Bible. One in 10 (9%) read it less than once a year and about the same number (11%) read it only once or twice a year,

---

251   Research commissioned by American Bible Society, conducted by Barna Group, *The State of the Bible | 2014,*
23, available at http://www.americanbible.org/uploads/content/state-of-the-bible-data-analysis-american-bible-society-2014.pdf (accessed March 3, 2015).

not including times when they are at a church service or church event. These three segments combined represent non-Bible readers (46%).[252]

Merely 15% said they read the Bible daily. That is catastrophic. If we truly believe Jesus' words that, "Man shall not live by bread alone, but by every word that comes from the mouth of God," (Mathew 4:4) then we must realize we are starving our spirit. What would happen to our physical bodies if we ate only once a week, or once a month, or once a year? Our disregard for the Word of God has reached such a state that our spiritual muscles are atrophied. It should be no surprise then that we don't even realize what is going on. It is no wonder to see in the report that even though, "More than four out of five US adults (81%) believe that morality is on the decline in America," only "One-quarter of US adults (29%) say the lack of Bible reading is the primary cause."[253]

The Book is key

Let us go back to the words of God to Joshua, after the passing of Moses:

> This Book of the Law shall not depart from your mouth, but you shall meditate on it day and night, so that you may be careful to do according to all that is written in it. For then you will make your way prosperous, and then you will have good success. Have I not commanded you? Be strong and courageous. Do not be frightened, and do not be dismayed, for the LORD your God is with you wherever you go" (Joshua 1:8-9).

The Scriptures are key. The Bible. The Word of God. We must search it, know it, and share it. The passage calls us to "meditate on it day and night." It says it should not depart from our mouth. It calls us to be careful to *do* as it commands, for knowledge alone is not enough. It is in *following* its commands that the essence of our success as individuals, families, communities, peoples and nations lies— a success that goes well above the material. The "American dream" is more than an opportunity to make more money, which unfortunately, many have reduced it

---

252   *Id.* at 11.

253   *Id.* at 24.

to. It is a dream of freedom, liberty and fulfillment, including vocational success, but going well beyond that. It is the pursuit of happiness, the pursuit of truth, the pursuit of the knowledge of God. We have forgotten that for the most part and that is the danger we face. Routinely, we hear of a movie or music star lost to suicide or drug addiction. Why would people who seemingly "have it all," as we say, end up as such emotional wrecks? The answer seems fairly clear, doesn't it? Sure, there are mental illnesses and out of control addictions, we would never want to minimize that. But we must also admit that having all the money, fame and success in the world is as hollow and empty a state as any other, apart from God. Yet, this continues to be our dream. It continues to be the model we elevate for our children. It seems to be what we all work for all our lives—that elusive road to fame and fortune. The Scripture calls us back to reality. Listen to Jesus: "Do not work for the food that perishes, but for the food that endures to eternal life, which the Son of Man will give to you. For on him God the Father has set his seal," (John 6:27-28). These are the truths we must pass on to the next generations if we are to preserve liberty. We must never forget them. That is where true "happiness" can be discovered. And more profoundly, joy can be attained.

No other source

The Psalmist had discovered this, the most precious resource available to all mankind: the Word of Almighty God. These excerpts from Psalm 119 paint the picture for us:

> Blessed are those whose way is blameless,
> who walk in the law of the Lord!
> Blessed are those who keep his testimonies,
> Who seek him with their whole heart…
> You have commanded your precepts
> to be kept diligently.
> Oh that my ways may be steadfast
> in keeping your statutes!
> Then I shall not be put to shame,
> having my eyes fixed on all your commandments…
>
> How can a young man keep his way pure?

By guarding it according to your word…
I have stored up your word in my heart,
that I might not sin against you…
With my lips I declare
all the rules of your mouth.
In the way of your testimonies I delight
as much as in all riches.
I will meditate on your precepts
and fix my eyes on your ways.
I will delight in your statutes;
I will not forget your word…

Open my eyes, that I may behold
wondrous things out of your law.
I am a sojourner on the earth;
hide not your commandments from me…
Even though princes sit plotting against me,
your servant will meditate on your statutes.
Your testimonies are my delight;
they are my counselors…

Put false ways far from me
and graciously teach me your law…

Incline my heart to your testimonies,
and not to selfish gain!
Turn my eyes from looking at worthless things;
and give me life in your ways…

I will also speak of your testimonies before kings
and shall not be put to shame…

When I think of your rules from of old,
I take comfort, O Lord.
Hot indignation seizes me because of the wicked,
who forsake your law.
Your statutes have been my songs
in the house of my sojourning…

Though the cords of the wicked ensnare me,
I do not forget your law…
I am a companion of all who fear you,
of those who keep your precepts…

Before I was afflicted I went astray,
but now I keep your word.
It is good for me that I was afflicted,
that I might learn your statutes.
The law of your mouth is better to me
than thousands of gold and silver pieces…

I know, O Lord, that your rules are righteous,
and that in faithfulness you have afflicted me…

All your commandments are sure…

Forever, O Lord, your word
is firmly fixed in the heavens…
If your law had not been my delight,
I would have perished in my affliction.
I will never forget your precepts,
for by them you have given me life…
I have seen a limit to all perfection,
but your commandment is exceedingly broad.

Oh how I love your law!
It is my meditation all the day.
Your commandment makes me wiser than my enemies,
for it is ever with me.
I have more understanding than all my teachers,
for your testimonies are my meditation.
I understand more than the aged,
for I keep your precepts.
I hold back my feet from every evil way,
in order to keep your word.
I do not turn aside from your rules,

for you have taught me.
How sweet are your words to my taste,
sweeter than honey to my mouth!
Through your precepts I get understanding;
therefore I hate every false way.

Your word is a lamp to my feet
and a light to my path.
I have sworn an oath and confirmed it,
to keep your righteous rules....

I hold my life in my hand continually,
but I do not forget your law...
Your testimonies are my heritage forever,
for they are the joy of my heart...

It is time for the Lord to act,
for your law has been broken.
Therefore I love your commandments
above gold, above fine gold.
Therefore I consider all your precepts to be right;
I hate every false way...

The sum of your word is truth,
and every one of your righteous rules endures forever...

Great peace have those who love your law;
nothing can make them stumble...

Let my cry come before you, O Lord;
give me understanding according to your word...
I have gone astray like a lost sheep; seek your servant,
for I do not forget your commandments.

The dangers of forgetting

Forgetting the commandments of God was the catalyst for the Israelites in Egypt. It is how they fell under oppression. If you remember, Joseph saved the Egyptians by interpreting Pharaoh's dream of seven years of bounty, followed by seven years of famine. Joseph counseled Pharaoh to save a tenth of the food of each year during the years of abundance in order to have enough food during the years of famine. Pharaoh put Joseph in charge of the operation and Joseph became only second to Pharaoh in command and stature. He saved the Egyptians and also his family, the Israelites, who came in search of food and settled with him there. But time passed and soon people forgot about Joseph and what the Lord had done through him. Exodus 1 has the progression for us:

> Now there arose a new king over Egypt, who did not know Joseph. And he said to his people, "Look, the people of the children of Israel are more and mightier than we; come, let us deal shrewdly with them, lest they multiply, and it happen, in the event of war, that they also join our enemies and fight against us, and so go up out of the land." Therefore they set taskmasters over them to afflict them with their burdens. And they built for Pharaoh supply cities, Pithom and Raamses. But the more they afflicted them, the more they multiplied and grew. And they were in dread of the children of Israel. So the Egyptians made the children of Israel serve with rigor. And they made their lives bitter with hard bondage—in mortar, in brick, and in all manner of service in the field. All their service in which they made them serve was with rigor (Exodus 1:8–14, NKJV).

Everything started with the rise of a king who did not know Joseph and who had not learned from his own history. The king does not realize that he exists because of what God had done through an Israelite. This has happened continually throughout history. The book of Judges is full of the accounts. After the great victories of Gideon, through whom God delivered the Israelites from the hand of Midian,[254] unbelievably, the people again forgot about God and His statutes: "As soon as Gideon died, the people of Israel turned again and whored after the Baals and made Baal-berith their god. And the people of Israel did not remember the Lord their God, who had delivered them from the hand of all their

---

254   Judges 6-8.

enemies on every side..." (Judges 8:33, 34).

Today in America, we elect leaders who do not know or appreciate our rich Christian history. Oh that we had a leader who would, say, call the nation to prayer and fasting to seek God's guidance as Washington and Lincoln did! No, our leaders have forgotten about the blessings of Providence. *We* have forgotten. And chains usually follow, as in the case of Joseph. We have forgotten, not only about where and from Whom the blessings we have come from, but also about the reason why many of our forefathers settled in American in the first place. Here is the introduction to the "Religion and the Founding of the American Republic" exhibition at the U.S. Library of Congress:

> Many of the British North American colonies that eventually formed the United States of America were settled in the seventeenth century by men and women, who, in the face of European persecution, refused to compromise passionately held religious convictions and fled Europe. The New England colonies, New Jersey, Pennsylvania, and Maryland were conceived and established "as plantations of religion." Some settlers who arrived in these areas came for secular motives--"to catch fish" as one New Englander put it--but the great majority left Europe to worship God in the way they believed to be correct. They enthusiastically supported the efforts of their leaders to create "a city on a hill" or a "holy experiment," whose success would prove that God's plan for his churches could be successfully realized in the American wilderness. Even colonies like Virginia, which were planned as commercial ventures, were led by entrepreneurs who considered themselves "militant Protestants" and who worked diligently to promote the prosperity of the church.[255]

Clearly, many of those who came to this country came looking for something more profound than earthly riches. The teachings of the Bi-

---

255   Religion and the Founding of the American Republic, America as a Religious Refuge: The Seventeenth Century, Part 1 at http://www.loc.gov/exhibits/religion/rel01.html (accessed Sept. 17, 2014).

ble are the only way of preserving a proper perspective of what our lives are about, even for those who refuse the existence of a creator. We have forgotten many of the Biblical lessons our forefathers knew. At first we just lost the source, even as we continue to teach the general principles of Christianity, but that development would turn out to be disastrous, for we must be grounded somewhere, especially in times of trials, if we are to stand firm. When our faith is tried and our beliefs come under attack, we must not only know the principles, but know where they come from and why they are true. The old serpent trick, "Did God really say…"[256] that precipitated the fall of man in the beginning is still the enemy's most powerful tool today. How we answer that question will determine whether we go the way of Adam and Eve, or the way of Jesus of Nazareth who time after time told the serpent, "It is written…" in order to withstand temptation. Can we talk in those terms? Do we approach the trials we face, first and foremost with, "It is written," with the Word of God, with Truth?

The value of truth

The Founding Fathers, whatever their personal faith, understood the value of Biblical principles. Even while many had deep questions and some doubts, they esteemed the Book above any other. This is vital, for as long as you maintain the standard, you will be able to correct any abuse of that standard and grow experientially on the implications of deviating from it. But if the standard is removed, as we have slowly allowed in our own lives, let alone on our culture and public policy, then there is no north. There is no point of reference, as Nietzsche vividly illustrated in "The Parable of a Madman."

Some secularists gleefully point to Thomas Jefferson to disparage his faith because he "created his own 'bible'" by taking out things he didn't agree with.[257] But just think about that. Which other book is so vital to someone's life that they would take the time and trouble to do such

---

256   "Now the serpent was more crafty than any other beast of the field that the Lord God had made.
He said to the woman, 'Did God actually say, 'You shall not eat of any tree in the garden'?'" Genesis 3:1.

257   Owen Edwards, How Thomas Jefferson Created His Own Bible, *Smithsonian Magazine* at http://www.smithsonianmag.com/arts-culture/how-thomas-jefferson-created-his-own-bible-5659505/.

an exercise? Most likely we discard a book if we don't find value in its content. Not that his position is defensible in any way, but there can be no question to the uniqueness and the high value placed in Scripture by our forefathers — even by those who seemed to have doubted it the most. It is more likely to see them say, as that loving father told Jesus, "Lord, I believe; help my unbelief!" (Mark 9:24 NKJV), than to somehow extrapolate from their small expressions that they did not believed at all in the Word of God. Benjamin Franklin said, "A Bible and a newspaper in every house, a good school in every district—all studied and appreciated as they merit—are the principal support of virtue, morality and civil liberty."[258] Daniel Webster delivered an address at the completion of the Bunker Hill Monument on June 17, 1843, where he said:

> [I]t is not to be doubted, that to the free and universal reading of the Bible, is to be ascribed in that age, ascribed in every age, that men where much indebted for right views of civil liberty. The Bible is a book of faith, and a book of doctrine; but it is also a book, which teaches man his own individual responsibility, his own dignity, and his equality with his fellow man.[259]

You can feel the high value placed on Scripture for the preservation of freedom and liberty. That belief went beyond personal faith, into practical public policy. And their belief was not irrational but well founded. It has been the experience shared by innumerable great men throughout history. "The Bible simply stands alone in human literature in its elevated conception of manhood, in character and conduct," said American clergyman and abolitionist Henry Ward Beecher (1813-1887), "the word of God tends to make large-minded, noble-minded men."[260] The great jurist and philosopher Francis Bacon (1561-1626) said, "There never was found, in any age of the world, either religion or law that did so highly exalt the public good as the Bible." Poet John Milton (1608-1674),

---

258   Forty Thousand Quotations: Prose and Poetical, comp. by Charles Noel Douglas. New York: Halcyon House, 1917; Bartleby.com, 2012. Available at http://www.bartleby.com/348/authors/195.html (accessed Sept. 17, 2014).

259   Daniel Webster, An Address Delivered at the Completion of the Bunker Hill Monument 17 (Tappan and Dennet 1843).

260   Henry Ward Beeche, Proverbs from Plymouth Pulpit 135 (William Drysdale ed. D. Appleton and Co. 1887).

author of the classic *Paradise Lost*, said, "There are no songs comparable to the songs of Zion, no orations equal to those of the prophets, and no politics like those which the Scriptures teach."[261] Many today would be absolutely taken aback to discover that the Bible actually teaches us about politics, among so many other things. But it makes perfect sense. The Bible is life. Scottish minister James Hamilton, said:

> The Bible is a treasure. It contains enough to make us rich for time and eternity. It contains the secret of happy living. It contains the key of heaven. It contains the title-deeds of an inheritance incorruptible, and that fadeth not away. It contains the pearl of great price. Nay, in so far as it reveals them as the portion of us sinful worms, it contains the Saviour and the living God Himself.[262]

Within the pages of Scriptures lies the answer to the pursuit of happiness; certainly for the Christian citizen, but beyond that for every living creature— for it is my great conviction that if you are not a Christian, you should be. It was the great truth asserted by John Locke, so influential in the development of the Founders' worldview, who said in a letter to Rev. Richard King:

> You ask me, "what is the shortest and surest way, for a young gentleman, to attain a true knowledge of the Christian religion, in full and just extent of it?"… to this I have a short and plain answer: ""Let him study the Holy Scripture, especially the New Testament." Therein are contained the words of eternal life. It has God for its author; salvation for its end; and truth, without any mixture of error, for its matter. So that it is a wonder to me, how any one professing Christianity, that would seriously set himself to know his religion, should be in doubt where to employ his search, and lay out his pains for his information; when he knows a book, where it is all contained, pure and entire; and

---

261   Philip Schaff, *Literature and Poetry* 77 (Charles Scribner's Sons 1890).

262   James Hamilton, *Works of the Late Rev. James Hamilton*. 1873. Reprint. London: Forgotten Books, 2013. 60-1.

wither, at last, every one must have recourse, to verify that of it which he finds any where else."[263]

No freedom apart from Scripture

We must conclude therefore, as the Founders and so many other great men have done before us, that there is no freedom apart from the Holy Scriptures, that unless we transmit the importance of this Book and its principles to the next generations, we will not be able to preserve the liberties we have come to enjoy for so many years. This is not mere inference; the Founders were crystal clear in this manner. Federalist Fisher Ames (1758–1808), a Representative from Massachusetts, said this in his oration on the sublime virtues of General George Washington: "Our liberty depends on our education, our laws, and habits, to which even prejudices yield ... it is founded on morals and religion, who[s]e authority reigns in the heart, and on the influence all the[s]e produce on public opinion before *that* opinion governs rulers. *Here* liberty is restraint..." (emphasis in original).[264] Charles Carroll, the delegate to the Continental Congress and senator from Maryland, said:

> Remove the hope and dread of future rewards & punishments, the most powerful restraint on wicked actions, & ye strongest inducement to virtuous ones is done away. Virtue may be said is its own reward; I believe it to be so and even in this life the only source of happiness; and this intimate & necessary connection between virtue & happiness here and between vice and misery in a future state of existence ... without morals a republic cannot subsist any length of time; they therefore who are decrying the Christian religion, whose morality is so sublime & pure, [which] denounces against the wicked eternal misery, & insured to the good eternal happiness are undermining the solid foundation of morals, the best security for

---

263   John Locke, *The Works of John Locke* Vol. X 306 (Thomas Davison, Whitefriars 1823).

264   Fisher Ames, *An Oration on the Sublime Virtues of General George Washington* 23 (Young & Minns 1800).

the duration of free governments.[265]

But the most beautiful exposition of this truth is given to us by Dr. D. James McHenry (1753-1816), who fought in the Revolutionary War under the command of George Washington, was a delegate to the Continental Congress, and who later served as Secretary of War under both Presidents Washington and Adams. He was a strong advocate of Bible literacy as the foundation for good leadership. Listen carefully to his extraordinary insight on the manner:

All Christians allow that the Old and New Testaments taken together, are the only books in the world which clearly reveal the nature of God, contain a perfect law for our government, propose the most powerful persuasions to obey this law, and furnish the best motives for patience and resignation, under every circumstance and vicissitude of life. Even those writers who deny their divinity, have yet acknowledge that the matters contained in them are, at least, calculated to make mankind wiser and better. These surprising and salutary effects the scriptures have unequivocally produced, and whenever they are read and attended to, will continue to produce. Facts so fully ascertained and so clearly demonstrating the great importance of circulating the sacred writings have (within these few years past) called the attention of men more particularly to this subject, and given rise to the establishment of Societies whose object is to encourage their circulation, by promoting the printing of them in all languages, and their distribution gratis, whenever they could not be otherwise obtained.

Neither in considering this subject, let it be overlooked, that public utility pleads most forcibly for the general distribution of the Holy Scriptures. The doctrine they preach, the obligations they impose, the punishment they threaten, the rewards they promise, the stamp and image of divinity they bear, which produces a convic-

---

265   Charles Carroll, *The Life and Correspondence of James McHenry* 474-75 (Bernard C. Steiner ed., The Burrows Brothers, 1907).

tion of their truths, can alone secure to society, order and peace, and to our courts of justice and constitutions of government, purity, stability and usefulness. In vain, without the Bible, we increase penal laws and draw [e]ntrenchments around our institutions. Bibles are strong [e]ntrenchments. Where they abound, men cannot pursue wicked courses, and at the same time enjoy quiet conscience.

Consider also, the rich do not possess aught more precious than their Bible, and that the poor cannot be presented by the right with anything of greater value. Withhold it not from the poor. It is a book of councils and directions, fitted to every situation in which man can be placed. Tis is an oracle which reveals to mortals the secrets of heaven and the hidden will of the Almighty. It is a power that can eject the heaviest burthen. It is an armory which furnishes a sure defense against oppression and calumny. It is the genuine balm for wounded hearts. It is an antidote to the poisons which lie concealed in the cup of pleasure. It is a mountain from whose summit are seen the height and depth, the bearings and the boundaries of sin and iniquity. It is a fountain of delight which no drought can dry up. It is a country lofty and serene, laid out into beautiful landscapes, the view of which never satiates or wearies. It is an estate, whose title is guaranteed by Christ, whose delicious fruits ripen every season, survive the worm, and keep through eternity.[266]

How many in leadership today would speak of the Word of God in these terms? How many anywhere in America? There can be no question we have lost something. Can we be surprised at the parallel moral decay of our culture? Indeed, what we have experienced only proves too well the wisdom of the Founders when they spoke as Dr. McHenry. We must recapture that divine vision of God and His Holy Word; that sense of awe and wonder at God's creation and His workings with man. We

---

266   Dr. D. James McHenry, *One Hundred and Ten Years of Bible Society Work in Maryland, 1810-1920* 13,14 (Bernard C. Steiner ed., Maryland Bible Society, 1921).

have lost the wisdom of men like Dr. Benjamin Rush, who said:

> The only foundation for a useful education in a republic is to be laid in religion. Without this there can be no virtue, and without virtue there can be no liberty, and liberty is the object and life of all republican governments.[267]

What Dr. Rush is identifying is that we need wisdom even more than knowledge, for it directs how we used the knowledge we acquire. He also said:

> We profess to be republicans, and yet we neglect the only means of establishing and perpetuating our republican forms of government, that is, the universal education of our youth in the principles of Christianity by the means of the Bible. For this Divine Book, above all others, favors that equality among mankind, that respect for just laws, and those sober and frugal virtues, which constitute the soul of republicanism.[268]

Notice it is not one of the means, but the *only* mean to maintain a republican form of government: by the perpetuation of Christian principles through the use of Holy Scripture. Let us recall the words of that great Supreme Court Justice Joseph Story (1779-1845) who showed so clearly the connections between the Word of God, Justice and Freedom. He said:

> Indeed, the right of a society or government to [participate] in matters of religion will hardly be contested by any persons who believe that piety, religion, and morality are intimately connected with the well being of the state and indispensable to the administrations of civil justice. The promulgation of the great doctrines of religion—the being, and attributes, and providence of one Almighty God; the responsibility to Him for all our actions, founded upon moral accountability; a future state

---

267   Benjamin Rush, *Essays, Literary, Moral and Philosophical* 8 (Thomas and William Bradford, 1806).

268   *Id.* at 93-94.

of rewards and punishments; the cultivation of all the personal, social, and benevolent virtues—these never can be a matter of indifference in any well-ordered community. It is, indeed, difficult to conceive how any civilized society can well exist without them.[269]

That intimate connection between the principles of God, the wellbeing of a nation, and the administration of justice is crucial for us. Many seek justice but look for it in all the wrong places. Without God's objective standards, any idea of justice is mere preference. But we know intuitively there is such a thing as justice (we thirst for it), apart from personal preference. In fact, if it were up to us, we would probably ease that standard a bit, since we fail so miserably. But we have seen justice, we have tasted it, we just have no idea where it comes from or how to attain it. We have lost the source.

Obedience, obedience, obedience

As we have alluded to already, there is much more to this topic than merely realizing the importance of the principles of God and His Word. We must obey and live by these principles if they are to have the desired effect on us and in our culture. Obedience to the principles found in the Bible must be our aim. This, no doubt, begins with a high view of Scripture but it must go beyond that. Listen to the way God spoke to the Israelites in Deuteronomy 11:1-32, after Moses delivered to them the second pair of tablets containing the Ten Commandments:

> Therefore you shall love the LORD your God, and keep His charge, His statutes, His judgments, and His commandments always. Know today that I do not speak with your children, who have not known and who have not seen the chastening of the LORD your God, His greatness and His mighty hand and His outstretched arm— His signs and His acts which He did in the midst of Egypt, to Pharaoh king of Egypt, and to all his land; what He did to the army of Egypt, to their horses and their chariots: how He made the waters of the Red Sea overflow them

269   Joseph Story, *A Familiar Exposition of the Constitution of the United States* 260, §442 (New York: Harper & Brothers, 1847).

as they pursued you, and how the Lord has destroyed them to this day; what He did for you in the wilderness until you came to this place; and what He did to Dathan and Abiram the sons of Eliab, the son of Reuben: how the earth opened its mouth and swallowed them up, their households, their tents, and all the substance that was in their possession, in the midst of all Israel— but your eyes have seen every great act of the Lord which He did.

Therefore you shall keep every commandment which I command you today, that you may be strong, and go in and possess the land which you cross over to possess, and that you may prolong your days in the land which the LORD swore to give your fathers, to them and their descendants, 'a land flowing with milk and honey.' For the land which you go to possess is not like the land of Egypt from which you have come, where you sowed your seed and watered it by foot, as a vegetable garden; but the land which you cross over to possess is a land of hills and valleys, which drinks water from the rain of heaven, a land for which the Lord your God cares; the eyes of the Lord your God are always on it, from the beginning of the year to the very end of the year.

'And it shall be that if you earnestly obey My commandments which I command you today, to love the Lord your God and serve Him with all your heart and with all your soul, then I will give you the rain for your land in its season, the early rain and the latter rain, that you may gather in your grain, your new wine, and your oil. And I will send grass in your fields for your livestock, that you may eat and be filled.' Take heed to yourselves, lest your heart be deceived, and you turn aside and serve other gods and worship them, lest the Lord's anger be aroused against you, and He shut up the heavens so that there be no rain, and the land yield no produce, and you perish quickly from the good land which the Lord is giving you.

Therefore you shall lay up these words of mine in your heart and in your soul, and bind them as a sign on your hand, and they shall be as frontlets between your eyes. You shall teach them to your children, speaking of them when you sit in your house, when you walk by the way, when you lie down, and when you rise up. And you shall write them on the doorposts of your house and on your gates, that your days and the days of your children may be multiplied in the land of which the LORD swore to your fathers to give them, like the days of the heavens above the earth.

For if you carefully keep all these commandments which I command you to do—to love the LORD your God, to walk in all His ways, and to hold fast to Him— then the LORD will drive out all these nations from before you, and you will dispossess greater and mightier nations than yourselves. Every place on which the sole of your foot treads shall be yours: from the wilderness and Lebanon, from the river, the River Euphrates, even to the Western Sea, shall be your territory. No man shall be able to stand against you; the LORD your God will put the dread of you and the fear of you upon all the land where you tread, just as He has said to you.

Behold, I set before you today a blessing and a curse: the blessing, if you obey the commandments of the LORD your God which I command you today; and the curse, if you do not obey the commandments of the LORD your God, but turn aside from the way which I command you today, to go after other gods which you have not known. Now it shall be, when the LORD your God has brought you into the land which you go to possess, that you shall put the blessing on Mount Gerizim and the curse on Mount Ebal. Are they not on the other side of the Jordan, toward the setting sun, in the land of the Canaanites who dwell in the plain opposite Gilgal, beside the terebinth trees of Moreh? For you will cross over the Jordan and go in to possess the land which the LORD your God is giving you, and you will possess it and dwell in it. And you shall be careful to observe all the statutes and judgments which I set before you today (NKJV).

The same challenge is before us today: a blessing and a curse. What determines the way we go is our obedience to Truth, our obedience to God's Word—His principles. The lives we live and the policies we enact are a reflection of who we are. Therefore, we must seek to establish laws that comport to Biblical principle, not as an end to themselves, but as a reflection of a people sincerely seeking after Truth. We don't seek "goodies" from God, we seek God Himself.

Prepared for opposition

The passage we just read called us to obedience in following the statutes and also in sharing the blessings of that obedience. Passing the blessings to the next generations is crucial because we and our progeny are sure to encounter opposition to these views. Guaranteed. In fact, the opposition is rapidly growing in our nation. They have caused incredible harm to liberty and freedom already, but we must blame ourselves, in many respects, for their success. We must do a better job of communicating these precious truths with a sense of urgency. Why would we leave our children helpless to discover these truths on their own, when we have gone through so much pain to learn them? The principles are true, so that even our continued disobedience serves to prove the principles right, time and again. We bear the scars of our disobedience; our history books are full of the stories of our imprudence. Why would we want to continue to struggle in the same manner, generation after generation? We should want to spare our children the same hurt. It is part of the reason I write to you today, hoping that the principles discussed will serve you in your pursuit of Truth.

Many secularists will disparage this approach, accusing us of "brainwashing" children. It is why they have taken aim at public schools. They say that many young people believe in God and His Word because they have learned these truths from their parents. That that is the only reason they believe them. It is "cultural," they say. C.S. Lewis is again helpful in exposing the fallacy of that argument. He compared it to the way we learn math. Sure we learn math from someone else (usually our parents), but that doesn't make math any less truthful. Two plus two equals four. No reason for each generation to discover the same principles of math that we have discovered on their own. That would be unproductive. They should learn from what we have learned and develop even further. That is how we can truly progress. Test them? Absolutely. But to reject them outright just because they have learned them from someone else is foolishness. And the type of costly foolishness we wouldn't apply to any other area of our lives. No need for me to be electrocuted to learn the dangers of electricity. We should not single out the principles of Scripture in this manner. Future generations should indeed test and correct our teachings if a violation of the principles is found. Slavery is the example we have discussed in previous chapters. But the goal is to continue to grow in truth, not to reject truth. Nor for each generation to construct its own version of "truth" in a fantastic way, paying for the consequences of ignoring what we already know to be real and good, making the same mistakes we've made over and over. That is stagnation, not progress; it is not freedom, but slavery. To ignore truth is always the opposite of freedom. As Jesus said, "Truly, truly, I say to you, everyone who practices sin is a slave to sin," (John 8:34). So living "free," as the world sees it, enslaves.

The opposition we encounter is not surprising for the Christian citizen. Listen to 2 Timothy 3:2-7:

> But understand this, that in the last days there will come times of difficulty. For people will be lovers of self, lovers of money, proud, arrogant, abusive, disobedient to their parents, ungrateful, unholy, heartless, unappeasable, slanderous, without self-control, brutal, not loving good, treacherous, reckless, swollen with conceit, lovers of pleasure rather than lovers of God, having the appearance of godliness, but denying its power. Avoid such people. For among them are those who creep into households and capture weak women, burdened with sins and

led astray by various passions, always learning and never able to arrive at a knowledge of the truth.

Doesn't it seem like an accurate display of modern day America? We are led astray by our own passions. We are not able to control our appetites. As Philippians 3:19 describes, "[our] god is [our] belly."

What can we to do? How are we to counter this paralyzing state? The answer comes to us right in the next chapter of 2 Timothy:

> I charge you therefore before God and the Lord Jesus Christ, who will judge the living and the dead at His appearing and His kingdom: Preach the word! Be ready in season and out of season. Convince, rebuke, exhort, with all longsuffering and teaching. For the time will come when they will not endure sound doctrine, but according to their own desires, because they have itching ears, they will heap up for themselves teachers; and they will turn their ears away from the truth, and be turned aside to fables. But you be watchful in all things, endure afflictions, do the work of an evangelist, fulfill your ministry (2 Timothy 4:1-5 NKJV).

Preach the word! This is our calling: to speak truth, to teach truth, from generation to generation, in every area of our lives. Let us be spent in this magnificent endeavor. Let us speak truth every day, in season and out of season; when they agree with us, as was the case at one point in our history, but also now when the majority seem to disagree with us and our call to purity will offend most. We are not called to comfort, but to sacrifice and it will be difficult. Did you catch the call to "longsuffering" in the passage, to "endure afflictions"? We do not worry about results; Paul tells Timothy the world does not listen because "they have itching ears." It is not because of the cleverness of the arguments we use that they don't listen, it is because they do what they want to do. They will set up and build up those who tell them what they want to hear. Have you notice recently the type of media we consume? What messages are they telling us? Is it not what we tolerate? Is it not what we pay for and support with our time and hard-earned dollars? The sort of debauchery we see in entertainment today could not exist without our full support. In many respects they have the tacit endorsement of the church, which tries to emulate it. Haven't you seen those churches? Those whose moral standard evolve with the culture's views? They prefer to create their own fables rather than to submit the truth of God and be seen as "hateful" or "judgmental." They tend to be offended if someone points this out, but they shouldn't be. It has nothing to do with them, and all to do with God, whom they reject. We need only remain "watchful in all things."

May we respond to that holy call in faithfulness to He who called us out of darkness into light. He who called us out of the world to testify of the surpassing joy that is found in Christ. May God's glory be displayed in our marriages, friendships, charity, workmanship, conflicts, worship, rest, vacations, laws, leadership, etc. May we look and smell of Christ. Unashamed. And may we teach and model these marvelous truths to our children, and our children's children. This is the key to freedom's survival: to be spent for God's principles in every area of our lives. It must start with you and me. We must live Christ. In doing so, we commit and commend God, reaping the blessings of liberty, until His return.

As Thomas Pain wrote, "When we are planning for posterity, we ought to remember that virtue is not hereditary."[270]

---

270   Thomas Paine, *Common Sense* 38 (Penguin 1996 (1776)).

CHAPTER TWELVE
The Christian Citizen and His Vote

One important area of public policy to stress to the next generation, because our current vision is so far off, is in the area of voting. Daniel Webster said:

> Impress upon children the truth that the exercise of the elective franchise is a social duty of as solemn a nature as man can be called to perform; that a man may not innocently trifle with his vote; that every elector is a trustee as well for others as himself and that every measure he supports has an important bearing on the interests of others as well as on his own.[271]

Taking an interest in voting is part of loving our neighbors. Knowing the incredible benefits of God's principles for every person, regardless of their personal faith, the Christian citizen must be bold in articulating those precious truths anywhere he or she is; not only as to personal character, but as to public policy too. Everyone benefits form attending

---

271   Daniel Webster, *The Works of Daniel Webster* (Boston: Little, Brown, and Company, 1853), Vol. II, p. 108, from remarks made at a public reception by the ladies of Richmond, Virginia, on October 5, 1840.

to God's principles when electing people for public office. We are not imposing a Christian worldview but advocating for it. There is a big difference.

By their fruits

One of the most frustrating things about working in public policy is the cynicism many Americans have developed towards our political leaders. It is a shame that so many of us think nothing of public officials cheating, lying and stealing in the "normal" course of business. "They all do it," we say. Even though the corruption of the human heart is nothing new for us if we follow the teachings of Scripture, we should never let our hearts grow cold to wrong doings and become indifferent to sin. It should always be appalling for us to see that type of behavior in any arena, and especially by people in leadership. Time and again we see our public servants breaking our trust, but, "That's just the way it is," right? Sadly, many Christian have also fallen into this trap. We have become cynic citizens instead of Christian citizens. Some by willingly compromising their beliefs in order to see the party they support grow in power, while others simply ignore or have become insensitive to the principles God gave us through His Word that we may be good judges of character and always seek to do good. We must demand and expect better. Though many fail and disappoint us, the standard should never change.

Whether to select men for public office, business associates, a mate, or in any other area, Christian citizens must let God and His principles guide them. We must strive to live by those principles personally and we must hold others accountable to them, especially those in leadership positions. Some argue that it is just impossible to ascertain the truth in a particular matter because each party or candidate will say whatever is politically expedient for them at any given time. Character, however, knows no party and we must look beyond mere words and the self-serving rhetoric of the campaign trail to try to ascertain a person's true character. We should never fall for the narrative that a leader "technically" didn't lie. We know what is happening and we must call things what they are.

Jesus gave us great guidance in this area when he spoke to us about false prophets. He simply said, "You will know them by their fruits," (Matthew 7:16, NKJV). No matter how many times a politician says that he is pro-life, that he really hates abortion and that he wishes no woman be faced with that decision, if he votes for bills that expand abortion "rights," give federal funds to pay for abortions, or limit a doctor's right of conscience, then you need not listen to his latest campaign speech to know where he stands. It is what we do more than what we say that defines who we are. Jesus said it beautifully, "A good tree cannot bear bad fruit, nor *can* a bad tree bear good fruit," (Matthew 7:18 NKJV). Which is more important for us when evaluating a candidate then, that he says he loves his wife or that he is faithful to her; for him to say he is a Christian or to see what type of church he attends; that he says he is a compassionate patriot or his support and concern for veterans? "Therefore by their fruits you will know them," (Matthew 7:20 NKJV).

That principle always brings to my mind Jesus' "Parable of the Two Sons:"

> A man had two sons. And he went to the first and said, 'Son, go and work in the vineyard today.' And he answered, 'I will not,' but afterward he changed his mind and went. And he went to the other son and said the same. And he answered, 'I go, sir,' but did not go. Which of the two did the will of his father?" (Matthew 21:28-31).

Ever heard a politician promise "free" this or that? Saying, "I go, sir?" Remember, we are to be "harmless as doves," but "wise as serpents," (Matthew 10:16, NKJV). It is time Christian citizens leave the world's cynicism behind and commence to hold our leaders accountable to the high standard we read in the Word of God. We must never let a politician's campaign speech dictate our vote. We have a guide; look at their fruits.

Choosing men and women of character

A person's "fruits" in adversity will perhaps offer the most insight to us. We always talk about wanting men and women of "character." Well, Paul talks about where that character comes from: "[W]e rejoice in our sufferings, knowing that suffering produces endurance, and endurance produces character, and character produces hope..." (Romans 5:3-4). It is through tribulation that we ultimately form our character. Should we not pay more attention to this aspect of a candidate's record then? This is one reason to favor seasoned leaders when considering who to vote for (though we know there are exemptions).[272] In general, they have experienced adversity; they have been tried and tested, giving us the opportunity to know their true character more easily.

In *Exodus* 18 God uses Jethro, Moses' father-in-law, to tell Moses he needs help in performing his leadership duties. God commanded him to "select from all the people able men, such as fear God, men of truth, hating covetousness," (Exodus 18:21, NKJV). That principle has been used by Christians citizens ever since, when selecting men for leadership. Noah Webster alluded to it when he said:

> In selecting men for office, let principle be your guide. Regard not the particular [party] of the candidate—look to his character…. It is alleged by men of loose principles or defective views of the subject that religion and morality are not necessary or important qualifications for political stations. But the Scriptures teach a different doctrine. They direct that rulers should be men 'who rule in the fear of God, able men, such as fear God, men of truth, hating covetousness.'[273]

I fear many Christians today have forgotten this basic principle. Therefore, it is no wonder we see little of its application. Can you imagine what would happen in our country if we applied this principle and only selected (1) able men, (2) who feared God, (3) were of truth, and (4) hated covetousness? Let us discuss each briefly.

Able

When we think of able men, we must inevitably ask, "Able for what?" The requirement wisely requires that we think of the task at hand, in order to look for the type of man necessary to accomplish that specific task. If constructing a skyscraper be the task, an architect will probably be best suited. It is just like the Bible to never ignore reality, but to affirm

---

272   David said, "I understand more than the aged, for I keep your precepts," (Psalm 119:100).

273   Noah Webster, *Letters to a Young Gentleman Commencing His Education: To Which is Subjoined a Brief History of the United States* pp. 18-19, Letter 1 (New Haven, S. Converse, 1823).

it and expand our understanding of it. In that sense, this is a common sense requirement. It puts a premium on experience, knowledge and wisdom—on trial and error, and overcoming obstacles. We definitely need able men. When thinking of selecting a president for example, it would be unwise to look for someone who is incredibly committed to follow the principles of God, but who is not a leader. If the candidate has no experience leading, indeed has not the gift of leadership, we would be fools to vote for them, barring some truly extraordinary circumstances.

Fearful of God

Scripture tells us that, "The fear of the LORD is the beginning of knowledge," (Proverbs 1:7) and "wisdom," (Proverbs 9:10). We have already discussed some of the many practical implications of believing and fearing God. There is simply no better way to ensure men's desire to do what is good and right, even when no one is looking. The fear of God curtails our natural selfishness and gives us an unbelievable incentive to serve and esteem others as better than ourselves.[274] The fear of the Lord makes us care for those in need and demands we remain humble in everything we do. The benefits are literally innumerable. Even when we don't live up to those standards, as we have discussed, the fear of the Lord will always make us reevaluate not only what we do but also our motives.

Of the truth

This takes us all the way back to the beginning of our discussion. Truth must be paramount. Without truth, anything goes and there is no standard from where to evaluate our decisions in order to correct our inevitable mistakes. As we have seen, there is no truth without God, so that the pursuit of truth will always takes us back to Him who is Truth. Again, we must emphasize that this is an objective, impartial truth and not the modern concept of a self-made truth that falls right back into the self-serving nature of the world. Truth demands impartiality. This is why truth is good for all, not only for those who profess a belief in God. Even when we have fallen away from the right path and make some mistakes, being truthful with ourselves is the shortest, surest, way to get back on track.

---

274   "Let nothing be done through selfish ambition or conceit, but in lowliness of mind let each esteem others better than himself," (Philippians 2:3, NKJV).

Hating covetousness

Finally, we need men who hate covetousness. But what is it? What is covetousness? I fear this is a foreign concept in modern-day America, yet our struggle with covetousness is a daily human reality. We touched on it in our previous chapter, when discussing the Tenth Commandment, but let us go a bit deeper here as it relates to leadership and selecting men and women for office. Covetousness encompasses much more than mere envy or avarice. It is driven by a desire to do better than anyone else—to be ahead. Paul calls it idolatry.[275] Notice also the robust language in the text, asking for someone who *hates* covetousness. This implies that a strong force is needed to match and oppose this intense impulse within us. The New Bible Dictionary explains the powerful grip of the desires envisioned in Scripture:

> The Hebrews visualized the soul as full of vigorous desires which urged it to extend its influence over other persons and things. There was ⊠āma⊠, to desire a neighbour's possessions (Dt. 5:21; Mi. 2:2), be⊠a', the desire for dishonest gain (Pr. 28:16; Je. 6:13) and 'āwâ, selfish desire (Pr. 21:26).[276]

A person who recognizes this and who hates these desires will be better equipped to handle the temptations that inevitably come with the grant of the power in leadership. The Bible talks much about the accepting of bribes, for example, and how a leader must be able to resist them and be impartial. There is the warning of Exodus 23:8, "And you shall take no bribe, for a bribe blinds the clear-sighted and subverts the cause of those who are in the right;" and the encouragement of Exodus 18:21, "Moreover, look for able men from all the people, men who fear God, who are trustworthy and hate a bribe, and place such men over the people as chiefs of thousands, of hundreds, of fifties, and of tens." It tells us it is indispensable for the administration of justice: "You shall not pervert justice. You shall not show partiality, and you shall not accept a bribe, for a bribe blinds the eyes of the wise and subverts the cause of the righteous," (Deuteronomy 16:19). This concept has its roots in the

---

275   "Put to death therefore what is earthly in you: sexual immorality, impurity, passion, evil desire, and covetousness, which is idolatry," (Colossians 3:5).

276   Wood, D. R. W., & Marshall, I. H. (1996), *New Bible Dictionary*. Leicester, England; Downers Grove, IL: InterVarsity Press.

character of God Himself, in whose image we were created. Listen to Deuteronomy 10:17: "For the Lord your God is God of gods and Lord of lords, the great, the mighty, and the awesome God, who is not partial and takes no bribe."

In 2 Chronicles 19, God gives us some more insight into this principle, as King Jehoshaphat gives instructions to the judges who served the people at the time. He told them:

> Take heed to what you are doing, for you do not judge for man but for the Lord, who is with you in the judgment. Now therefore, let the fear of the Lord be upon you; take care and do it, for there is no iniquity with the Lord our God, no partiality, nor taking of bribes (2 Chronicles 19:6-7, NKJV).

It goes back to that standard we talked about in chapter four (*God's Established Authority*), which stands in judgment of leaders, as they know what they ought to do even if they chose another path. Stubborn leaders should take note; they will not "get away with it." This is big. These ideals are real. They are not vague, abstract or hypothetical concepts. These are practical and basic principles that will have an immediate impact in our lives and culture. The standard is not to be dismissed as unattainable, but desired by those aspiring public service, and demanded by those who willingly give their consent to be governed. There was a time when most Americans understood that. William Bross (1813-1890), a prominent American journalist and the co-publisher of the *Chicago Tribune*, was once asked in an interview to give his observations about the cause of failure in leadership. He answered, "Want of integrity, careless of the truth, reckless in thought and expression, lack of trust in God, and a disregard of the teachings of His Holy Word, bad company, and bad morals in any of their many phases."[277] How I wish we had Mr. Bross today. Can you imagine a member of "the media," no less, holding those in leadership to a high standard of excellence and recognizing that, just as in the case of our country, what is most important in a person's life is what lies at the foundations? Mr. Bross' wisdom is desperately needed today.

---

277   Dr. Richard G. Lee, *The American Patriot's Bible* 563 (Thomas Nelson, 2009).

So that the people rejoice

If we as Christian citizens apply these principles when exercising our right to vote, America would have a better chance of continuing to be that "city set on a hill."[278] Remember what the Proverbs say, "When the righteous are in authority, the people rejoice; but when a wicked *man* rules, the people groan." America's groans are heard all over the world today. We have become perpetual complainers. But if we would take these Biblical principles to the voting booth, the impact would be transformative. If we were on the lookout for men and women of character, instead of looking for who will promise us more "goodies," we would reap a bountiful harvest. Even in this area of our lives, the Christian citizen is to be selfless, not looking for his own benefits but looking onto the benefit of his neighbors.[279] We must vote so that the people may rejoice. We must be and look for that type of leaders.

George Washington embodied many of these characteristics. In a letter that Thomas Jefferson wrote to a Dr. Walter Jones on Jan. 2, 1814, he described what he thought of Washington:

"I think I knew General Washington intimately and thoroughly; and were I called on to delineate his character, it should be in terms like these.

His mind was great and powerful, without being of the very first order; his penetration strong, though not so acute as that of a Newton, Bacon, or Locke; and as far as he saw, no judgment was ever sounder. It was slow in operation, being little aided by invention or imagination, but sure in conclusion. Hence the common remark of his officers, of the advantage he derived from councils of war, where hearing all suggestions, he selected whatever was best; and certainly no general ever planned his battles more judiciously.... He was incapable of fear, meeting personal dangers with the calmest unconcern. Perhaps the strongest feature in his character was prudence, never acting until every circumstance,

---

278   Matthew 5:14 (NKJV).

279   "Let each of you look not only to his own interests, but also to the interests of others," (Philippians 2:4).

every consideration, was maturely weighed; refraining if he saw doubt, but, when once decided, going through with his purpose, whatever obstacles opposed. His integrity was most pure, his justice the most inflexible I have ever known, no motives of interest or consanguinity, of friendship or hatred, being able to bias his decision. He was, indeed, in every sense of the words, a wise, a good, and a great man…

These are my opinions of General Washington, which I would vouch at the judgment seat of God, having been formed on an acquaintance of thirty years.[280]

Abigail Adams (1744-1818), wife of President John Adams had this to say about Washington, "No Man ever lived, more deservedly beloved and Respected…. Possesst of power, posest [possessed] of an extensive influence, he never used it but for the benefit of his Country…. If we look through the whole tennor of his Life, History will not produce to us a Parrallel…."[281] This virtuous character in Washington was not "just the way he was." He knew the value and indeed the absolutely essential nature of personal integrity. In a letter to his young nephew George Steptoe Washington on December 5, 1790, he counseled:

This reflection must shew the necessity of an unremitting application to your studies. To point out the importance of circumspection in your conduct, it may be proper to observe that a good moral character is the first essential in a man, and that the habits contracted at your age are generally indelible, and your conduct here may stamp your character through life. It is therefore highly important that you should endeavor not only to be learned but virtuous. Much more might be said to shew the necessity of application and regularity, but when you must know that without them you can never be qualified to render service to your country, assistance to your

---

280   Thomas Jefferson, *The Life and Selected Writings of Thomas Jefferson*, 173-174. (Adrienne Koch and William Peden ed. (Random House 1944)).

281   Abigail Adams, *Letter to her sister Mary Cranch*, December 22, 1799, available at http://www.ushistory.org/presidentshouse/history/quotesja.htm (accessed Sept. 12, 2014).

friends, or consolidation to your retired moments, nothing further need be said to prove their utility.[282]

We need more men like Washington who not only embody these principles, but also who take it upon themselves to impart that wisdom on future generations, demanding its application. That means we also need many "Jeffersons" and "Abigails," recognizing these qualities in others and supporting them in their leadership. Virtue should be upheld as good, desirable and attainable. Examples as that of Washington are vital. We should think of this pursuit as one of the responsibilities of the Christian citizen, both as to the development of our own character, but also as applied to the wisdom we use in selecting men and women for public office. The quality of our leaders not only depends on them but on "we the people" who must be absolutely diligent in selecting them. President James Garfield (1831-1881) said it best:

> [P]eople are responsible for the character of their Congress. If that body be ignorant, reckless, and corrupt, it is because the people tolerate ignorance, recklessness, and corruption. If it be intelligent, brave, and pure, it is because the people demand these high qualities to represent them in the national legislature. ... [I]f the next centennial does not find us a great nation... it will be because those who represent the enterprise, the culture, and the morality of the nation do not aid in controlling the political forces.[283]

Unfortunately, many Christians today think of politics as unholy— as "dirty politics." Our cynicism has gotten the best of us and it has made us not only cynics as to men in leadership, but also as to the principles God has given us to help in this area and the responsibility He has placed on us through His Word. Many think of getting involved in politics as somehow "beneath" the Christian citizen. Well, we may disregard

---

282   George Washington, *Writings of Washington*, Vol. 31, available at http://memory.loc.gov/mss/mgw/mgw2/017/3220318.jpg.
http://etext.virginia.edu/etcbin/ot2www-washington?specfile=/texts/english/washington/fitzpatrick/search/gw.o2w&act=surround&offset=38919743&tag=Writings+of+Washington,+Vol.+31:+To+GEORGE+STEPTOE+WASHINGTON&query=December+5,+1790&id=gw310164, (accessed Sept. 12, 2014).

283   James Garfield, *The Atlantic Monthley*, Volume 40, 63 (The Riverside Press 1877).

the principles of God but we do not control the consequences of our choices. We will reap what we sow,[284] for in disregarding or minimizing the ministry of voting and politics, we fail to do everything as unto God, as we are commanded. Ignoring the Word of God in this area will have tremendous negative consequences for every aspect of our lives, including the life of the church. We will render an account to God for all our lives, including in our role as citizens. My prayer is that God will allow His Church to open its eyes in this area of the Christian life, that we may stand up as one and be the Church of God, the light of the world, the salt of the earth in the public arena. I hope you feel the practicality of God's wisdom for everything we do: in marriage, in business, in friendship and yes, even in the way we govern. It is not too late for us to recover this vision. If we turn to God and ask for His guidance to obey Him in this area, relying on His Word and working for His glory, there is no limit to what God can do through us in America. May it be so.

But we are far from that vision. In his book *How Would Jesus Vote?* Dr. D. James Kennedy describes our times:

> Just a few decades ago it was reported that 50 percent of Christians were not registered to vote, and 50 percent of those who were registered did not vote. I'm reminded of the old anecdote about two Christians. One of them said, "The main problem in our nation today are ignorance and apathy, don't you agree? The other replied, "I don't know, and I don't care."[285]

Dr. Tim LaHaye, the famous pastor and *New York Times* best-selling author, who was so instrumental in mobilizing Christians to engage in public policy throughout his life and ministry, tells the story of being inspired by Dr. Francis Schaeffer (1912-1984), the famous theologian and philosopher, as he was dying of cancer, addressing thousands of people in Washington, D.C., bringing them to their feet as he said, "He that will not use his freedom to preserve his freedom will loose his freedom.

---

284   "Do not be deceived: God is not mocked, for whatever one sows, that will he also reap. For the one who sows to his own flesh will from the flesh reap corruption, but the one who sows to the Spirit will from the Spirit reap eternal life," (Galatians 6:7-8).

285   Dr. D. James Kennedy, Jerry Newcombe, *How Would Jesus Vote?: A Christian Perspective on the Issues* 31 (WaterBrook Press 2008).

And neither his children or his grandchildren will rise up to call him blessed."[286]

The ministry of politics

Let us change the way we look at politics then. Let us engage joyfully, knowing it is a worthy service to the glory of God. The greatest men in history recognized that the principles of worthy politics are born from a Biblical worldview. Here are the wise words from Frederick Douglas:

> I have one great political idea. . . . That idea is an old one. It is widely and generally assented to; nevertheless, it is very generally trampled upon and disregarded. The best expression of it, I have found in the Bible. It is in substance, "Righteousness exalteth a nation; sin is a reproach to any people" [Proverbs 14:34]. This constitutes my politics - the negative and positive of my politics, and the whole of my politics. . . . I feel it my duty to do all in my power to infuse this idea into the public mind, that it may speedily be recognized and practiced upon by our people.[287]

Charles Finney (1792-1875), the great leader of the Second Great Awakening, said, "[T]he time has come that Christians must vote for honest men and take consistent ground in politics... Christians seem to act as if they thought God did not see what they do in politics. But I tell you He does see it..." May we join that call today. A call for the men and women of God, the Christian citizen, the body of Christ, the Church, to rise up and show its willingness to be spent for the Gospel in every area of our lives, including in the way we elect people to positions of leadership. Whatever we do in the coming elections will decide the course of liberty and freedom in American History.

As Chief Justice John Jay (1745-1829), one of our Founding Fathers said, "Providence has given to our people the choice of their rulers, and

---

286   Dr. Tim LaHaye, *Dr. Tim LaHaye's 2012 Election Call to Action*, September 17, 2012, available at https://www.youtube.com/watch?v=S0JyARq7k7A (accessed March 3, 2015).

287   Frederick Douglass, *The Frederick Douglass Papers*, Vol. 2, p. 397 (John Blassingame ed., Yale University Press 1982), from a speech delivered at Ithaca, New York, October 14th, 1852.

it is the duty, as well as the privilege and interest of our Christian nation, to select and prefer Christians for their rulers." Let us never be ashamed of that. The Christian citizen should proudly prefer the true Christian man or woman for office, for again, a true Christian has a clear standard to abide by, a standard to which he or she can be held accountable. Knowing that he or she will fall short of that standard should encourage us to both support and remind him or her. This does not mean the Christian citizen cannot support anything but a Christian for office and neither does it mean that the Christian citizen cannot hold non-Christians to that high Biblical standard. It only means something that is already difficult would be an impossible task for anyone not living by the high, noble, objective principles of Christianity, but who instead holds him or herself to his or her own subjective vision of right and wrong. Let us stress the urgency of the matter with an excerpt from an 1803 sermon by Matthias Burnette Tallmadge (1774-1819), pastor of the First Baptist Church in Norwalk:

> Consider well the important trust… which God… [has] put into your hands… To God and posterity you are accountable for [your rights and your rulers]… Let not your children have reason to curse you for giving up those rights and prostrating those institutions which your fathers delivered to you… [L]ook well to the characters and qualifications of those you elect and raise to office and places of trust… Think not that your interests will be safe in the hands of the weak and ignorant; or faithfully managed by the impious, the dissolute and the immoral. Think not that men who acknowledge not the providence of God nor regard His laws will be uncorrupt in office, firm in defense of the righteous cause against the oppressor, or resolutely oppose the torrent of iniquity… Watch over your liberties and privileges - civil and religious - with a careful eye.[288]

May we recapture that vision. The Christian citizen is free to engage in politics in the confidence of God. What joy! This should not be a burden for us. I suspect much of the internal struggles we have in terms

---

288   Matthias Burnett, *An Election Sermon* 27-28 Preached at Hartford, on the Day of the Anniversary Election, May 12, 1803 (Hudson & Goodwin, 1803).

of our political engagement come from our prideful hearts. We like to win. We want people to like us. And since we have lost the art of communicating with one another, it is difficult to engage each other respectfully. We don't want to "fight," yet this is mostly what we do. But we need not fight in order to speak truthfully and lovingly. There is another way. Applying 1 Corinthians 10:24, for example, "Let no one seek his own good, but the good of his neighbor." This is truly revolutionary. Let us, therefore, not let the world keep us silent and divided. We have hope; the world is hopeless. It is up to us to share the joy of freedom in Christ. This will inevitably translate into blessings for this desperate world that cries out for what it does not, indeed cannot see. Our eyes are open. Let us speak boldly, respectfully and lovingly. This is a new kind of politics (for many of us), defined by God's truth and not man. This is the precious contribution of the Christian citizen. We do not conform to the world, but we bring the transformative principles of God as applied to our hearts and minds, and governments and cultures.

CHAPTER THIRTEEN

JOY THROUGH ADVERSITY

Through it all, we are not naïve. As we have discussed, we do not look for heaven on earth. Life is hard. Therefore, we must end with perhaps the biggest challenge facing the Christian citizen wherever he is: our Lord's call to a life of suffering. The concern was probably on your mind as you read through some of the areas in the book, so I'd be remiss if we didn't provide some clear principles to deal with all of this. It is a fact that when we engage the world, many will reject our message. This is also to the glory of God. Americans have been incredibly blessed for a long time, almost sheltered among men and women who agreed, at least in principle, with some type of faith. Our Lord's warning that we would suffer for His name's sake was therefore a bit attenuated. Today however, in an increasingly secularized America, we are feeling the pressures of those who not only reject Christ, but who actually despise all He represents. This, contrary the immediate American impulse, is not out of the ordinary.

The providential role of suffering

Few things are clearer in Scripture than our call to suffer, just as Christ suffered. Jesus said it time and again, "If anyone desires to come after Me, let him deny himself, and take up his cross, and follow Me," (Matthew 16:24, NKJV); "And whoever does not bear his cross and come after Me cannot be My disciple," (Luke 14:27, NKJV); "If they persecuted Me, they will also persecute you," (John 15:20, NKJV). There is no way around it; the world will reject us. Jesus explained why this would happen:

> If the world hates you, know that it has hated me before it hated you. If you were of the world, the world would love you as its own; but because you are not of the world, but I chose you out of the world, therefore the world hates you (John 15:18-19).

This is the reason we are hated; we are not of this world. Never forget that. God chose us out of the world to accomplish His purposes and this is repugnant to the unbelieving world. "Who do you think you are?" they cry. We are the light of the world[289] and the light exposes the darkness. Have you ever been in a dark room for a long time and then suddenly gone outside to the bright sun? Not very comfortable, is it? Our righteousness makes the ungodly much more uncomfortable. I should say God's righteousness, for it is His righteousness that we bare. But that is no distinction at all, as far as the world is concerned. The message of the Cross is foolishness to them.[290] So John said, "Do not be surprised, brothers, that the world hates you," (1 John 3:13). Peter also:

> For to this you have been called, because Christ also suffered for you, leaving you an example, so that you might follow in his steps. He committed no sin, neither was deceit found in his mouth. When he was reviled, he did not revile in return; when he suffered, he did not threaten, but continued entrusting himself to him who judges justly (1 Peter 2:21–23).

---

289 "You are the light of the world. A city set on a hill cannot be hidden. Nor do people light a lamp and put it under a basket, but on a stand, and it gives light to all in the house. In the same way, let your light shine before others, so that they may see your good works and give glory to your Father who is in heaven," (Matthew 5:14-16).

290 "For the word of the cross is folly to those who are perishing, but to us who are being saved it is the power of God," (1 Corinthians 1:18).

It is interesting that those words came from Peter who wanted to fight back when the Pharisees came to arrest Jesus.[291] Here is the scene. Jesus knows the hour is at hand and goes to prepare Himself through prayer at Gethsemane. He tells the disciples, "Sit here, while I go over there and pray," (Matthew 26:36). He then takes Peter, James and John with Him and tells them, "My soul is very sorrowful, even to death; remain here, and watch with me," (Matthew 26:38). He goes even further then and prays one of the most fascinating prayers that have ever been recorded. He says, "My Father, if it be possible, let this cup pass from me; nevertheless, not as I will, but as you will," (Matthew 26:39). Here is Jesus in distress, knowing full well the path that is ahead of Him, and pleading with His Father, while in full submission that His will be done. This is the preparation He needs. This is what we all need. Not a denial of our feelings– Jesus was clearly afflicted—but full submission. We need complete submission to God, while in full acknowledgment of the task before us, even in full awareness of the suffering before us. Jesus goes back to His disciples but finds them sleeping and says, "[C]ould you not watch with me one hour? Watch and pray that you may not enter into temptation. The spirit indeed is willing, but the flesh is weak," (Matthew 26:40-41). But they could not comply. Jesus went back to pray and came back to find them asleep again and says, "Sleep and take your rest later on. See, the hour is at hand, and the Son of Man is betrayed into the hands of sinners. Rise, let us be going; see, my betrayer is at hand," (Matthew 26:45-46). Keep this in mind as we approach Peter's reaction to Jesus' arrest. Peter will not be prepared for it and this helps us understand why. Jesus, having spent that intimate time with the Father, was prepared. He is in complete awareness of the Father's will and in full submission. The disciples are not so in tune. Therefore,

> While he was still speaking, Judas came, one of the twelve, and with him a great crowd with swords and clubs, from the chief priests and the elders of the people. Now the betrayer had given them a sign, saying, "The one I will kiss is the man; seize him." And he came up to Jesus at once and said, "Greetings, Rabbi!" And he kissed him. Jesus said to him, "Friend, do what you came to do." Then they came up and laid hands on Jesus and seized him. And

---

291   Matthew 26:51, John 18:10.

behold, one of those who were with Jesus stretched out his hand and drew his sword and struck the servant of the high priest and cut off his ear. Then Jesus said to him, "Put your sword back into its place. For all who take the sword will perish by the sword. Do you think that I cannot appeal to my Father, and he will at once send me more than twelve legions of angels? But how then should the Scriptures be fulfilled, that it must be so?" (Matthew 26:47–54).

Peter was the one who struck the servant[292] and he did a most reasonable thing in the world's eyes; he wanted to save Jesus form suffering. Jesus, on the other hand, showed him another way: full submission to the Father's will, even through suffering. I love the way John put it, he quotes Jesus saying, "[S]hall I not drink the cup that the Father has given me?" (John 18:11). It is a hard principle to follow. Christ, tells the Apostle, not only suffered to the point of death, but He did not revile in return.[293] There is no bitterness in Christ, only love. "Father, forgive them, for they know not what they do," he prayed from the cross (Luke 23:34). His meekness was unparalleled; His obedience beyond comparison. That doesn't happen in a vacuum. He accomplished it by cultivating a relationship with God and surrendering to the Father's will. We are all called to be like Him—like Jesus. Let us "turn the other cheek" and "love our enemies," yea, even "pray[ing] for those who persecute [us]," (Matthew 5:38–44):

> For if you love those who love you, what reward do you have? Do not even the tax collectors do the same? And if you greet only your brothers, what more are you doing than others? Do not even the Gentiles do the same? You therefore must be perfect, as your heavenly Father is perfect (Matthew 5:46–48).

---

292   *See* John 18:10.

293   "When he was reviled, he did not revile in return; when he suffered, he did not threaten, but continued entrusting himself to the him who judges justly," (1 Peter 2:23).

Sanctification road

We are perfected through suffering. It is the work of God in our lives. Paul says we "are being transformed into the same image from one degree of glory to another," (2 Corinthians 3:18.) As gold is purified through fire, said Peter:

> In this you rejoice, though now for a little while, if necessary, you have been grieved by various trials, so that the tested genuineness of your faith—more precious than gold that perishes though it is tested by fire—may be found to result in praise and glory and honor at the revelation of Jesus Christ (1 Peter 1:6–7).

Life is extremely difficult and complex, the trials are hard, but we are stronger than gold through the power of Christ in our lives. Jesus said, "In the world you will have tribulation. But take heart; I have overcome the world," (John 16:33). "[S]orrowful, yet always rejoicing," (2 Corinthians 6:10) was the way Paul described the Christian walk. I find it hard to come up with better words to describe it. We do indeed suffer, but our joy is ever present; it is never-ending. It is a profound and sweet mystery. We experience joy through everything. Not only at the end of it all, but *through* it all. That is the answer to the often-asked "how" question: How can we do this? Only through the joy that is found in Jesus Christ; only through the power of the Holy Spirit within us. That's how Christ did it! Hebrews 12:1-2:

> [L]et us run with endurance the race that is set before us, looking to Jesus, the founder and perfecter of our faith, who for the joy that was set before him endured the cross, despising the shame, and is seated at the right hand of the throne of God.

Jesus endured the cross "for the joy that was set before Him." Incredible! We too have a joy set before us that is more precious than life itself. It is more valuable than all our sufferings. A joy that, like a massive boulder, is immovable. It is an unshakable joy that serves as an anchor that we can always hold on to when the tempestuous winds of life come passing through. For they will pass. "[T]hough now for a little while," read the passage we just discussed. That is a most precious promise too. Whatever you are going through, it will pass. But that joy will never pass! Oh that joy will be there once this stormy season passes by. Indeed it will surpass this life and take us into eternity. He, Christ, is our joy and our salvation! Jesus said:

> When a woman is giving birth, she has sorrow because her hour has come, but when she has delivered the baby, she no longer remembers the anguish, for joy that a human being has been born into the world. So also you have sorrow now, but I will see you again, and your hearts will rejoice, and no one will take your joy from you (John 16:21-22).

"No one" means no one. Though many will try, "no one will take your joy from you." This joy will follow you all the days of your life, and beyond. It is part of that Kingdom focus again, isn't it? "Consider it all joy, my brethren, when you encounter various trials," says James, "knowing that the testing of your faith produces endurance," (James 1:2-3, NASB). Some precious truths come through suffering. As 1 John 3:16 tells us, "By this we know love, that he laid down his life for us, and we ought to lay down our lives for the brothers." We know love through suffering. It is why those who are completely focused on not getting hurt find it extremely difficult to find true love. Love makes us vulnerable, and we are called to love. Therefore, our call makes us vulnerable. We are called to love to the point where we are willing to lay down our lives as Christ laid down His life. We are called to live outwardly, as we already touched on. We are called to spend and be spent. The question is, "Are we willing to accept the call?" Are we willing to accept the reality that we need to be sanctified and purified in this manner— through sufferings and various trials?

> Beloved, do not be surprised at the fiery trial when it comes upon you to test you, as though something strange were happening to you. But rejoice insofar as you share Christ's sufferings, that you may also rejoice and be glad when his glory is revealed. If you are insulted for the name of Christ, you are blessed, because the Spirit

of glory and of God rests upon you. But let none of you suffer as a murderer or a thief or an evildoer or as a meddler. Yet if anyone suffers as a Christian, let him not be ashamed, but let him glorify God in that name. For it is time for judgment to begin at the household of God; and if it begins with us, what will be the outcome for those who do not obey the gospel of God? And

> "If the righteous is scarcely saved,
> what will become of the ungodly and the sinner?"

Therefore let those who suffer according to God's will entrust their souls to a faithful Creator while doing good (1 Peter 4:12-19).

I find it interesting how we are always willing to do everything and anything for God, except that which He has called us to do. We must realize obedience is doing what our Father calls us to do, not doing what we want to do for Him. Jesus said, "If you love me, you will keep my commandments," (John 14:15).

Standing for Truth

We don't get to make our own truth and we do not get to choose where the enemy attacks us either. We can only be ready for his every attack. We are to, "Put on the whole armor of God, that [we] may be able to stand against the schemes of the devil," as Paul tells us in Ephesians 6:11. We must be on high alert in every area, because it would make sense that the enemy will want to attack us where we are most vulnerable. Where we are most weak in the Word of God. His trick has always been the same: "Did God really say...?"[294] He wants us to doubt and therefor deny He who is Truth. At bottom, it is not the principles he calls into question, but He who gave us the principles. His aim is for us to doubt God. This is why we must not stand in judgment of God's principles. We do not get to choose from among the principles God has established in Scripture those we wish to stand up for at any given time. Martin Luther

---

294   "Now the serpent was more crafty than any other beast of the field that the LORD God had made. He said to the woman, 'Did God actually say, 'You shall not eat of any tree in the garden'?'" (Genesis 3:1).

had a wonderful thought on this regard:

[I]t does not help that one of you would say: "I will gladly confess Christ and His Word on every detail, except
that I may keep silent about one or two things which my
tyrants may not tolerate, such as the form of the Sacra-
ments and the like." For whoever denies Christ in one detail or word has denied the same Christ in that one detail
who was denied in all the details, since there is only one
Christ in all His words, taken together or individually.[295]

Denying God's Word is denying Him—denying Christ. Distorting His
Word is no improvement.[296] Therefore, we must stand for His principles, whatever the cost. We must leave everything behind, as Jesus
told us. "So therefore, any one of you who does not renounce all that he
has cannot be my disciple," (Luke 14:33). He also said, "[E]veryone who
acknowledges me before men, I also will acknowledge before my Father
who is in heaven, but whoever denies me before men, I also will deny
before my Father who is in heaven," (Matthew 10:32-33). May we stand
boldly before the world in representation of God and His ways. We must
not only believe all, the fullness of God's counsel as found in Scripture,
but we must live it all too. We fail, of course, but that is our aim. President Theodore Roosevelt placed his hand on that famous verse in James
1:22, as he took his oath in 1905, "But be doers of the word, and not
hearers only, deceiving yourselves." That is a big part. We must take these
truths from the theory to the practice. That's where the blessings flow
from.

I mentioned that it makes sense that the devil would attack us where
we are weakest. The other side of that picture that is even more important for us is that in our weakness, God shows Himself Mighty. The
words of Paul to the Corinthians are most enlightening here: "Therefore
I will boast all the more gladly of my weaknesses, so that the power of
Christ may rest upon me. For the sake of Christ, then, I am content with

---

295   D. Martin Luther's Werke : kritische Gesamtausgabe (Weimarer Ausgabe) :
[3. Band] Briefwechsel, ed. (Weimar: H. Boĭˆhlaus Nachfolger, 1933), 81-82.
http://www.dennyburk.com/the-apocryphal-martin-luther/ (accessed Sept. 17, 2014).

296   For more on this topic see Distortion: How the New Christian Left is Twisting
the Gospel and Damaging the Faith by Chelsen Vicari (Frontline 2014).

weaknesses, insults, hardships, persecutions, and calamities. For when I am weak, then I am strong," (2 Corinthians 12:9–10). Paul's confidence in Christ is so steady, so cemented in faith and truth that he actually boasts in his weakness, for of course that's when Christ has to do most. It makes perfect sense. It is in those things that we are in most need, that He is able to meet our needs most. He is the strong One. He, the all-knowing One. He, the all-powerful One. And He loves us with a love like no other. It is a true, pure and perfect love.

The love of God, our joy

God tells us, "A thousand may fall at your side, ten thousand at your right hand, but it will not come near you," (Psalm 91:7); "[F]ear not, for I am with you; be not dismayed, for I am your God; I will strengthen you, I will help you, I will uphold you with my righteous right hand," (Isaiah 41:10); that He "will supply every need of yours according to his riches in glory in Christ Jesus," (Philippians 4:19); and that He will not withhold any good thing, "from those who walk uprightly," (Psalm 84:11). Those are just a few of the thousands of promises He has given us throughout Scripture. The Hebrew writer even exalts the hope of Christ through God's discipline:

> Consider him who endured from sinners such hostility against himself, so that you may not grow weary or faint-hearted. In your struggle against sin you have not yet resisted to the point of shedding your blood. And have you forgotten the exhortation that addresses you as sons?
>
> > "My son, do not regard lightly the discipline of the Lord, nor be weary when reproved by him. For the Lord disciplines the one he loves, and chastises every son whom he receives."
>
> It is for discipline that you have to endure. God is treating you as sons. For what son is there whom his father does not discipline? If you are left without discipline, in which all have participated, then you are illegitimate

children and not sons. Besides this, we have had earthly fathers who disciplined us and we respected them. Shall we not much more be subject to the Father of spirits and live? For they disciplined us for a short time as it seemed best to them, but he disciplines us for our good, that we may share his holiness. For the moment all discipline seems painful rather than pleasant, but later it yields the peaceful fruit of righteousness to those who have been trained by it (Hebrews 12:3–11).

Let us be weary then if we fail to see God's discipline in our lives, not when we suffer through it. He whom God loves He disciplines. When we hurt after doing wrong, we are loved. He disciplines for our own good. Every mother and father reading this understands it perfectly. Oh, how I dislike disciplining my children (at least as often as I must do it). It is not fun. I wish I did not have to do it. But I know how important it is for them. I know how important discipline was in my childhood. I love my children too much to allow them to do whatever they want without an understanding of the proper consequences of their actions in relation to themselves and others. Thank God for His discipline on us, where would we be without it?

It is through adversity that our spiritual maturity is exposed. Thomas Pain said during the American Revolutionary War, "I love the man that can smile in trouble, that can gather strength from distress, and grow brave by reflection. 'Tis the business of little minds to shrink; but he whose heart is firm, and whose conscience approves his conduct, will pursue his principles unto death."[297] He describes a characteristic of the Christian faith. For the Christian citizen, the joy on the other side of the struggle, indeed through the struggle, cannot be properly expressed. Nothing compares to the joy of faithfulness through trial. Thomas Paine knew the joy of freedom is never free. He wrote, "Those who expect to reap the blessings of freedom, must, like men, undergo the fatigues of supporting it."[298]

---

297   Thomas Paine, *The American Crisis*, No. 1 (December 19, 1776) http://www. ushistory.org/PAINE/crisis/singlehtml.htm (accessed Sept. 17, 2014).

298   Thomas Paine, *The American Crisis*, No. 4 (September 11, 1777)

Towards what end?

The Christian citizen never suffers in vain. We can see this clearly in the life of Christ. As Isaiah put it:

[H]e was pierced for our transgressions;
he was crushed for our iniquities;
upon him was the chastisement that brought us peace,
and with his wounds we are healed (Isaiah 53:5).

Christ most definitely did not die in vain. And we can see this in our sufferings too. Listen to the words of Paul while he suffered in prison:
I want you to know, brothers, that what has happened
to me has really served to advance the gospel, so that
it has become known throughout the whole imperial
guard and to all the rest that my imprisonment is for
Christ. And most of the brothers, having become confident in the Lord by my imprisonment, are much more
bold to speak the word without fear (Philippians 1:12-
14).

This is the divine perspective we seek. Paul sees beyond his immediate circumstances and delights in his obedience to God. Here is his recount of what he has experienced for the sake of Christ:
Five times I received at the hands of the Jews the forty
lashes less one. Three times I was beaten with rods. Once
I was stoned. Three times I was shipwrecked; a night and
a day I was adrift at sea; on frequent journeys, in danger
from rivers, danger from robbers, danger from my own
people, danger from Gentiles, danger in the city, danger
in the wilderness, danger at sea, danger from false brothers; in toil and hardship, through many a sleepless night,
in hunger and thirst, often without food, in cold and ex-
posure. And, apart from other things, there is the daily
pressure on me of my anxiety for all the churches (2 Corinthians 11:24-28).

That is just part of the story of his sufferings. Yet his conclusion is extraordinary: "Therefore I will boast all the more gladly of my weaknesses, so that the power of Christ may rest upon me. For the sake of Christ, then, I am content with weaknesses, insults, hardships, persecutions, and calamities. For when I am weak, then I am strong," (2 Corinthians 12:9-10). He continually says things like, "I am overflowing with joy in all our affliction," (2 Corinthians 7:4, NASB). Or "Now I rejoice in my sufferings for your sake," (Colossians 1:24). This is the same man of God who writes Philippians 4:

> Rejoice in the Lord always; again I will say, rejoice. Let your reasonableness be known to everyone. The Lord is at hand; do not be anxious about anything, but in everything by prayer and supplication with thanksgiving let your requests be made known to God. And the peace of God, which surpasses all understanding, will guard your hearts and your minds in Christ Jesus.

> Finally, brothers, whatever is true, whatever is honorable, whatever is just, whatever is pure, whatever is lovely, whatever is commendable, if there is any excellence, if there is anything worthy of praise, think about these things. What you have learned and received and heard and seen in me—practice these things, and the God of peace will be with you.

> I rejoiced in the Lord greatly that now at length you have revived your concern for me. You were indeed concerned for me, but you had no opportunity. Not that I am speaking of being in need, for I have learned in whatever situation I am to be content. I know how to be brought low, and I know how to abound. In any and every circumstance, I have learned the secret of facing plenty and hunger, abundance and need. I can do all things through him who strengthens me.

> Yet it was kind of you to share my trouble. And you Philippians yourselves know that in the beginning of the gospel, when I left Macedonia, no church entered into

partnership with me in giving and receiving, except you only. Even in Thessalonica you sent me help for my needs once and again. Not that I seek the gift, but I seek the fruit that increases to your credit. I have received full payment, and more. I am well supplied, having received from Epaphroditus the gifts you sent, a fragrant offering, a sacrifice acceptable and pleasing to God. And my God will supply every need of yours according to his riches in glory in Christ Jesus. To our God and Father be glory forever and ever. Amen (Philippians 4:4–20).

Joy is not only an emotion, as we tend to believe, it is the makeup of the Christian citizen. We have joy. It is who we are, whatever life may bring. I love the way the psalmist approaches difficult times:

Vindicate me, O God, and defend my cause against an ungodly people, from the deceitful and unjust man deliver me! For you are the God in whom I take refuge; why have you rejected me? Why do I go about mourning because of the oppression of the enemy? Send out your light and your truth; let them lead me; let them bring me to your holy hill and to your dwelling! Then I will go to the altar of God, to God my exceeding joy, and I will praise you with the lyre, O God, my God. Why are you cast down, O my soul, and why are you in turmoil within me? Hope in God; for I shall again praise him, my salvation and my God (Psalm 43:1-5).

He, Christ, is our exceeding joy. He is our joy no matter the circumstances, and perhaps especially in difficult times. Therefore Christ said:

"Blessed are you who are poor, for yours is the kingdom of God.
"Blessed are you who are hungry now, for you shall be satisfied.
"Blessed are you who weep now, for you shall laugh.
"Blessed are you when people hate you and when they

exclude you and revile you and spurn your name as evil, on account of the Son of Man! Rejoice in that day, and leap for joy, for behold, your reward is great in heaven; for so their fathers did to the prophets (Luke 6:20-23).

We are blessed. Let us display that blessing to all around us in our nation, for freedom's sake and to His glory. Let us spend and be spent for Christ, and each other.

Amen.

CPSIA information can be obtained at www.ICGtesting.com
Printed in the USA
BVOW08s1235021115

424681BV00002B/3/P

9 781927 684245